# 草原瑰宝

## 内蒙古文物考古精品

# Treasures on Grassland

### Archaeological Finds from the Inner Mongolia Autonomous Region

上海博物館

Shanghai Museum

**展览策划**　　陈燮君　　汪庆正　　李朝远
*Exhibition Management*　　Chen Xiejun　Wang Qingzheng　Li Chaoyuan

**展览协调**　　周志聪　　杭　侃
*Exhibition Coordinator*　　Zhou Zhicong　Hang Kan

**展览设计**　　李蓉蓉　　侯　立　　董卫平
*Exhibition Design*　　Li Rongrong　Hou Li　Dong Weiping

**主办**　内蒙古自治区文化厅
　　　　上海博物馆
**承办**　内蒙古自治区文物考古研究所
　　　　内蒙古自治区博物馆
**协办**　赤峰市博物馆
　　　　哲里木盟博物馆
　　　　巴林右旗博物馆
　　　　巴林左旗博物馆
　　　　乌兰察布盟博物馆
　　　　宁城辽中京博物馆
　　　　阿鲁科尔沁旗博物馆
　　　　敖汉旗博物馆
　　　　翁牛特旗博物馆
　　　　喀拉沁旗王府博物馆

**图录执笔人**　　乌　兰　　冯　雷　　丛艳双　　赵爱军　　李　义
　　　　　　　　霍树梅　　苏　东　　贾鸿恩　　于海燕　　包冬梅
　　　　　　　　于潜慧　　蒙景新　　唐彩兰　　孙建华　　黄雪寅

# 目　录
## *Contents*

# 前　言

　　"草原瑰宝——内蒙古文物考古精品展"经过上海博物馆和内蒙古自治区文物考古工作者近两年的精心准备,终于与广大观众见面了。在这样一个内容丰富多彩的展览中,我们可以欣赏到长期居住在内蒙古的先民们创造的高度的物质文明及其文化精神,从中可以领略到这种文明与整个华夏文明之间血脉相连的骨肉关系。

　　提起内蒙古,那首"天苍苍,野茫茫,风吹草低见牛羊"的乐府民歌,就在耳旁悠悠回荡。的确,辽阔的草原为北方民族的崛起提供了广袤的空间,"生生之资,仰给畜牧",骑马民族在这里成长壮大,并融入历史的滚滚洪流之中。一幅幅波澜壮阔的历史画面,足以让我们认识到草原文明对世界文化交流所做出的贡献。这次展览,重点展现了骑马民族在将"马上行国"与"农业城国"相结合的过程中所创造的辉煌成就。处于农牧交错带上的内蒙古地区,历来都是多种文化的相互碰撞地带,出土文物中有距今八千年前的兴隆洼文化的大型石锄、陶器、玉饰件和石雕女神像,昭示着原始农耕和宗教信仰在内蒙古地区的出现。距今

　　五六千年以前的红山文化的玉龙,来自于内蒙古的东部地区,反映出中华民族源远流长的龙崇拜的历史。由于有了历史与文化的沉思,我们驻足于展品前,就不会惊诧于辽代灿烂辉煌的物质文化成就,就容易理解为什么在中原文明发达的两宋时期,北方民族相继崛起于大漠之中,并与宋王朝相抗衡;也就容易理解为什么辽人对于宋人称其为"夷"十分反感,认为契丹"吾修文物,彬彬不异于中华"。也正是这种华、夷界限的消弭,使得民族之间的冲突,并没有让中国走向长久的分裂,而迎来了元、明、清时期空前规模的大一统局面。北方民族在祖国民族大家庭中,做出了自己卓越的贡献。

　　本次展览得到了内蒙古自治区文化厅、内蒙古自治区文物考古研究所、内蒙古自治区博物馆和赤峰市及其他诸县旗文博单位的热情帮助,谨致以深切的谢忱。

上海博物馆常务副馆长

陈燮君

# *Foreword*

**Treasures of Grassland — Archaeological Finds from Inner Mongolia Autonomous Region** is finally open to the public after two years of meticulous preparations by archaeologists from the Shanghai Museum and Inner Mongolia Autonomous Region. In such a diverse exhibition, we can appreciate the advanced civilization both in material and in culture created by the ancestors who had lived long ago in Inner Mongolia. Moreover, we can experience the close kinship between the civilization of Mongolian nationalities and the whole Chinese civilization.

When speaking of Inner Mongolia, a folksong still rings in our ears, which reads: "A blue canopy of sky over a wilderness where cattle and sheep can be seen when the wind blows through the grass." The vast grassland, indeed, provided a spacious expanse for the growth and prospers of the northern tribes. Making a living on animal husbandry, the horse-riding tribes were founded here, and then merged into the ever-progressing human history. Spectacular historical scenes make us understand the contributions made to the world by the grassland civilization. This exhibition highlights the remarkable achievements made by the horse-riding tribes in the process of combining the livestock husbandry with agriculture. Located in the overlapping area of agriculture and animal husbandry, Inner Mongolia has always been a place of cultural interchange. These unearthed relics including large stone hoes, pottery wares, jade decorative objects and stone-carved goddess, characteristic of the Xinglongwa Culture over 8,000 years ago, demonstrate the birth of a primitive farming and religious beliefs in Inner Mongolia. The jade dragon of the Hongshan Culture over 5,000 to 6,000 years ago, unearthed in the east of Inner Mongolia, reflects the venerable history of dragon adoration which is characteristic of Chinese culture. Have meditated on history and culture, we will not marvel the extraordinary material and cultural achievements of the Liao Dynasty when stopping in front of the exhibition case. We can also acquire a better understanding that along with the advanced civilization of the Central Plains the northern tribes grew up and strengthened successively from the desert during the Northern and Southern Song Dynasties. And they competed against the two Song dynasties. We will have no difficulty in understanding why the people of the Liao Dynasty had a strong aversion to the name "Yi" (a non-Han nationality or its people), given to them by the people of the Song Dynasty, and why the former deemed that the historical relics of the Qidan nationality were on the same par as those of the Song Dynasties. It was the elimination of the bounds between the Han and Yi nationalities that prevented whole China from splitting even by conflicts between different nationalities. Instead, it led to the unprecedented unification in the succeeding Yuan Dynasty, Ming Dynasty and Qing Dynasty. The northern nationalities made outstanding contributions in the midst of the great family of Chinese nationalities.

Heartfelt acknowledgments should be made to the Department of Culture of Inner Mongolia Autonomous Region, the Institute of Historical Relics and Archaeological Research of Inner Mongolia Autonomous Region, Inner Mongolia Autonomous Region Museum, Chifeng City, and various counties in Inner Mongolia, all of whom have offered their great support to this exhibition.

*Chen Xiejun*
Executive Deputy Director of the Shanghai Museum

# 祝 辞

　　来自祖国北疆内蒙古大草原的文物精品展览，在上海博物馆马承源先生的倡导下，经过上海和内蒙古两地文化、文物部门两年多的精心筹划和准备，在上海博物馆如期与广大观众见面了。这是世纪之交两地文博界合作与交流的一件盛事。在此，我们对所有为这一展览做出努力和贡献的领导、专家和同志们表示衷心的感谢！

　　内蒙古大草原，地域辽阔，历史悠久，生息和繁衍在这块热土上的古代先民，以其聪明和睿智、豪爽和剽悍，创造了极其灿烂和独树一帜的草原文化，并为缔造伟大的中华文明做出了独特的贡献。这次展出的二百多件文物精品，有孕育了中华文明的新石器时代红山文化的玉器和彩陶，也有匈奴、鲜卑、契丹、蒙古这些叱咤风云、彪炳史册的马背民族创造的游牧文明，上下几千年，琳琅满目、熠熠生辉，洋溢着浓郁的芳草气息。带着乳香的草原文化，将把观众带入草原文明由产生到成长壮大并与中原文明、世界文明交融的神奇的历史画卷之中。这批文物展品，多数为考古发掘所得，有确切纪年和地层，其中有不少堪称国宝级的文物，有些还是首次面世，弥足珍贵。内蒙古的文物精品，这样集中、系统、高品位的展示，在国内外尚属首次。

　　上海是国际大都市，我国最大的城市，特别是近年来的迅猛发展，越来越为世界瞩目，为国内外人们所景仰、所神往。上海博物馆这颗国际大都会中的璀璨明珠，以其自身的努力和自身的形象，已经跻身于世界一流博物馆的行列。内蒙古文物精品，能在上海这样的国际大都会，能在上海博物馆这样的世界一流博物馆与国内外观众见面，是内蒙古文博界的一大幸事。

　　两年多的精诚合作，不仅使我们增进了友谊，建立了深厚的感情，也使两地文博界达成了长期合作优势互补的共识。展览会期间，双方专家学者还将就共同关心的学术问题开展深入的研讨和交流。这无疑会进一步推动两地文博事业的发展，进而带动两地经济和文化的交流和繁荣。

　　预祝展览圆满成功！

内蒙古考古博物馆学会理事长
内蒙古自治区文化厅副厅长
赵芳志

# *Introduction*

The exhibition of the cultural relics from the Inner Mongolia steppe in the northern border area of our motherland is being held at the Shanghai Museum as scheduled. Suggested and initiated by Mr. Ma Chengyuan, this exhibition went through careful preparation and planning by the cultural relics institutions in Shanghai and Inner Mongolia. This is a great event for the museums and institutions in these two areas at the turning of the century. We'd like to extend our sincere thank to all the leaders, experts and colleges who have contribute efforts to this exhibition.

The steppe of Inner Mongolia covers a vast area and has a long history. The ancient Mongols, who lived in this region, created a brilliant and unique steppe culture with their intelligence, knowledge, and straightforward personality. They contributed toward the establishment of the great Chinese civilization with their special achievements. Among the over two hundred exhibits, there are jade and painted pottery pieces from the Hongshan Culture in the Neolithic period, which was the beginning of the Chinese civilization. There are pieces from the nomadic cultures of the Xiongnu, Xianbei and Qidan as well. The Mongol nationality once was a dominant and powerful nation in history. This colorful and fragrant exhibition, covering a history of thousands of years through various magnificent artifacts, brings visitors into a picture of the evolution of the steppe civilization from its emergence to its success mixing with the cultures of Central Plains and the rest of the world. Most of the exhibits are newly excavated pieces with confirmed dating and layering. Many of them are national treasures shown in public for the first time. This is a very rare opportunity that comes only once in a thousand years. The gems of cultural relics from Inner Mongolia are being exhibited for the first time home or abroad in such concentration and broad scale and in high quality.

Shanghai, the largest city in China, is an international metropolis. In recent years, she has become more and more attractive to the world due to her rapid development. Shanghai has become a city with respect and admiration from the world. One brilliant pearl of this metropolitan city, is the Shanghai Museum who has stepped into the realm of world class museums with its continuous improvement. It is the good fortune of the Inner Mongolian museums that the cultural relics of Inner Mongolia can be exhibited in the Shanghai Museum for visitors from home and abroad.

After two years of cooperation, we have not only strengthened our friendship but also come to a mutual understanding that museums from both areas shall have a long-term cooperation in giving full play to the superiority of both places. During the exhibition, experts and scholars from both places will discuss and exchange ideas on academic issues pertaining to common interests. This exhibition and discussion will definitely promote the development of museum courses in both regions and bring about the exchange and prosperity of the economy and culture.

*Zhao Fangzhi*

Director of the Museum of the Archaeology
Association of Inner Mongolia
Vice Director of the Department of Culture,
Inner Mongolia Autonomous Region

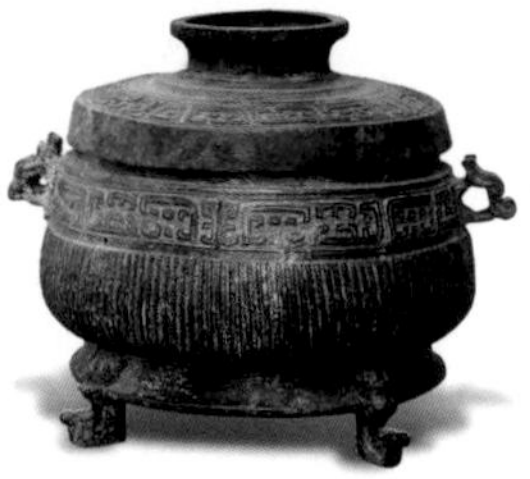

# 师道簋铭文考释

## *Interpretation of the Inscriptions on the Shi Dao Gui*

李朝远　（上海博物馆）
Li Chaoyuan　(Shanghai Museum)

师道簋1996年出土于内蒙古宁城县小黑石沟，现藏宁城县博物馆。1985年在小黑石沟曾清理过一座石椁墓，发现20件青铜礼器，其中有著名的刖人守门方鼎、许季姜簋、滕盉等器[1]，为学界所重。1992年—1993年该地又有重要发现[2]。1996年的发掘再获重要成果。后两次的发掘报告尚未发表，此次承蒙内蒙古同道的厚谊，将未发表的小黑石沟出土的青铜器先行送至上海展出，师道簋即为其中之一。现以师道簋铭文及其相关问题略述己见，就教于方家学者。

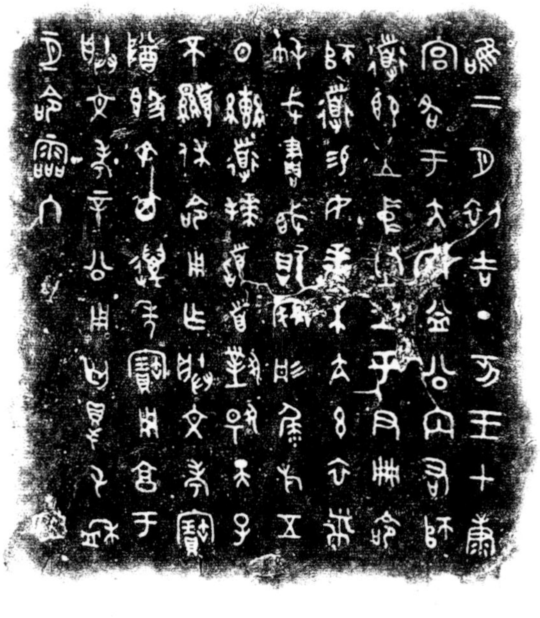

### 一　铭文考释

师道簋铭文铸于器内，共10行94字，属于赏赐铭文。按其行次，释文如下：

唯二月初吉丁亥，王才（在）康
宫，各（格）于大室。益公内（入），右（佑）师
道，即立（位）中廷。王乎（呼）尹册命
师道，易（赐）女（汝）桒朱亢（黄）、玄衣黹
屯(纯)，戈:彇(琱)戓、歆(緱)鉍(柲)、彤屎、
旂五
日，辔。道捧(拜)韻(稽)首，对䚄(扬）天子
不（丕）显休命，用乍朕(朕）文考宝
隮毁(簋)，余其迈（万）年宝用亯(享）于
朕文考辛公。用匃𦥑(得）屯盉，
亘（恒）命冬霝(终)。

下面对簋铭逐句进行考释与说明。

**唯二月初吉丁亥**

“唯”字从口，在金文中少见于不从口之“隹”。

**王才（在）康宫，各（格）于大室**

康宫为康王之庙，大室即太室，太庙中央之室。《尚书·洛诰》“王入太室祼”，孔颖达疏:“太室，室之大者，故为清庙。庙有五室，中央曰太室。”格，《尔雅·释诂》:“至也。”

**益公内（入），右（佑）師道，即立（位）中廷**

益公是西周中期一位重要的执命大臣，曾与当时地位极高的邢伯、荣伯等共传王命。在申簋（恭王或懿王时器）、王臣簋（懿王）、询簋（恭王）、走马休盘（恭王）、师永盂（恭王）铭文中均有益公辅佑大臣接受册命的记载。

师道，道为其名，师为其官职。道作“衜”，从亘从行。貉子卣铭文中有“王令士道”，士道与师道是否为一人，待考。中廷，王国维认为:“诸器文系中廷于入门后，自当为门内之廷。……中廷当为太室之廷。”[3]陈梦家认为:“中廷在大室之南、门之北。”[4]廷通庭，“礼经中言庭，皆谓自堂下至门之庭”[5]，故以陈氏之言为是。

**王乎（呼）尹册命师道**

尹，有时作“尹氏”，如《克鼎》“王乎尹氏册

命善夫克"，尹、尹氏均为作册尹，其主要职掌之一即为天子的册命官。铭文言"册命"，然并无册命授职的记录，故该铭文只能视为赏赐铭文。

**易（赐）女（汝）秦朱亢（黄）**

秦，当通"贲"，强运开认为："秦当读为贲，秦从喘声，贲亦从喘声。《说文》：籨或从贲作馈。秦、贲自可通假。……容庚说如此，精确可从。"[6]

秦在此作形容词。贲，《说文·贝部》："饰也，从贝，喘声。"《诗·小雅·白驹》："皎皎白驹，贲然来思。"朱熹注："贲然，光彩之貌也。"《广雅·释诂》："贲，美也。"

朱亢即朱黄，《害簋二》："易女秦朱黄。"亢、黄上古可通假，黄是阳部匣纽字，亢是阳部见纽字。两字叠韵，见匣旁纽。吴大澂认为："黄，古横字，同作黄，今经典多作衡。"[7] 刘心源："黄，横省，经传作衡，亦作珩。"[8] 横与珩亦为阳部匣纽平声字，与黄双声叠韵，故黄、亢均释为珩。《说文·玉部》："珩，佩上玉也，从王行，所以节行止也。"韦昭注《国语·晋语》曰："珩，佩上饰也，珩形似磬而小。"（图一）

图一

**玄衣黹纯（纯）**

《说文·黹部》："黹，箴缕所紩衣也。从㡀，丵省，象刺文也。"

纯，一般作屯，孳乳为纯。《诗·召南·野有死麕》："白毛纯束。"郑笺："纯读如屯。"《左传·哀公十八年》："执孙蒯于纯留。"《汉书·地理志》引纯留作屯留。《广雅·释诂》："纯，缘也。"《说文·糸部》"缘，衣纯也，从糸"，"纯，丝也，从糸，屯声"。纯同缘，段注"礼之纯释为缘，实即缘之音近假借也"，"缘其本字，纯其假借字"。黹、屯两字，唐兰在前人研究的基础上，根据《书·顾命》"敷重篾席，黼纯"和《仪礼·士丧礼》中之"缁纯"，将之释为"黹纯"[9]。从巾之"帕"字为首见，巾，《说文》"佩巾也，从冂，丨象糸也"。古文字中从巾从糸一也。屈万里《释黹屯》指出："玄衣黹屯，便是玄色衣服而用黹形花纹饰着它的边沿。从金文资料看，有黹形花纹的衣服是由天子所特赐的。"并用殷墟侯家庄所出的石雕来证明何为黹形花纹的衣服[10]（图二）。

图二

**戈：肅（琱）戒、畞（缑）䣄（柲）、彤屖**

肅一般作禹、琱、雷，从玉，为雕。《史记·酷吏列传》"斫雕而为朴"，《汉书·酷吏传》中雕作琱；《汉书·郊祀记》"赐尔旂鸾黼黻琱戈"，颜师古注："琱戈，刻镂之戈也，琱与雕同。"雕又与彤同，《周礼·考工记》"雕人"，《释文》"雕，本作彤"。段注《说文》彤字曰："凡琱琢之成文曰彤，故字从彡。今则彫、雕行而琱废已。”师道簋中的𦘒字不从玉而从聿，极为罕见。玉与聿的今音为双声叠韵，而上古音，玉为屋部疑组字，聿为质部喻组字，两字的声、韵全不同，故不得通假。然琱与𦘒文例相同，其义亦应通。彫有文饰、彩绘之义；聿为笔，用笔绘之。吴大澂认为“画古文从聿从爻从周。爻，交也，象手执笔画于四周，文相交错与彫同意”[11]。所以，王臣簋铭文中同样的句子作“戈：画戠”。画作畫形。而在五年师旋簋铭文中有：“盾生皇画内，戈琱戠。”作畫形的“画”与作𦘒形的“琱”同时存在，两者的区别显而易见。

关于戠字，有诸多不同意见。郭沫若正确地指出该字：“从戈从内，字形之非戟字，较然可见。……琱戠恒与戈连文，知必属于戈。”但又提出“余谓戠当是戈之援……戈琱戠乃戈援有花纹之戈”的猜测。戠，当是戈之内而非戈之援。马承源认为，戠从戈肉声。肉、内古皆从入声，金文内即入。肉、内声符相同音近而假借。[13]内（Nei）为之部泥组入声字，内(Na)为缉部泥组入声字，入字为缉部日组入声字，肉字为屋部日组入声字。之、缉通转，泥、日准双声。戈琱戠当是内上镶嵌绿松石的戈。

欳字从厚从欠，厚声，当读为緱，厚为侯部匣组，緱（Gou）为侯部见组。两字叠韵，见匣旁组，可通假。《说文 · 糸部》：“緱，刀剑緱也。”《广韵 · 侯韵》：“緱，刀剑头缠丝为緱。”考古发现中，见有剑茎为緱者，但尚未见戈有緱者。

𡨋字从“冖”从二戈，裘锡圭认为“戈”是必的象形初文，《说文》说必字从弋声，是有问题的。弋、必两字古韵不同部，声母又远隔，无从相谐。“弋”的字形与“必”字所从的戈有相当明显的区别。“弋”和“柲”的象形初文戈是两个字。事于曾鼎亦有从“宀”从二戈的𡨋字，古文字偏旁单复往往不别，故林义光释为“宓”（质部明组入声）是可信的。[14]“必”字所从的戈，正是柲的形状（图三）。

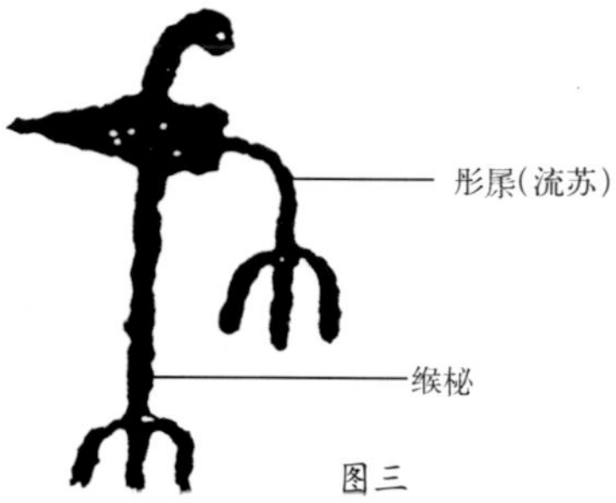

图三

柲为质部帮组入声字，柲、宓双声，帮、明旁组，故宓假借为柲。或可解为形声字，二戈为形，宀为声。宀(Mian)，有覆盖之义，而 冖（幂）字亦有覆盖义，故该字所从之⌒形，亦可隶为冖。 读为Mi，从师道簋的该字看，与其将之视为宀，不如将之视为Mi。

屎字从尾从小，为会意字，小尾之义。裴骃集解：“苏，尾也。”马承源认为，从尾从小的字当是流苏之苏的本字[15]，彤尾当为红色的流苏。铭文中有戈的图形文字，十分形象[16]，见图三。

**旂五日，䜌**

金文中一般作“䜌旂五日”，如王臣簋、师耤簋、辅师嫠簋等，亦常见有“䜌旂”连用者。金文中也有单称“旂”者，如师奎父鼎、师俞簋。“旂五日”，张政烺认为是指旂旗上图绘的五个日形。[17]古文献中多有古代旂旗上绘有日形图案的记载，河南汲县山彪镇曾出土一青铜鉴，其水陆攻战纹中即有上画五日图形的旂旗（图四）。[18]此旌飘扬在戈之柲上，而不是如常论所认为的那样为车舆之旌。此鉴虽为战国时器，然亦可略见一斑。

图四

绊，金文常以"绊乘"相连，如九年卫鼎"帛绊乘"、贸鼎"马绊乘"等。"绊乘"指四马之绊，此地单用"绊"，则指单马之绊。《说文·丝部》："绊，马绊也，从丝，从夤，与连同义。"《诗·邶风·简兮》"有力如虎，执绊如组"，朱熹《集传》"绊，今之缰也"。

**道捧（拜）頴（稽）首，对飙（扬）天子不（丕）显休命，用乍脪（朕）文考宝尊殷（簋），余其迈（万）年宝用亯（享）于朕文考辛公**

"宝"前似少铸一"永"字，金文中常见"永宝用享"、"永保用享"、"永用享"等，尚未见有"宝用享"者。

**用勾晕（得）屯盉（和），亘（恒）命霝冬（终）**

勾，经典皆假为介，《诗·七月》"以介眉寿"，郑玄笺"助也"；《尔雅·释诂下》"介，右也"。勾与介上古音中均为月部见纽入声字，两字双声叠韵。但是，《说文·匄部》"匄，气也"。段注："气者，云气也，用其声假借为气（乞）求，俗作丐。"《广韵·泰韵》："匄，乞也，丐，上同。"《左传·昭公六年》"不强匄"，《经典释文》"匄，本或作丐。音盖，乞也"。所以，此地还是以读为本字为好，为乞求之义。

得，《说文·见部》有导字："取也，从见寸。寸，度之，亦手也。"《说文·彳部》"得"的古文省彳为导。师道簋中的晕字从贝从手，从财富之取的意义上看，从贝恐更为正确，故疑《说文》"从见寸"之"见"乃"贝"字之误。

《玉篇·屮部》："屯，厚也。"《广雅·释诂一》："屯，满也。"《易·序卦》："屯者，盈也。""得屯"为得而满盈。

盉，同和。徐锴《说文解字系传》："《诗》曰'亦有盉羹'，今诗作'和'，借也。"[19] 引和为盉。《玉篇·皿部》："盉，调味也，今作和。""得屯盉"在金文中罕见，其义相当于金文中常见的"得屯亡敃"（如师望鼎、克鼎、梁其钟、虢叔旅钟等器铭）和"得屯无敃"（如史墙盘铭）。《说文·攴部》"敃，强也"，有强暴、顽悍之义。《易·乾》"保合大和乃利贞"，王弼注："不和而刚暴。"和为和谐、协调，即"无敃"之义。

"亘（恒）命霝冬（终）"句，"亘"即恒，《说文·二部》："恒，常也。…… 古文恒，从月。诗曰：如月之恒。"商承祚认为甲骨文和金文"皆从月，既云古文从月，又引《诗》释之，则原本作亘。"[20] "亘（恒）命"即金文中常见的"永命"。"霝"，令也，善也；"冬"即终。"霝冬"即善终。

## 二．器的时代及其他

师道簋通高23.4、口径19.6、底径20.6厘米。从器形上看，该器的器腹下垂，腹部较深，双耳为兽头衔环式（所衔之环已失），圈足外撇，圈足下置三个兽面象鼻形扁足，上有盖，与器子母合口，盖捉手为圈状。器腹部饰直条沟纹，口沿下和盖沿饰变形兽面纹（图五）。一般的变形兽面纹多为双目式，如大克鼎口沿的纹饰，而师道簋口沿下的变形兽面纹则是四目式。这或许启发我们,这一类的纹饰的分组,可能并不一定是以中隔的左右为一组,也可能是中隔的两边各为一组。

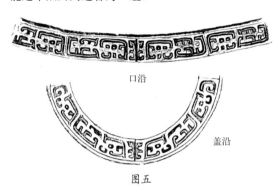

口沿

盖沿

图五

簋铭中见有益公,其主要生活在恭王和懿王初年。懿王时器牧簋有铭曰:"佳王七年十又三月既生霸甲寅……用作朕皇文考益白(伯)。"益伯即益公[21],可见懿王七年时益公已故。孝王时器毕鲜簋铭文"毕鲜作皇且(祖)益公尊簋",可知益公的孙子已是孝王时人了。又,盠方彝、盠方尊铭曰"用作朕文祖益公宝尊彝",知盠与毕鲜为兄弟,盠器亦为孝王时器。益公的出现决定了该簋的年代在西周恭王至懿王七年之前。

师道簋的器形和主纹与长安张家坡出土的五年师旋簋相似,后者通高23、口径18.7厘米,尺寸也极为近似。五年师旋簋的时代一般认为是懿王五年器。综合器形、铭文字体、纹饰以及益公的系名,师道簋的时代可推定为懿王早年。

古本《竹书纪年》载"懿王元年天再旦于郑",如果"天再旦"是一次日全食,且通过科学计算,懿王元年为公元前899年的推论是正确的话,那么,在懿王前七年中,符合师道簋"二月初吉丁亥"要求的只有公元前893年,即懿王七年。这一年的二月合朔日为甲申,丁亥为二月的第四日,在初吉之内。这样,师道簋的时代便可得到进一步的推定。

小黑石沟位于内蒙古东部赤峰市最南端的宁城县甸子乡,为内蒙、辽宁和河北的交界处。这一地区可以称为中原周文化的北进通道。这一地区北部的林西县曾发现了年代相当于商周之际的大井古铜矿遗址,60年代初在宁城稍北的赤峰药王庙、夏家店的发掘,又揭示了该地区富有特色的青铜文化的面貌,并以之命名了"夏家店下层文化"和"夏家店上层文化";同为宁城县属且距离小黑石沟不远的南山根于1958年发现了71件青铜器;1963年发掘的101号石椁墓又出土了大量的青铜器[22]。宁城东南的辽宁咯左也曾出土了相当数量的西周青铜器,虽多为周初的燕国器,但很可能是周文化北进的基地。这些地区出土的青铜器中既有中原的周代礼器,亦有当地文化色彩的铜器群,表现出复杂的多元结构。这一地区作为古文化通道的地位、意义、内涵,以及文化传播和交融的过程、中原政权与地方的关系、与周代青铜器共存器的时代问题,都是值得深入研究的课题,已非此篇小文所能涵盖,容当日后详论。无论如何,这一地区颇有特色的青铜器的不断出土,已经并将继续突破旧的以地域疆界、文化疆界为限的思维疆界和认识局限,为青铜器研究的深入和扩展开辟了新的道路。不管从哪个角度来审视周代的历史,都不能忽视这一地带的历史创造性。林沄曾指出:"要以放眼于整个东北亚地区来搞中国东北考古。"[23] 同样,研究中国北方考古和北方青铜器也须放眼于整个大北方地区。

**参考文献**:

[1] 项春松、李义《宁城小黑石沟石椁墓调查清理报告》,

《文物》1995 年第 5 期。

[2] 郭素新、田广金《源远流长的北方民族青铜器文化》附注[9]，《中国青铜器全集》第 15 册，文物出版社 1995 年版，第 37 页。

[3] 王国维《明堂庙寝通考》，《观堂集林》第一册，中华书局 1959 年版，第 136 页。

[4] 陈梦家《西周铜器断代·三》，《考古学报》1956 年第 1 期，第 105 页。

[5] 同注[3]，第 135 页。

[6] 强运开《说文古籀三补》，商务印书馆 1935 年，第 10 卷第 6 页。

[7] 吴大澂《说文古籀补》光绪年间刻本，第 33 页。

[8] 刘心源《颂鼎考释》，《奇觚室吉金文述》鼎文二，第 20 页。

[9] 唐兰《古文字学导论》下编，齐鲁书室 1981 年版，第 173 页。

[10] 《屈万里全集》第 14 木《书佣论学集》，联经出版事业公司 1984 年版，第 348、351 页。

[11] 同注[7]，第 15 页。

[12] 郭沫若《殷周青铜器铭文研究》，科学出版社 1961 年版，第 173、174、184、185 页。

[13] 马承源《商周青铜器铭文选》，文物出版社 1988 年版，第三册第 134 页。

[14] 裘锡圭《释"柲"》，《裘锡圭自选集》，大象出版社 1994 年版，第 27—31 页。

[15] 马承源《商周青铜器铭文选》，文物出版社 1988 年版，第三册第 151 页。

[16] 参见注[12]，第 180、181 页。

[17] 张政烺《王臣簋释文》，《古文字研究论文集》（《四川大学学报》丛刊第十辑）。

[18] 郭宝钧《山彪镇与琉璃阁》，科学出版社 1959 年版，第 21 页图十一[3]。

[19] 丁福保《说文解字诂林》，医学书局刊本，第 2127 页。

[20] 商承祚《说文中之古文考》，上海古籍出版社 1983 年版，第 114 页。

[21] 马承源《商周青铜器铭文选》，文物出版社 1988 年版，第三册第 188 页注[8]。

[22] 《宁城县南山根的石柄桪墓》，《考古学报》1973 年第 2 期。

[23] 林沄《林沄学术文集》，中国大百科全书出版社 1998 年版，第 8 页。

# 师道簋铭文考释
## *Interpretation of the Inscriptions on the Shi Dao Gui*

李朝远 （上海博物馆）
**Li Chaoyuan** (Shanghai Museum)

The *Shi Dao Gui*, with a height of 23.4 cm, a mouth diameter of 19.6 cm and a base diameter of 20.6 cm, unearthed in 1996 from Xiaoheishigou, Ningcheng County, Inner Mongolia, is now in the collection of the Ningcheng County Museum. The *Gui* has a drooping deep belly. The two animal-head shaped handles have rings through the mouth. (The rings are missing). It has a flared ring foot supported by three flat feet each of which is decorated like an animal with an elephant trunk. The *Gui* has a matching cover with a circular handle. Vertical groove designs decorate the body while underneath the rim there are stylized animal patterns. According to the shape of the vessel, the inscription style, the decorative patterns on the vessel and the name of the official who was present at the ceremony, this *Shi Dao Gui* is dated to the early King Yi reign of the Western Zhou (ca. 9th century BC).

The ninety-four inscriptions in ten-lines on *Shi Dao Gui* can be interpreted as that: one day in February, the King of the Zhou, in his family temple, granted awards to Shi Dao. These awards included a very beautiful cinnabar-painted jade pendant, a black jacket edged with lace, a *Ge* tied with a red tassel on the rope-bound post, a banner with a five-sun design and a bridle for horse riding. Shi Dao was very grateful to the King. Therefore he had this *Gui* made so he could offer sacrifices to his father.

Xiaoheishigou is located in Dianzi Township to the south of Ningcheng County in the eastern part of Chifeng City, Inner Mongolia, and at the conjunction of Inner Mongolia, Liaoning and Hebei provinces. This region is the northern corridor of the culture of the Western Zhou dynasty in the Central Plains. The *Shi Dao Gui*, discovered in this area, has a special historical significance.

# 绚丽多彩的北方民族青铜文化
## Ever Lasting Bronze Culthure of the Northern Nationalities

郭素新 （内蒙古文物考古研究所）
Guo Suxin （Institute of Archaeology, Inner Mongolian Autonomous Region)

在中国北方，从西辽河流域经燕山南北、阴山、贺兰山至陇山这一弧形狭长地域，其地理环境属半湿润区向干旱区过渡的半干旱区。自古以来，这里不仅是自然环境演变的敏感地区，也是物质文化演变的活跃地带。在距今三千五百年左右，因受干冷气候影响，一些原来宜于农耕的地区，逐渐发展起了畜牧业。这里很早就创造了适宜其经济活动和生活习俗的青铜文化，即北方民族青铜文化，西方学者称之为"斯基泰—西伯利亚"风格。在中国，因鄂尔多斯地区出土的青铜器早在20世纪初就已享誉海内外，被称之为"鄂尔多斯式"。这些以各种动物纹为题材的青铜器，分布范围广泛，沿用时间很长，但大体上集中于中国北方的燕山南北长城地带，因此可统称之为"北方系青铜器"。它们的族属，应该是史籍所载的北方和西北方的戎狄—匈奴族系。

## 北方民族青铜器的发现和研究

北方民族青铜器，前后延续一千六百余年，经历了几个重要发展阶段。

（一）商周时期（公元前15世纪—前11世纪）

北方民族青铜文化滥觞期和形成期。主要分布于内蒙古中南部、山西和陕西北部的黄河两岸、燕山南北，以及陕西西部和甘肃、青海东部地区。

在内蒙古中南部除零散发现外，主要是1983年在鄂尔多斯的朱开沟墓葬中发现了早商时期的青铜短剑、铜刀、铜鍪及装饰品等。[1]这是目前发现时代较早的成组的北方民族青铜器。

在山西、陕西北部的黄河两岸，发现有成组的商代晚期青铜器。其中以典型的北方民族青铜器为主；也有中原式青铜器，如鼎、簋、甗等礼器和直内戈等兵器；还有中原式与北方式青铜器风格相结合的器物。通过对陕西清涧李家崖古城的发掘，上述遗存可归属于"李家崖文化"。[2]

在燕山以北，70年代在赤峰西牛波罗、克什克腾旗天宝同曾出土有铜甗。1981年在翁牛特旗头牌子又出现了一甗二鼎。苏赫先生指出这些大型铜器应属于夏家店下层文化[3]，时代相当于商代前期(或殷墟早期)和晚期。

这里有必要提到的是，在夏家店下层文化大甸子墓地发现的陶鬲、爵和彩绘陶器。[4]其中陶鬲、爵上还装饰有成排的泥质铆钉，推测其很可能是仿自铜器。大量彩绘陶器上的云雷纹、变形饕餮纹等彩绘图案与商代早期青铜器纹饰密切相关，应是商代青铜器及其纹饰的重要源头。[5]

（二）西周晚期至春秋早、中期（公元前10世纪—前7世纪）

北方民族青铜器的发展期。比较集中地发现于西辽河流域，学术界称之为"夏家店上层文化"，属山戎遗存。较重要的地点是宁城县南山根[6]和小黑石沟[7]。出土的青铜器表现出多元结构的特点，除了具有本身特征的銎柄剑、齿柄铜刀外，既有鄂尔多斯式直刃剑系器物群，也有东北夷曲刃剑系器物群。更重要的是，由这两个系统所衍生出的具有当地特征的器物群。另外，还有各种马具，特别是青铜容器，既有仿自当地陶器的器物，还有中原青铜礼器。上述情况表明，山戎文化是将多种文化之精华融于一体，成为当时北方民族青铜文化中最发达的一支。

（三）春秋中晚期至战国时期（公元前6世纪—前3世纪）

北方民族青铜器的鼎盛时期。重要发现主要集中于鄂尔多斯、燕山南麓和以陇山为中心的宁夏南部、甘肃东部三个区。

在鄂尔多斯地区，继发掘桃红巴拉墓地之后，又发现了阿鲁柴登、西沟畔、玉隆太等墓葬。[8]另外，在阴山地带又发掘了呼鲁斯太[9]、崞县窑子[10]和毛庆沟墓地[11]。尤其是通过对毛庆沟墓地出土资料的深入研究，对该文化的内涵和特征有了更深刻的认识，"鄂尔多斯式青铜器"应属狄—匈奴族系文化。

在燕山南麓的重要发现，首推北京延庆军都山地区玉皇庙、葫芦沟和西梁垙三处墓地，发掘者认为属山戎文化。[12]韩嘉谷先生据器物群文化谱系、延续年代和分布范围，结合文献记载提出："军都山墓葬属白狄，不属山戎。"[13]类似的文化遗存还有河北宣化小白杨[14]、张家口白庙[15]、怀来甘子堡[16]等。翟德芳提出上述滦河流域及张家口地区发现的以直刃匕首式铜剑为代表的文化遗存，属"东胡"遗存。[17]

在以陇山为中心的黄土高原，发现有固原杨郎墓地、撒门村墓地，中卫狼窝子坑和中宁倪丁村墓地，甘肃宁县袁家村墓地等。许成和罗丰认为，这些遗存应属"西戎文化"。[18]

（四）秦汉时期（公元前2世纪—公元1世纪）

战国晚期以后进入了衰落期，许多典型器类，如短剑、刀及动物纹装饰品等多为铁制品所取代。

由于匈奴的强大，征服和统一了大漠南北草原地带各部族，黄土高原的某些西戎部族可能亦加入了匈奴联合体。所以，秦及两汉时期的匈奴文化遗存，主要分布在鄂尔多斯及向西南走向的黄土高原、前苏联外贝加尔和蒙古草原三个地区。

两汉时期最能代表匈奴传统文化的青铜艺术品，是由各种动物纹饰牌组成的"胡带"，其中长方形动物纹饰牌，造型比较规范，特点亦鲜明。

## 北方民族青铜器的类别和特征

按其功用可分为兵器和工具、装饰品、生活用具和礼器、车马具等四大类。

（一）兵器和工具类

有短剑、刀、管銎斧、戈、钺、匕、锥和觿等。其中，短剑和刀最具代表性。短剑又分为兽首和铃首短剑、动物纹柄首短剑、銎柄剑和触角式短剑等。

1.短剑、刀

目前发现最早的短剑是朱开沟早商墓葬中出土品，不规则扁环首，扁柄，舌状格外突，剑柄用麻绳缠绕，便于握持。伴出遗物有刀、护胸牌饰和中原式直内戈。

兽首和铃首短剑，造型较一致。柄部稍弯曲，上饰成排短线纹，柄端装饰有圆雕的鹿、马和羊等动物头像；有的柄首铸成铃形，内置弹丸，摇之声响。柄首一侧多有环扣，便于携带。剑格宽厚呈一字形，剑脊隆起呈柱状。此种短剑在山西和陕西北部黄河两岸、河北北部多有出土，时代相当于商代晚期。至西周，宽厚的一字形格变成舌状格，剑柄亦渐趋伸直，并出现蕈状首。

銎柄剑，柄端有銎，中空，翼状格下斜，剑身一般较长，有直刃和曲刃两种，是夏家店上层文化（山戎文化）最具代表性的器型。克什克腾旗龙头山出土有銎柄直刃剑，时代相当于西周早期。小黑石沟不仅出土有直刃的，还出土有双联鞘銎柄曲刃剑，应是受到东北夷曲刃剑影响而产生的，时代相当于西周晚期至春秋早期。

动物纹柄首短剑，柄端或柄部、剑格装饰有各种动物纹，有直刃和曲刃两种，应是吸收西部区狄系和东北夷系文化而创

造，并成为夏家店上层文化有代表性的器物。小黑石沟出土有鹿纹柄、双涡纹首和动物纹直刃剑，有的柄首还附带金环。其中动物纹直刃剑，柄端和剑格均装饰有双鸟头，扁平柄部装饰四对卧豹纹，其图案与共出的双豹纹饰牌相似，特别是剑身中间还装饰一排呈伫立状的短尾动物（似熊），比较特殊。另外，南山根还出土有立人柄曲刃剑，柄部两面分别铸男女裸体像，形象逼真，有人称"阴阳剑"。此种剑可能与宗教礼仪活动有关，实属难得之珍品。

T形柄曲刃剑，柄身分铸，短茎，柄端T形把手附有石质枕状加重器，应是东北系铜剑代表性器物。南山根出土的此类剑，则是柄身联铸，铜质加重器变成半圆形并与椭圆形盘联为一体。整体造型厚重规整，格及盘上还镶嵌绿松石，是曲刃剑中之精品。

触角式短剑，剑首呈双鸟（兽）头相对回首状，有的双鸟头相背联接，有的相对呈环状。主要流行于张家口以西地区，是鄂尔多斯式（狄系）青铜器最具代表性器物。毛庆沟墓地出土的双鸟首短剑最为典型，时代相当于春秋晚期。剑首为双鸟头相对联接呈"触角式"，剑格规整呈翼状，直刃有柱状脊。从造型看，触角式短剑的前身应是双动物柄首短剑，如玉皇庙、甘子堡、小白杨出土的双熊、双虎、双豹首短剑。另外，在由双兽首向双鸟首的演化中，双鸟的喙部变长内勾的造型，与斯基泰文化的鸟纹近似，应是受其影响所致。至战国早期以后，剑首多变形呈双或单环状，并出现了造型相似的铁短剑。

青铜刀，是北方民族惯用的工具，其柄首和柄部往往装饰有动物纹。早期的刀刃、柄间还有突出的栏。

朱开沟出土的环首弯柄刀，柄两侧起棱，有舌状栏。整体造型还显得薄轻，没有装饰。至商代晚期流行的铃首、兽首刀，首下有环扣、柄、刃间有突出的一字形栏，造型厚重，装饰讲究。这种器物在整个北方长城地带，东起辽宁兴城杨河，西至新疆哈密[19]，北达河北北部山地至西辽河流域，南到安阳殷墟，均有出土。至西周早期，兽首和铃首逐渐演变成蕈状首，栏和环扣也逐渐消失。

西周中期至春秋早期的刀与短剑一样，在柄部装饰有各种动物纹饰。有的在柄首铸一伫立形动物，有的在柄部装饰成排动物纹和几何纹。小黑石沟出土的铜刀柄端一侧还附有金质的豹头饰，是较为罕见的珍品。至春秋中期以后开始流行环首刀，其变化规律与触角式短剑相一致。春秋晚期以后亦出现了铁刀。

另外，在小黑石沟还出土有齿柄长刀和骨柄刀。齿柄刀短柄内侧铸一突齿，便于按柄，刀身装饰重三角纹带，长达37厘米，是齿柄刀中最长的一件。骨柄刀柄铸两突齿，两骨片夹住刀柄，上有六个穿孔，有的孔内尚存骨楔（铆钉），柄端两穿孔可用以系绳佩带。此类短柄带齿需另加刀柄的铜刀，应是夏家店上层文化中具有代表性的器物，与西部区鄂尔多斯式铜刀柄身联铸有别。

2. 管銎斧、戈、钺

中原地区的斧、戈、钺等传统兵器均是直内，利用内或援上的穿孔缚绳固定木柲。在朱开沟出土的直内戈，内上装饰有虎纹。商代晚期以后，北方地区流行的则是内上带管銎，其按柄方式是以纳柲，使握柄更为牢固，增强杀伤力。小黑石沟出土有銎内戈、管銎钺和斧。西周和春秋时期，这三种器物在北方地区仍很盛行，但其细部有所变化。

（二）装饰品类

有头饰（包括耳坠）、项饰、垂饰和腰带饰等。

由于北方民族过着逐水草随畜牧而转移的游牧生活，除了随身佩带的兵器和工具外，身上的装饰品就成为身份和地位的重要标志。

头饰，在夏家店上层文化遗址中发现有将联珠状饰成排钉缀在丝毛织物上的头带饰，而在鄂尔多斯的阿鲁柴登则发现重达一千余克的鹰形金冠饰。冠顶有一展翅雄鹰，双爪踏在一半球体上，其上有四组狼咬羊图案。冠带由三条绳索状金条以榫卯连接组成，在近人耳部有半浮雕卧式虎、狼、羊图案。这是迄今为止发现的唯一的"胡冠"标本。其制作工艺之精，令人叹为观止。

项饰，阿鲁柴登和西沟畔发现的金项圈长达一米余，重五百余克。在速机沟和玉隆太发现有银项圈，后者一端装饰有虎咬羊纹。而一般情况下，都是由各种料珠组成的串珠项饰。

腰带饰，是北方民族青铜器中最富特征、最为精彩的部分，主要流行于西部狄—匈奴文化分布区。

带扣和动物纹饰牌，是腰带上的钩挂构件，腰带饰的主要组成部分。目前在甘子堡发现较早的带扣是椭圆环状鸟形带扣，侧视似展翅欲飞的鸟，时代相当于春秋中晚期。稍晚扣环呈圆形，环面多装饰有联点纹、弧线交错纹和S形纹等。至战国晚期扣环逐渐缩小，装饰加大，变成各种动物纹带扣，如宁夏固原出土的卧兽纹、双虎纹、双豹纹和双兽搏斗纹带扣，以及鄂尔多斯发现的牛首纹、鹿纹和虎噬羊纹带扣等，装饰图案形象逼真，造型极富动感。

B（或P）形饰牌，多以猛兽吞噬弱小动物为题材。主体一般为伫立形猛兽（以虎为多数），外形轮廓多为B字形，故名。毛庆沟春秋战国之际墓地出土的虎纹带饰，整体造型古朴，仅表现伫立形虎。西吉陈阳川出土的虎噬羊纹带饰，则虎的造型形象生动，并且是左右（2件）配套使用。杨郎战国晚期墓出土的二件虎噬驴纹带饰，造型已接近P形，其图案也是左右对称，驴的后半身翻转搭在虎的背部，作挣扎状，创意新颖。至汉代以后则演变为真正P形，有人称刀把形。装饰图案内容丰富，不仅有表现飞禽与猛兽为争夺食物（小动物）而搏斗的场面，还有表现人物活动的场面，如骑士捉俘、骑士驱车出猎等，是草原牧人现实生活的艺术再现。此类饰牌在西方斯基泰和萨尔马特文化中也普遍流行。[20]

长方形饰牌，其特征是饰牌围有边框，框内装饰有各种动物纹。其中群兽纹小型饰牌，可能是从动物纹柄短剑或刀柄部流行的成排动物纹发展而来的。如小黑石沟出土的双豹纹、三兽纹饰牌，桃红巴拉出土的三马纹饰牌等，形体较小，一般不及5厘米，图案简单，造型古朴。至战国晚期以后，才普遍流行较大型的长方形饰牌，一般长10厘米左右，并多是成对出土，替代了带扣的作用。此类饰牌的动物纹有双牛、双马、双鹿和双驼等。一般构图对称严谨，动物头部或相对或相背，或相互纠结。还有表现多个动物或动物搏斗纹的，如阿鲁柴登和西沟畔出土的虎牛、虎豕搏斗纹金饰牌，前者还配有成排的虎鸟纹金饰牌，构成一副金碧辉煌的腰带。

从考古发现看，凡出土成对青铜动物纹腰带饰的墓，均是有较高身份的贵族墓；凡出土成对金饰牌的，墓主身份更高，可能是部落首领或者王；而出土小型带扣者，则是一般平民墓。特别像阿鲁柴登墓主，头带鹰形金冠带、耳佩金耳坠、颈挂金项圈，腰佩虎牛搏斗纹和虎鸟纹金饰牌组成的腰带饰，衣服上还缝缀着各种动物纹的金扣饰，等等，富丽堂皇、威武无比。这就是当时活动在鄂尔多斯地区林胡部落的王。

（三）生活用具和礼器（容器）类

北方民族由于地近中原，在商代晚期就大量使用中原式礼器。在山西、陕西北部黄河两岸发现的青铜礼器中，有相当数量具地方特征，如石楼桃花庄出土的龙纹觚、三鱼涡纹盘、竖直线纹簋、带铃觚，曹家垣的铎形器，清涧解家沟的龟鱼纹盘等。[21]

两周之际，出土礼器的重要地点是燕山南北地区。南山根和小黑石沟出土的礼器分属两个系统，一是中原式礼器，有鼎、簋、盂、罍、匜等；二是仿自当地陶器，如双耳鼎、兽耳鬲、立兽饰豆、联体豆、鋬手四足盘、六联罐及祖柄勺、鼓形器等。其中带铭文的师道簋、许季姜簋以及刖人守门方鼎等，其原属地远在河南许昌、南阳的许国和周原等地。特别是刖人守门方鼎，从造型特征看，与庄白窖藏微氏家族铜器群的同类器相似。关于在北方地区出土的大量中原青铜礼器的来源问题，很早就引起学术界的关注，有人提出是北方民族进犯中原掠夺而来。但是，也不排除因政治上的某种需要由中原以友好方式直接或间接传入塞北的。

铜鍑，体近筒形或鼓腹，口外有双耳，便于携带，是北方民族特有的炊器。目前，最早的发现是在延庆西拨子和怀来甘子堡，时代在两周之际。其后随着游牧化的发展而广泛流行，从鄂尔多斯至蒙古、外贝加尔和中欧等地均有发现，沿用时间很长。鄂尔多斯的铜鍑时代为汉代，扎赉诺尔鲜卑墓出土的铜鍑属东汉时期，北魏时期亦有出土品。

（四）车马具类

北方民族使用车大约在春秋早期，如南山根出土的狩猎纹骨板，刻画有驾车行猎场面；小黑石沟出土一件特大型车軎，重达十余公斤。军都山和甘子堡以及西部区也出土有马车零件。

至战国晚期，匈奴墓中出土的马车配件，才真正显示出北方民族风格。如玉隆太和速机沟出土的圆雕盘羊首辕饰，马、狻猊、鹤头形等竿头饰及铜鹿等，器体中空，有銎，多数成对出土。制作工艺精致，动物形象生动逼真，是这个时期青铜器的精华。车具如此豪华讲究，代表了车主的身份，应与礼器涵义相同。

马具的出现，标志着骑马术的普及。南山根出土的锚头形马衔，显示出驯马初期对马衔的刻意加工。春秋中期以后，各地出土的马衔均为两节直棍式，另附有各种造型的马镳，特别是注重对马的装备，如马面饰和节约等，说明骑马用具更讲究简便实用，反映出骑士的重要地位。正如《史记·匈奴列传》所载："士力能弯弓，尽为甲骑。其俗，宽则随畜，因射猎禽兽为生业，急则习战功以侵伐，其天性也。"

## 小　结

北方民族青铜器动物纹饰伴随着畜牧、游牧经济的发展而繁荣、发展，并始终与中原传统文化有着密切的联系。随着游牧化的发展，北方民族活动范围更加广泛，可以说早在张骞通西域之前，草原"丝绸之路"已经沟通，中西方文化交流、影响速度之快是惊人的。战国晚期，匈奴在发扬传统文化艺术的基础上，吸收了西方艺术之精华，使其动物纹造型艺术达到顶峰。各种写实性动物搏噬纹的大量出现，正是剽悍尚武的匈奴民族处于上升阶段意识形态的真实写照。汉武帝以后，北方广阔草原上处于稳定的和平发展阶段，故各种动物纹，如双马、双牛、双驼、双鹿等，均以花草树木为衬托，表现动物悠闲自得的心态，呈现出和平的自然景观。

公元 1 世纪以后，北匈奴西迁，南匈奴入塞归汉，鲜卑乘机南迁和西进，占据了匈奴故地。从此，匈奴文化被鲜卑文化继承下来。

丰富多彩的北方民族青铜文化，显示出长城地带是畜牧、游牧文化和中原农业文化相交汇、融合的重要地域。可以说民族文化的交融，也是历史发展的一种动力。

**参考文献:**

[1] 内蒙古文物考古研究所《内蒙古朱开沟遗址》，《考古学报》1988 年第 3 期。

[2] 田广金《中国北方系青铜器文化和类型的初步研究》，《考古学文化论集》第四辑，文物出版社 1997 年版。

[3] 苏赫《从昭盟发现的大型青铜器试论北方的早期青铜文明》，《内蒙古文物考古》第 2 期，1982 年。

[4] 中国社会科学院考古研究所《大甸子》，科学出版社 1996 年版。

[5] 郭大顺《赤峰地区冶铜考古随想》，《内蒙古文物考古文集》第一辑，中国大百科全书出版社 1994 年版。

[6] 中国社会科学院考古研究所东北工作队《宁城南山根的石椁墓》，《考古学报》1973 年第 2 期。

[7] 赤峰博物馆等《宁城小黑石沟石椁墓调查清理报告》，《文物》1995 年第 5 期。

[8] 田广金等《鄂尔多斯式青铜器》，文物出版社 1986 年版。

[9] 同[8]。

[10] 内蒙古文物考古研究所《凉城崞县窑子墓地》，《考古学报》1989 年第 1 期。

[11] 同[8]。

[12] 北京市文物研究所山戎文化考古队《北京延庆军都山东周山戎部落墓地发掘纪略》，《文物》1989 年第 8 期。

[13] 韩嘉谷《从军都山东周墓谈山戎、胡、东胡的考古学文化归属》，《内蒙古文物考古文集》第一辑，中国大百科全书出版社 1994 年版。

[14] 张家口市文物事业管理所、宣化县文化馆《河北宣化县小白杨墓地发掘报告》，《文物》1987 年第 5 期。

[15] 张家口市文物事业管理所《张家口市白庙遗址清理简报》，《文物》1985 年第 10 期。

[16] 贺勇、刘建中《河北怀来甘子堡发现的春秋墓群》，《文物春秋》1993 年第 2 期。

[17] 翟德芳《试论夏家店上层文化的青铜器》，《内蒙古文物考古文集》第一辑，中国大百科全书出版社 1994 年版。

[18] 许成等《东周时期戎狄青铜文化》，《考古学报》1993 年第 1 期；罗丰《近年来以陇山为中心甘宁地区春秋战国时期北方青铜文化的发现与研究》，《内蒙古文物考古》1993 年 1-2 期合刊。

[19] 新疆维吾尔自治区社会科学院考古研究所《新疆古代民族文物》，文物出版社 1985 年版。

[20] 杜正胜《欧亚草原动物纹饰与中国古代北方民族之考察》，(台湾)《历史语言研究所集刊》第六十四本，1993 年。

[21] 晋中考古队《山西娄烦、离石、柳林三县考古调查》，《文物》1989 年第 4 期。

# 绚丽多彩的北方民族青铜文化
# Ever Lasting Bronze Culture of the Northern Nationalities

郭素新　（内蒙古文物考古研究所）
Guo Suxin　（Institute of Archaeology, Inner Mongolian Autonomous Region）

Between the Xiliao River Valley and the Yanshan, Yinshan, Helanshan and Longshan areas is a narrow curved strip of land belonging in a semi-dry region for that is an environmentally sensitive area as well as a hotbed for civilization and cultural evolution. Its economic activities and lifestyle resulted in a bronze culture that became the bronze culture of the northern nationalities. The bronzes with various animal motifs had wide spread popularity in this area and lasted for a long time. This style of bronze can be regarded as "bronzes of the northern region."

The bronze age of the northern nationalities lasted for 1600 years passing-over several important periods. The Shang and Zhou periods were the beginning and formative periods. From the Zhukaigou tomb in Ordos, Inner Mongolia, we have found an early Shang bronze dagger, a broad sword, a bronze Ao (cooking vessel) and pendants. These are the earliest group of bronzes ever found from the northern nationalities. In the lower level of the Xiajiadian Culture, a great number of painted pottery vessels were decorated with cloud and thunder design and stylized animal mask patterns. These decorative patterns were closely related to those on the early Shang bronzes. It is possible that these decorative patterns are the origin of the Shang bronzes and their decorative patterns.

From the late Shang period to the early and mid Western Zhou period was the developing period of the bronze of the northern nationalities. Most of the bronze objects of this period were found in the Xiliao River Valley which was the "upper level of the Xiajiadian Culture", regarded to be the Shanrong remains. The unearthed bronzes appeared to have diversified styles; they had the Ordos-styled straight blade swords and also the Dongbei Yi-styled curved swords. The most important aspect of these bronzes is that they combine local features with these two very different styles.

The mid and late Spring and Autumn period (771 - 481 BC) to the Warring States (480 - 221 BC) was the flourishing era of the northern bronze culture. Most of the unearthed bronzes were centered in Ordos, southern Yanshan, and also in Longshan, southern Ningxia and eastern Gansu. These areas respectively represented the Di-Xiongnu Culture, the Sanrong remains and Xirong Culture.

After the late Warring States, the bronze culture of the northern nationalities came into decline. Many typical types of bronze objects such as the dagger, sword and animal-shaped pendants were replaced by iron pieces.

According to their functions, the bronzes of the northern nationalities can be divided into four categories:

1) Weapons and tools: Small daggers, swords, axes with a socket handle, Ge, Yue, dagger, awl and Xi (tool). Small daggers and broad swords are the best examples of northern craftsmanship; such as daggers with animal head hilts, daggers with ring hilts, dagger hilt decorated with animal patterns, antenna-styled small daggers and swords with socket hilts.

2) Garments and pendants: Headdresses, earrings, necklaces, girdles and belts. Belts are most gorgeous and are representative of the bronzes of the northern nationalities. Mainly they were popular with the western Di-Xiongnu Culture. The belts decorated with various animal motifs truly reflect the life on the prairie.

3) Daily utensils and ritual vessels (containers): The bronze *Fu* had been a unique cooking vessel of the northern nationalities for a long time. Northern nationalities started to use ritual vessels with the Central Plain's style even in the late Shang period. Where did these Central Plains bronzes come from? This question has attracted many concerns from the academy circle for years. The bronzes found in Shanxi and along the Huanghe River in northern Shaanxi carry a distinct local feature.

4) Chariot fittings and harnesses: The northern nationalities started to use chariots in the early Spring and Autumn period. The emergence of harness marked the beginning of horse riding.

The animal patterns used to decorate the bronzes developed along with the flourishing of animal husbandry and nomadic economy. The bronze culture was closely related to the traditional culture of the Central Plains. With the development of the nomadic lifestyle, the northern nationalities living territory extended to a much larger area. We can say before Zhang Qian (? -114 BC) started the trade with the Western countries, the "Silk Road" on the prairie had already begun. The cultural exchanges between China and the Western world developed at an astonishing speed. During the late Warring States period, the Xiongnu continued traditional art and culture; at the same time they were influenced by West art; decorative animal patterns reached its peak. There appeared a great number of various realistic decorations of animals fighting and devouring each other. These patterns clearly show the bellicose nature and ideology of the Xiongnu people. But after the Wudi reign of the Han dynasty, the northern steppe entered a period of peace and stability. As a result, all kinds of animals such as horses, cattle, camels and deer have been seen in pair with background patterns of flowers, trees and forest, that reflects the natural scenery of peace by the leisure and the carefree mood of animals.

After the first century, the northern Xiongnu moved to the west and the southern Xiongnu surrendered to the Han dynasty. At that moment, the Xianbei nationality seized the opportunity to move southwest and to occupy the homeland of the Xiongnu. From then on, the Xiongnu culture was carried on by the Xianbei culture.

The rich and colorful bronze culture of the northern nationalities indicates that the area along the Great Wall was very important for the fusion of animal husbandry and nomadic culture with agriculture from the Central Plains. The exchange of cultures between different nationalities was also a driving force for development.

# 红山诸文化的构成及相互关系

## The Composition of Hongshan Culture and its Relations

郭治中 （内蒙古文物考古研究所）

Guo Zhizhong （Institute of Archaeology, Inner Mongolian Autonomous Region）

红山文化的发现和确立，经历了将近二十年的时间。从30年代日本人开始发掘赤峰红山后到新中国建立的最初几年，考古发掘和研究工作进展缓慢。因此，在1954年尹达生先生提出"红山文化"这一概念的时候，学术界对红山文化的认识可谓知之甚少。通行的观点是将红山文化看作是仰韶文化的一个地方变种[1]，或者把它纳入所谓的北方细石器文化系统。而对于红山文化之前或之后存在于同一地域的其他史前文化，几乎是一无所知。直到60年代初中国社会科学院考古研究所内蒙古工作队发掘巴林左旗富河沟门遗址并提出富河文化的命名之后，这种停滞不前的研究状况才有所改观。进入80年代以来，辽西区史前考古工作取得了突破性进展，相继确立了具有重要意义的兴隆洼文化和赵宝沟文化，以及根据敖汉旗小河沿遗址、翁牛特旗大南沟墓地的发现而命名的"小河沿文化"。与此同时，相关的研究工作也都取得了可喜的成果。

目前所知，红山文化分布的范围，涉及今内蒙古赤峰市全境，哲里木盟的大部，辽宁省的西部以及河北北部和京津地区，学术界习惯上称之为"辽西区"。燕山两侧的西拉木伦河、老哈河流域和大小凌河流域，是红山文化形成和发展的中心地带。兴隆洼文化、赵宝沟文化、小河沿文化也大体不出这一区域，唯富河文化集中在红山文化的偏北部。

上述诸考古文化遗存有几个显著的共同点：（1）房址皆作长方形或方形半地穴式，且成排分布；聚落的外围都有围沟，聚落的中部一般都有大房址。（2）生产工具中磨制石器和细石器共存，但各文化中细石器所占的比重则有所不同。（3）陶器的基本器类是一种口大底小、状如编篓的筒形罐，典型纹饰是压印的短线交叉纹或连续之字纹。（4）墓地的地表有明显的积石遗迹，敛尸以石板为棺，流行随葬玉器。（5）作为原始宗教的崇拜物，多见石雕或泥塑的裸体女像。以上诸要素共同构成了本地区史前文化的基本特征，故苏秉琦先生称之为红山诸文化，并一度将它们表述为前红山（早于红山文化）、后红山（晚于红山文化）、红山前（红山文化的早期）和红山后（红山文化的晚期）等概念。[2]

兴隆洼文化在红山诸文化中是年代最早的一种，约当公元前六千年后段至公元前五千年初。其分布范围也相当广阔。根据目前的发现，可将该文化区别为四个不同的地方类型，即：以敖汉旗兴隆洼遗址为代表的兴隆洼类型[3]，以林西县白音长汗遗址为代表的白音长汗类型[4]，阜新的查海类型[5]和北京的上宅类型[6]。上宅的资料很少，但近年发现的河北迁西县东寨遗址可资补充[7]。各类型之间存在着一定差异，但共性是主要的。

兴隆洼文化的陶器皆为夹砂陶，泥质陶极其罕见，而且仅限于该文化的晚期。器形以瘦高的筒形罐为主，皆有一定数量的敛口罐和少量的钵、碗类器物。纹饰以压印的短线交叉纹或连续之字纹为主，一般通体饰纹，密集繁缛。采用"三段式"布局的施纹方法为兴隆洼文化所独有，即器物的上三分之一饰凹弦纹，凹弦纹以下为一周压划几何纹的凸泥带，泥条以下饰交叉纹或之字纹直至器底，此为主体纹饰。纹饰种类纹样和施纹方法的消长变化，具有指示分期的意义；特别是泥条带上的几何纹，被认为是赵宝沟文化几何纹的源头。

兴隆洼文化的聚落址多选择在临河不远的坡冈上，坡度平缓，背风向阳，适于营造居室。在兴隆洼遗址发现了极其罕见的居室内墓葬。而在白音长汗遗址内出土的石、骨制作的生产工具和动植物遗骸分析，兴隆洼文化的农耕种植业仍处于不发达的农耕阶段，采集和渔猎经济依然是人们谋生的主要手段。

最能代表兴隆洼文化技术水平的是玉器的制作。其种类有玦、管、蝉、锥、匕形器等，皆小型件，但制作精细。切割、钻孔、打磨、抛光，工序齐备。虽然钻孔仍采用较原始的对钻法，但抛光技术已臻完善，手感光滑圆润。所选玉质多为半透明的淡绿色玉，具有一定硬度。这是目前所知中国最早的具备成熟形态的玉器制品，为后来红山文化发达的玉器制作奠定了基础。

兴隆洼文化的另一引人注目之处是它的女神崇拜。

在内蒙古的林西县、克什克腾旗和巴林右旗等地，陆续发现了一批石雕的裸体女像，已知有8件，皆为裸体孕妇的形象，最大的高60多厘米，小者30厘米左右，雕琢古朴稚拙。根据白音长汗的出土情况可知，这类雕像被安置在室内火塘的近旁，具有灶神、生殖女神等多种神格。[8]女神崇拜作为一种原始宗教形式，早在8千年前的兴隆洼文化时期已普遍存在于辽西大地，其后的红山文化出现大型女神庙也就无足为怪了。这是本地区区别于黄河流域的一个十分耐人寻味的历史现象。

进入公元前五千年以后，发达一时的兴隆洼文化开始走向衰落。值此之时，辽西区同时兴起了若干支不同的考古学文化：在西拉木伦河以北有富河文化，河北北部和北京地区分布着上宅文化，从渤海北岸到西拉木伦流域有赵宝沟文化，它和努鲁儿虎山以北的早期红山文化呈交错分布态势。上述几种文化虽兴起的前后略有不同，延续的时间有长有短，但在很长一段时间内，几种文化是平行发展的。从前一阶段兴隆洼文化的几个类型进而分化演变为若干不同的考古学文化，其区域差异和发展的不平衡性，进一步凸现出来。

此阶段赵宝沟文化的地位似较显著，不但分布广泛，遗存也甚为丰富。该文化的突出特征是陶器上装饰着发达的几何形纹饰。还有一部分被神化了的动物图形，有猪首、鹿首和鸟首三种，躯干蜷曲盘转，如神龙遨游于云际。陶器种类除传统的筒形罐之外，新出现了一部分泥质陶器，红顶钵、圈足碗、尊形器、器盖和椭圆底罐，形成一套别具特色的器物组合。赵宝沟文化的泥质陶多为灰色或橘黄色，不施纹彩，这同黄河流域的泥质陶系以红陶为主的特征大相径庭。另一方面，赵宝沟文化中圈足器类的大量出现，与黄河流域前仰韶时期圈足的流行具有异曲同工之妙。它的红顶钵，也和拒马河流域北福地诸遗址[9]的同类器以及稍后的后岗一期文化之红顶钵，有着密切的关系。有一种观点认为赵宝沟文化起源于燕山以南的渤海沿岸是不无道理的，因为这里正是黄河流域经华北平原向辽西区输入影响的中介地带。可以说，赵宝沟文化在联系内地与东北的文化交往中，起着一种关键的纽带作用。

赵宝沟文化中存在着大量磨制精良的舌形石铲（耜）。此外，还有形制比较固定的石磨棒和磨盘，表明当时的农业生产较之前一阶段已经取得了长足的进步。正是由于农业的发展，促进赵宝沟文化的居民一步步向北推移，将农业垦殖的范围扩大到遥远的西拉木伦河以北，为辽西区史前时代农耕种植业的发展打下了基础。

富河文化是由兴隆洼文化分化形成的一个旁支，分布范围主要集中在西拉木伦河以北。这里是辽西区的最北边，地势高寒，宜于畜牧和狩猎。从遗址中出土的大量野生动物骨骼和细石器来看，渔猎经济占有相当比重[10]，这种经济形态和生产方式的存在，在很大程度上受到地理环境和自然条件的制约或支配。

富河文化的房址仍作长方形，内设石板围砌的四方形火塘，此点与兴隆洼文化白音长汗类型的石板灶别无二致。陶器以夹砂陶为主，器类仅见筒形罐和圈足钵。[11]压印的篦点式竖排之字纹是比较常见的纹饰。关于富河文化的年代，以往的看法比较晚，认定其为红山文化之后的一种史前遗存。近年不少学者对此提出质疑。事实上，富河文化的筒形罐，口底比例差别不大，腹壁弧度不明显，在筒形罐序列中，显然属于一种较早的形态。所见圈足钵与赵宝沟文化同类器完全一样。篦点纹和横压竖排之字纹，还有石板灶在白音长汗阶段就已经产生，这些因素应是形成富河文化的主要渊源。这也表明两者之间的年代不会相去太远。富河文化的年代当处于兴隆洼文化之后，上限与赵宝沟文化的出现差不多或略晚一点，下限至少不晚于红山文化。

红山文化的形成与兴隆洼文化有着更为密切的关系。在赵宝沟文化由盛转衰的时候，也正是红山文化发展壮大之时。换句话说，红山文化的兴起正是导致赵宝沟文化走向衰亡的一个直接原因。红山文化的筒形罐无论陶质、纹饰还是器形，无疑都是前阶段兴隆洼文化的直接延续。它的陶器纹饰中不见赵宝沟式几何纹,器形中也没有赵宝沟文化习见的圈足器、尊形器和椭圆底器。红山文化中泥质陶的产生虽然有可能受到过赵宝沟文化的启发,但器形种类、彩绘纹饰乃至制法皆仿中原;早期为后岗一期因素,晚期为庙底沟文化因素,完全摒弃了赵宝沟文化的传统形式。两者唯一具有共同点的器物是形制奇特的斜口器和口沿呈砖红色的红顶钵。此外,赵宝沟文化舌形石铲和红山文化的桂叶形石耜,形制上颇相近似,后者显然承袭了前者的传统作风和工艺技术。通过以上分析似乎可以得出这样的结论:赵宝沟文化绝非红山文化的直接祖先,在红山文化的早期阶段,两者曾有过较为频繁的接触和交流。

根据目前的发现,大致可将红山文化划分为从早到晚三个大的时期。早期以夹砂陶为主,泥质陶也占一定比重。饰之字纹的筒形罐仍然是最常见的器物,同时也见斜口器。泥质器类有曲腹钵、小口尖底瓶、敛口厚唇盆、红顶钵等。此时的红山文化已出现彩陶,有红、黑两色,图案主要为平行竖线纹、平行线组成的三角形纹、鳞纹等。陶器装饰纹样除了之字纹外,新出现成组划纹、乳钉纹、泥条堆纹等。如前所述,红山文化的主要成分来源于前一阶段的兴隆洼文化,但红顶钵、红彩彩陶以及部分彩陶图案等都与后岗一期文化相似。故此可知红山文化早期的年代,大致同后岗一期相当,上限可与赵宝沟文化相近。红山文化的中期仍大量使用夹砂陶筒形罐,但泥质陶显著增多,折腹钵大量存在。彩陶流行黑彩,图案以菱形纹、涡纹、平行斜线和弧边三角等纹样为主,显然受庙底沟文化影响较深,其年代也应与庙底沟文化相当。这一时期是红山文化大发展的时期,不但赵宝沟文化开始消退,南边的上宅文化和东边的新乐下层文化,都开始走向衰落,红山文化呈现出一枝独秀的局面。红山文化的晚期遗存主要发现于大小凌河流域,除继承上一阶段的主要特点外,专门用于祭祀的筒形器甚为流行,新出现豆和三足或四足小陶器。彩陶图案以错叠三角纹、方块纹和宽带纹为主,

并出现一部分内彩。错叠三角纹和方块纹也见于西部地区庙子沟文化。[12]庙子沟文化与半坡四期同时,故红山文化晚期的年代应当与半坡四期文化接近。目前已有8组碳14测定数据可供参考,三期的年代跨度大体在公元前4710—公元前2920年之间。

红山文化石工具多与农业生产有关,其中突出的有用于深翻土地的大型石耜和收割用的穿孔石刀,加工谷物的磨盘和磨棒也十分普遍。农业的高度发展,同时也带动了建筑业、手工制作业、冶铜技术乃至社会形态和宗教艺术的划时代变革和进步。通过对红山文化玉器群、龙题材、女神像、大型祭祀遗迹和冶铜铸铜技术的研究和分析,我们从中窥见的是一幅幅独特的古国风情画卷,在距今五千多年以前的西辽河流域,最先放射出了"文明时代的新曙光"。

小河沿文化在红山诸文化中,习惯上被视为后红山文化之一种。事实上,小河沿文化至迟在红山文化的晚期阶段就已经形成了,经过同红山文化的一段平行发展之后,小河沿文化得以延续下来,而红山文化则过早地结束了。从这个意义上说,把小河沿文化看作是后红山文化之一种,就不够准确。另外,该文化的主要特征,也同传统的红山文化面貌背离甚远。唯一保留的是筒形罐这类器形,但体积开始变小,纹饰中压印的之字纹也为拍印线纹所取代。完全没有纹饰的素面陶也占有一定比例。泥质陶有红、灰、黑三种颜色。器类有钵、盆、豆、双耳小口罐、侈口鼓腹罐,还有数量虽少但别具特色的陶尊、器座、鸟形壶和双口壶等。彩陶的颜色有黑红两色或黑红相间,图案以错向平行线或错向半重环纹最为常见,少数八角星纹、动物纹、回折几何纹等。

构成小河沿文化的成分十分复杂,但大致可归纳为三个方面:一是来自南边大汶口文化的影响,如豆座上的三角形镂孔和八角星的彩陶图案;二是来自西边河套地区的影响,如拍印绳纹和线纹错向斜线纹的彩陶图案、侈口鼓腹罐、深腹罐等,同时在西部河套地区

的准格尔旗、岱海和黄旗海地区都发现有同小河沿文化类似的筒形罐；三是来自本地区上一阶段赵宝沟文化的影响，两者之间目前虽然存在着时间上的缺环，但确有不少因素存在着继承性，如陶尊和回折儿何形纹样。以上三种关系中，同大汶口文化的交流是单向的，与西部河套地区的交流则是双向的，赵宝沟和小河沿文化之间应该是一种间接继承的关系，尽管两者之间存在缺环，但这一缺环相信在今后的工作中会得到弥补。综合以上分析，可推定小河沿文化的年代基本上不出仰韶晚期阶段，与红山文化的晚期处于同一时代；但两者在谱系上比较远，小河沿文化的逐步发展和红山文化的渐次消亡，是一个非常值得重视的历史现象，它标志着一个大动荡、大融合的时代开始了。

本地区新石器时代各考古文化的时空框架和相互关系大致可表述如下：

红山文化是本地区贯穿始终且脉络清楚的一条文化主线。其分布地域主要在西拉木伦河和大小凌河之间，晚期的活动中心有向大小凌河移动的趋势。富河文化区域特征明显，属红山文化以北的一支文化。由于工作开展得比较少，富河文化之前和之后甚至富河文化本身，尚有许多问题没有得到解决。赵宝沟文化和小河沿文化的生成都同南边的文化因素介入有关，基本上属红山文化以南的一支文化。中原对西拉木伦流域的影响，大约都得力于这两支文化的传播。毫无疑问，兴隆洼文化在本地区发生较早，而且广为流布，对其后出现的诸考古学文化影响甚大。但兴隆洼文化也绝非无本之木。目前本地区普遍发现的一种以素面陶为特征的遗存，就极有可能是兴隆洼文化的祖先。

这里需要对红山文化的去向作一点推测。笔者认为，红山文化的最后结局是一分为二：一部分向北移动，加入到富河文化的系统，成为"走向草原深处的牧人"；而一部分则融入到小河沿文化的系统，固守着农业民族的传统，并经过夏家店下层文化的洗礼，最终成为燕文化的重要组成部分。

**参考文献:**

[1] 佟柱臣《试论中国北方和东北地区含有细石器的诸文化问题》，《考古学报》1979年第4期；安志敏《略论三十年来我国的新石器时代考古》，《考古》1979年第5期。

[2] 苏秉琦《辽西古文化古城古国》，《辽海文物学刊》1986年创刊号。

[3] 中国社会科学院考古研究所内蒙古工作队《内蒙古敖汉旗兴隆洼遗址发掘简报》，《考古》1985年第10期。

[4] 郭治中等《林西县白音长汗遗址发掘述要》，《内蒙古东部区考古学文化研究文集》，海洋出版社1991年版。

[5] 辽宁省文物考古研究所《阜新查海新石器时代遗址试掘简报》，《辽海文物学刊》1988年第1期。

[6] 北京市文物研究所等《北京平谷上宅新石器时代遗址发掘简报》，《文物》1989年第8期。

[7] 河北省文物研究所《河北省迁西县东寨遗址发掘简报》，《文物春秋》1992年增刊。

[8] 郭治中《论白音长汗发现的女神像及其崇拜性质》，《青果集》，知识出版社1993年版。

[9] 拒马河考古队《河北易县涞水古遗址试掘报告》，《考古学报》1988年第4期；北京市文物研究所《北京市拒马河流域考古调查》，《考古》1989年第3期。

[10] 中国社会科学院考古研究所内蒙古工作队《内蒙古巴林左旗富河沟门遗址发掘简报》，《考古》1964年第1期。

[11] 刘观民《不同文化之间交叉现象释例》，图一.20，《中国考古学论丛》，科学出版社1993年版。

[12] 内蒙古文物考古研究所《内蒙古察右前旗庙子沟遗址考古纪略》，《文物》1989年第12期。

# 红山诸文化的构成及相互关系

## The Composition of Hongshan Culture and its Relations

郭治中 （内蒙古文物考古研究所）

Guo Zhizhong （Institute of Archaeology, Inner Mongolian Autonomous Region)

The excavation of the late Hongshan site in Chifeng began in 1930s. In the Liaoxi region, the archaeological excavation of the prehistoric period has greatly developed since 1980s. This region was home to the significant Xinglongwa Culture, Zhaobaogou Culture and Xiaoheyan Culture. In these archaeological cultural sites there are several obvious common features: (1) The sites of the houses were all in a rectangular or square shaped pit. They were all arranged in rows. Ditches surrounded all of the settlements. In the center of each of the settlements there was a larger house. (2) Fine stone tools and grounded stone tools co-existed, but the number of fine stone tools varied from one culture to another. (3) The basic form of pottery vessels were bucket-shaped vessels with a large mouth and a small base, like a shoulder basket. Pressed "X" designs and continuous zigzag patterns were typical decorative patterns on the pottery. (4) On top of the tombs, there was a gathering of stones. Bodies were buried in stone coffins made of stone slabs. Jade were popular burial objects. (5) Primitive religious idols were mostly stone sculptures or clay nude female figures. The above mentioned factors formed the basic features of prehistoric cultures. Scholar Mr. Su Binqi verified these cultures as various cultures of Hongshan. He categorized his results into pre-Hongshan Culture, post-Hongshan Culture, early Hongshan Culture and late Hongshan Culture.

Xinglongwa Culture is the earliest culture among the Hongshan Culture (ca. late 6000 BC to 5000 BC). The main pottery vessels of this culture are the bucket-shaped pottery jars. The three-section layout of the decorative patterns is unique. Jades are the best examples of the craftsmanship of Xinglongwa Culture. Small in size, but exquisitely made, these jades laid the foundation for advanced jades of the Hongshan Culture. There are altogether eight pieces of nude sculpture found from Xinglongwa Culture, which all appeared to be pregnant women carved in a simple and primitive style.

The Xinglongwa Culture, once well developed, but declined in the fifth century BC. At that time, several archaeological cultures emerged. Among them, the Zhaobaogou Culture was dominant. The pottery vessels were decorated in geometric patterns as well as deified animal designs. Zhaobaogou Culture has a great number of well-ground stone farm tools, which indicated agriculture had been well developed by this time.

The Fuhe Culture, a branch of the Xinglongwa

Culture, spread mainly in the north of the Xilamulun River. This area, located in the far north of Liaoxi in high altitudes and cold temperatures, was suitable for animal husbandry and hunting. From a large amount of animal bones and refined stone tools excavated from archaeological site, we can conclude that fishing and hunting occupied an important place in the economy of that time.

The early period of the Hongshan Culture was the continuation of the Xinglongwa Culture. Hongshan Culture can be divided into three periods spanning from 4710 to 2920 BC. Highly developed agriculture of the Hongshan Culture brought with the development of architecture, handicrafts, and bronze smelting together with the epoch-making changes in social structure and religious art. Through further study and analysis of the jades, dragons, female deities and large-scale archaeological sites for ritual ceremonies, we can picture the unique lifestyle of ancient Chinese.

The Xiaoheyan Culture came into existence in the late period of the Hongshan Culture. They paralleled to each other for a while, then the Xiaoheyan Culture continued after the Hongshan Culture ended.

The structure and relations of the archaeological cultures in this area can be summarized as follows:

The Xinglongwa Culture was the earliest one and spread over a wide area. It had a great influence on the other cultures. Located over the Xilamulun River and Linghe River, the Hongshan Culture was the dominant culture in this area. In the late period, the center shifted to the big and small Linghe Rivers. Fuhe Culture, a branch of the Hongshan Culture in the north, had a distinguished regional feature. The Zhaobaogou Culture and Xiaoheyan Culture were regarded as a branch of the Hongshan Culture in the south, because of its overlapping cultures of the southern region. The Xilamulun River Valley was influenced by the culture from Central China through these two cultures.

# 内蒙古近年辽代考古的发现与研究
## Recent Archaeological Finds and Studies of the Liao Dynasty from the Inner Mongolia Autonomous Region

**孙建华** （内蒙古文物考古研究所）
**Sun Jianhua** （Institute of Archaeology, Inner Mongolian Autonomous Region）

内蒙古自治区幅员辽阔，历史悠久。水草丰美的大草原自古以来就是中国历代北方游牧民族繁衍生息的地方。活跃于内蒙古西拉木仑河、老哈河流域，建立国家达二百年之久的契丹族，在中国历史的发展进程中曾作出过重大贡献，因而辽代考古在中国考古学方面占有重要地位。

近十几年，内蒙古地区随着全区文物普查工作的深入开展，以及配合基本建设所进行的一些抢救性发掘工作，大批的辽代遗址、墓葬被发现，同时有一些重大考古发现，为辽代考古和研究工作提供了许多珍贵的实物资料。

一

1986年，由内蒙古文物考古研究所主持发掘的辽陈国公主和驸马合葬墓，是目前所见最完整、出土文物最丰富的契丹皇族墓葬，墓内随葬品达三千余件，均属辽代文物精品。[1]

陈国公主墓位于内蒙古自治区哲里木盟奈曼旗青龙山镇东北十公里的南山坡上，墓地为群山所环抱。系砖木结构的多室壁画墓，由墓道、天井、前室、东、西耳室、后室组成，全长16.4米。墓门门额以上用雕砖建造仿木结构的屋檐，并加饰彩画。耳室和后室均为圆形穹隆顶，形同契丹人居住的毡帐。在墓道两壁和前室两壁绘有壁画，画面用简练概括的写实手法，突出了公主夫妇出则骑从拥行、入则奴仆供奉，侍卫森严的生活场景。

陈国公主与驸马的尸体安置于后室的尸床上，头枕金花银枕，身着银丝网络葬衣，脸覆金面具，脚穿金花银靴，胸佩琥珀璎珞。公主腰系金銙丝带，驸马腰束金銙银鞢躞带，身上还佩带着各种金、银、玉、珍珠、玛瑙以及琥珀饰件，头部各放置一件鎏金银冠。两套完整的殡葬服饰，真实地展示了契丹皇族的特有葬俗，使我们第一次了解到契丹大贵族独特葬俗的全貌。

银丝网络是用细银丝编制的特制葬衣。其形制是根据人体结构分头、臂、手、上身及下肢、脚等部位编结成型，穿戴包裹在内衣之外，再用银丝将衔接处连结缀合成一个整体，外面再穿套上外衣，束腰带，戴面具，穿银靴，佩戴手饰等。公主和驸马的金面具，是根据死者真容，用薄金片打制。死者戴面具穿网络葬衣是辽代契丹族独有的殡葬习俗，这种葬俗只是在契丹贵族中实行。从考古资料所知，辽代的金属面具按质地有金、银、铜三种，银质和铜质面具中有的还用鎏金。网络葬衣目前所知有银丝、铜丝、鎏金铜丝三种。从这些不同材料制作的面具和网络上可以看出，契丹贵族使用面具和网络的葬俗，是有等级之分的。陈国公主和驸马的金面具和银丝网络，代表了皇家规格葬俗。

鎏金银冠，工艺精湛。公主的银冠为高翅圆顶，镂空刻花，冠顶缀饰一件道教人物的鎏金银造像。驸马的银冠用16片镂花薄银片连缀组成，冠正面刻饰一道教人物。这两顶银冠，代表了契丹贵族妇女和亲王贵戚们的冠帽形制，将道家人物饰于帽端，反映出陈国公主夫妇对道教的尊崇。陈国公主和驸马身上束系的腰带以及随葬的几条腰带，是目前所见到的辽代最为完整的腰带，有契丹族的鞢躞带，有汉服腰带。鞢躞带在《辽史》和《契丹国志》中称为鞢躞带。我国古代北方民族习惯在腰带上佩挂弓、箭、刀等狩猎用具以及刀子、解锥、针筒、砺石等随时备用的生活用具。所以鞢躞带是北方游牧民族的传统服饰。陈国公主墓出土的银冠和腰带，为研究辽代冠服制度提供了珍贵的资料。

据墓志记载，陈国公主是辽景宗的孙女，秦晋国王皇太弟耶律隆庆正妃所生。辽制："皇子嫡生者，其女与帝女同。"[2]《辽史·礼志》还规定，公主下嫁，"选公主诸父一人为婚主，凡当奥者，媒者致词之仪，自纳币至礼成，大略如纳后仪"，连同公主死后的"送终之具，至覆尸仪物咸在。赐其婿朝服、四时袭衣、鞍马，凡所需无不备。选皇族一人，送至其家"。陈国公主是皇子耶律隆庆正妃萧氏所生，因此享有与帝女同等的待遇，出土实物印证了史书的记载。陈国公主死于辽圣宗开泰七年（1018），此时正当辽代中期政治、经济、文化繁荣昌盛之时，殷实的经济基础，也为陈国公主的厚葬提供了充足的条件。公主死时年仅18岁。驸马萧绍矩，职任"泰宁军节度使、检校太师、驸马都尉"，是圣宗仁德皇后之兄，先公主而逝。公主死后祔葬于驸马先茔。

陈国公主墓内除了死者身上的穿戴之外，还随葬许多生活用具和两套完备的马具。生活用具中的瓷器有定窑的白瓷、越窑和耀州窑的青瓷，还有辽国自己烧制的瓷器。几件玻璃器均来自中亚地区，其产地主要是伊朗一带，这些玻璃器皿是通过聘使或贸易关系从西域各国输入辽国，亦或是由回鹘商人从中亚贩卖转运而来。回鹘商人，在辽朝特别受到重视，并给予优厚的待遇，在辽上京的汉城中，建有"回鹘营"，专门招待回鹘商人。这些来自中亚的物品证实了契丹族与西方诸国相互交往的密切关系，为研究中西文化的交流提供了珍贵的资料。

两套完备的马具虽非实用之物，但形制大小与实用马具相同。墓内还随葬有木弓、弓囊、银刀、刺鹅银锥、驾鹰的玉臂鞲等畋猎用具，真实地反映出契丹族的生活习俗。契丹族早期以游牧经济为主，圣宗以后逐渐汉化，转入定居生活，但仍然保留着传统的游猎生活习俗，不废鞍马骑射，保持尚武之风，故有四时捺钵制度，列为国之礼仪常典。契丹人对马具的制作非常讲究，据宋·太平老人撰《袖中锦》记载，契丹鞍与端砚、蜀锦、定瓷被并列为"天下第一"。辽朝还以制作精美的"涂金银龙凤鞍勒、红罗匣金线绣方鞯"等来贺宋朝皇帝生辰。[3]陈国公主墓出土的两副马鞍，鞍桥为木制，外侧镶包錾花鎏金银饰和贴金银饰，制作精致美观。这些游猎用具和马具代表了契丹族的传统文化因素，为研究契丹族的社会生活提供了实物资料。陈国公主墓的发掘，是辽代考古学方面的一次重大发现，因而被评为"七五"期间全国十大考古发现之一。

二

90年代以来，内蒙古辽代考古与研究工作又有了长足的进展。先后清理了巴林右旗辽庆陵之东陵，发现过去未曾报道过的墓道南部两壁壁画；清理发掘了阿鲁科尔沁旗辽耶律羽之及其家族墓地[4]；发掘了宁城县境内辽秦晋国大长公主后人萧氏家族墓地[5]；在巴林右旗辽怀陵陵区内清理了两座大型贵族壁画墓；发掘了阿鲁科尔沁旗宝山辽墓[6]，以及敖汉旗境内的辽代壁画墓[7]；还重点发掘了赤峰地区辽初就开始烧造瓷器的缸瓦窑遗址等。这些发掘工作，获得了许多重要资料，极大地推动了辽代考古与研究工作。

耶律羽之（890—941），是辽代早期的皇族宗亲，为创建辽王朝曾立下赫赫战功。其家族墓地位于内蒙古赤

峰市阿鲁科尔沁旗罕苏木苏木朝克图山，1992年在发掘了耶律羽之墓之后，又对其家族墓地进行了大规模的抢救性发掘，清理了十座墓葬，其中有耶律羽之子甘露、孙元宁、重孙道清等人的墓葬。出土的四盒墓志，为研究耶律羽之及其家族史提供了珍贵的资料。耶律羽之墓其墓室结构特殊，规模宏大，主室全部用绿色琉璃砖装饰，在辽墓中尚属首见。数百件随葬品做工精湛，有錾刻精细的金花银器，有烧造细腻的青、白瓷器，酱釉瓷器，还有皇帝御赐的"万岁台"砚盒，以及工艺精湛、制作精美的摩羯形金耳坠和玛瑙水晶璎珞等。瓷器中釉色莹润、造型优美的白瓷盘口穿带瓶，可谓是稀世珍宝。这些随葬物品再现了辽早期政治经济、文化艺术等方面所取得的成就，反映出契丹文化除了传统因素，也包含诸多外来因素，展示了契丹民族昔日的辉煌和丰采。一千二百余字的墓志，记述了耶律羽之的家世，史料丰富。耶律羽之生于唐大顺元年（890），契丹迭剌部人。墓志中特别提到"其先宗分估首，派出石槐，历经汉魏隋唐已来世为君长"。这是首次发现的有关契丹族与鲜卑族关系的明确记载。耶律羽之的曾祖勤德、祖曷鲁、父金云大王洄思都曾历任迭剌部夷离堇。勤德也就是后来追谥的辽懿祖，曷鲁则是耶律阿保机的祖父、辽玄祖均德实的兄长，耶律羽之与辽太祖阿保机是堂兄弟，早年常参预军政，为阿保机所器重。耶律羽之墓的发掘，对契丹族早期历史的研究提供了重要的资料，因而被评为1992年全国十大考古发现之一。

赤峰市阿鲁科尔沁旗东沙日台乡的宝山辽墓，位于契丹族繁衍发展的腹地。墓地以茔墙围护，并设有南门和东门，规模壮观。1994年10月内蒙古文物考古研究所对墓地内两座较大的辽墓进行了抢救性发掘。据1号墓题记，墓主人名勤德，系"大少君"次子，年仅14岁，下葬于辽太祖天赞二年（923），这是迄今所知时代最早的有纪年的契丹贵族墓。墓室构筑采用砖雕、影作仿木结构，建筑构件均施彩绘，装饰华丽。墓门外以门楼与侧墙组成宽敞的庭院。穹庐式的墓室内又用几块大型石板构筑一座方形石房，两室之间彩柱倚立，阑额环绕，斗栱高挑，宛若回廊。外室的周壁和室内的四壁满饰壁画，内容以契丹贵族日常生活及神话故事为题材的画面，工笔细腻，色彩浓艳，具有典型的唐代绘画风格。其中2号墓内的《寄锦图》和《颂经图》中的仕女装束，犹如唐代侍女画的翻版。宝山辽墓壁画，堪称辽早期绘画艺术宝库，为中国绘画史的研究又增添了新的内容，获1994年全国十大考古发现之荣。

赤峰市松山区猴头沟乡的缸瓦窑遗址，辽初就已开始烧造瓷器，是一处大型瓷窑场，占地面积约二平方公里。1995、1996和1998年，内蒙古文物考古研究所连续三次对缸瓦窑遗址进行了发掘工作，发现了烧造三彩器的辽代官窑作坊区。辽代陶瓷业烧造技术，上承唐、五代以及宋，陶瓷工匠也多来自中原。缸瓦窑早期受定窑影响以烧制白瓷为主，在器形上也有许多仿定窑产品。辽代遗址和墓葬中出土的瓷器种类繁多，形制各异的鸡冠壶，造型优美的三彩壶、三彩砚，以及不同釉色的长颈瓶、盘口瓶、碗、盘、罐等等，有的就产自缸瓦窑。缸瓦窑所在地，蕴藏着丰富的优质瓷土，乌尔图河为其提供了充足的水利资源。因此,缸瓦窑遗址是辽、金时期北方草原烧造瓷器的重要基地,在中国陶瓷史上占有重要的地位。

缸瓦窑遗址的发掘和研究,对我国北方瓷系的研究将会产生重要影响。该遗址现为全国重点文物保护单位。

1988至1992年,在对位于赤峰市巴林右旗索布日嘎苏木的辽庆州释迦佛舍利塔进行维修工程中,在塔刹内发现一批辽代佛教文物。[8]这是辽代佛教考古的重大发现,为研究辽庆州释迦佛舍利塔的建造历史和辽代佛教文化提供了重要的实物资料。释迦佛舍利塔位于庆州城内西北隅,为八角七层楼阁式,高约七十余米。据建塔碑铭记述,释迦佛舍利塔是为"大契丹国章圣皇太后特建",辽兴宗重熙十六年(1047)二月十五日启土开工,"至十八年六月十五日及第七级,并随级内葬讫舍利,当年七月十五日于相肚中安置金法舍利,并四面安九十九本桎竿陀罗尼及诸供具"。全部工程于当年完成,历时两年。建塔碑铭还详细记述了有关释迦佛舍利塔建造工程的组织情况,以及参与营建工程的职官姓名,为勘补辽史又提供了新的资料。碑铭称塔之覆钵为"相肚",这是塔刹中安置遗物的主要部位。出土文物约六百余件,有造相、佛经、金银器、瓷器、漆器以及丝织品等。其中安置于相轮堂五室内的109件法舍利塔,塔内秘藏陀罗尼咒,是研究佛教文化的珍贵资料。庆州释迦佛舍利塔建于兴宗重熙年间,正是佛教在辽国极盛之时。章圣皇太后是圣宗钦哀皇后,兴宗生母。圣宗死后,她欲总揽朝政,以谋反之罪加害仁德皇后,自立为皇太后,重熙三年(1034)又企图废兴宗立少子重元,因事未成而获罪。"帝收太后符玺,迁于庆州七括宫",让她"躬守庆陵"[9],几年之后,兴宗悔悟,又将章圣皇太后迎回朝中。庆州释迦佛舍利塔的兴建,与章圣皇太后在庆州守陵敬佛,有直接的关系。

综上所述,近年来内蒙古辽代考古工作出现前所未有的喜人景象,大批实物资料的出土,极大地丰富和拓宽了辽代考古学的研究领域,一批专题论述和研究报告相继发表,引起国内外学术界的关注。内蒙古地区是契丹族的故乡和发祥地,辽代考古与研究工作将会有更为广阔的前景。

**参考文献:**

[1] 内蒙古文物考古研究所等《辽陈国公主墓》,文物出版社1993年版。

[2] 《辽史·地理志》,渭州,中华书局版。

[3] 宋·叶隆礼《契丹国志》卷二十一,上海古籍出版社1985年版。

[4] 内蒙古文物考古研究所等《辽耶律羽之墓发掘简报》,《文物》1996年第1期。

[5] 内蒙古文物考古研究所等《宁城县埋王沟辽代墓地发掘简报》,《内蒙古文物考古文集》第二辑,中国大百科全书出版社1997年版。

[6] 内蒙古文物考古研究所等《内蒙古赤峰宝山辽壁画墓发掘简报》,《文物》1998年第1期。

[7] 《内蒙古文物考古》(敖汉旗辽墓壁画专辑),1999年第1期。

[8] 德新、张汉君等《内蒙古巴林右旗庆州白塔发现辽代佛教文物》,《文物》1994年第12期。

[9] 《辽史·列传第一》后妃,中华书局版。

# 内蒙古近年辽代考古的发现与研究
## *Recent Archaeological Finds and Studies of the Liao Dynasty from the Inner Mongolia Autonomous Region*

孙建华 （内蒙古文物考古研究所）
**Sun Jianhua** （Institute of Archaeology, Inner Mongolian Autonomous Region）

The archaeological studies of the Liao Dynasty (AD 916 -1125) play an important role in Chinese archaeology. A large number of cultural relics unearthed in the past dozen years have enriched the research in this field and broadened its range.

The tomb of the Princess of the Chen State in the Liao Dynasty, excavated in 1986, is the best-preserved grave among those of the Qidan royal families. Its funeral objects amounts to over 3,000 pieces. Built with bricks and wood, this 16.4m. long tomb consists of different structures including a entrance passage, a shaft, an antechamber, east and west chambers, and a back chamber as well. Murals in the entrance passage and the antechamber briefly depict the life of the princess and her consort who went out with many attendants, while at home, were heavily guarded and carefully waited upon.

The couple was sleeping in the back chamber on a silver pillow with gold patterns. Each was wearing a shroud knitted with silver threads, a gold mask, a pair of silver shoes with gold patterns, and an amber necklace. The princess wore a silk belt with gold ornaments around her waist and her consort wore a silver leather belt with gold ornaments. Each had a gold-gilt silver crown on their heads. They also had various ornaments on the body, such as gold, silver, jade, pearl, agate and amber. The two shrouds and ornaments have revealed the distinctive funeral culture of the Qidan royalty and have provided valuable data for the study of the official-dress system of the Liao Dynasty.

Besides the clothing of the deceased there were also two sets of complete horse wares and many daily-use porcelains found in this tomb. The glassware from the Middle Asia proves that Qidan people had close contact with western countries. Hunting gear in this tomb, including a wooden bow, a bow case, a silver knife and an awl as well as a jade arm protector for falcons to rest on, virtually reflected the life and customs of Qidan. Qidan equestrian wares are so exquisitely made that the Qidan saddle, together with Duanxi ink-slab, Sichuan brocade and Ding porcelains, were considered to be the best in China. These hunting gear and equestrian wares, as part of Qidan tradition and culture, provide material objects for the study of Qidan society.

The Tomb of Yelu Yuzhi, excavated in 1992, is specially structured, with its major chamber fully decorated with green glazed bricks. Hundreds of funeral objects of excellent workmanship portray the Qidan achievements in politics, economy, culture and art in the early Liao Dynasty. These objects have shown that the Qidan culture not only had its own tradition, but also borrowed a lot from foreign cultures. It was the first time to find an epitaph telling about the relations between the two ancient Chinese nationalities, the Qidan and the

Xianbei. Yelu Yuzhi, as a member of the Early Liao royal family, once won brilliant military successes in the establishment of the dynasty. The large-scale excavation of his tomb has furnished valuable new data for the study of both him and his family.

Murals painted with high artistic skills have been found in the Liao tomb at Baoshan, Alukerqin Banner of Chifeng City. Qin De, the occupant of Tomb No. 1, was the second son of Da Shao Jun and was buried in the second year of Tianzhan Reign (AD 923). This is the earliest Qidan nobles' tomb with a chronological record that we have found. The murals tell something about both nobles' daily life and mythology. Figures and horses are painted in a realistic and simple style; and folklore and mythology are all rendered with fine brush-work and in bright colors, representing the typical Tang dynasty painting style. Especially, the dresses worn by court ladies in the murals of Tomb No.2 are just like reproductions of Tang Dynasty paintings. In this respect, the Baoshan tombs can be regarded as a treasure house of murals, which provides a new subject for the study of Chinese painting history.

The Gangwa kiln in Chifeng City started to produce porcelain at the beginning of the Liao Dynasty. There were official workshops of poly-chrome porcelain found in the excavation site of Gangwa kiln in 1990s. Among the various porcelains unearthed from the Liao Dynasty sites and tombs, some have been confirmed to be produced by this kiln.

More than 600 pieces of Buddhist relics were found in the pagoda of Sakyamuni in Qingzhou when it was being renovated. It was the Qidan king's mother who had this pagoda built. The inscription on the stone tablet records in great detail the construction of the pagoda and the names of officials involving in this engineering project. The relics found there include Buddhist statues, sutra, gold and silver wares, porcelains, lacquer wares and silk textiles. The 109 tower-shaped containers, laid in the laksta, have hidden incantations of Dharani inside. In summery, the excavation of this pagoda provides important concrete data of its construc-tion history and the Liao Buddhist culture.

# 辽代早期贵族墓墓制所反映的汉化问题

## The Han Influence on the Aristocratic Tomb System in the Early Period of the Liao Dynasty

**杭侃** （上海博物馆）
**Hang Kan** （Shanghai Museum）

本文的辽代早期指太祖、太宗、世宗、穆宗、景宗五朝，自公元916年到981年。"契丹早期遗迹遗物的探索是颇引人注目的问题"[1]，近年来随着一些考古新发现的公布，材料较之以前丰富了。在契丹早期文化的探索方面，早期贵族的汉化问题是一个重要课题，利用考古材料对它的探索也是多方面的。墓制特指墓地的选择、茔域的建造、坟垄的分布、墓仪、墓室结构、棺椁制度、墓志和壁画内容等墓葬营建规律。限于篇幅，本文的讨论重点放在墓室结构和壁画内容两方面的变化上。

契丹民族有着自己独特的丧葬习俗，原有的安葬方式是所谓的树葬。《北史》卷94《契丹传》谓契丹人"父母死而悲哭者，以为不壮。但以其尸置于山树之上，经三年后，乃收其骨而焚之。因酹酒而祝曰：冬月时，向阳食；夏月时，向阴食；若我射猎时，使我多得猪鹿"。《旧唐书》卷199下《北狄传》仍记载着契丹人实行树葬，谓"其俗，死者不得作冢墓，以马驾车送入大山，置之树上，亦无服纪。子孙死，父母晨夕哭之。父母死，子孙不哭"。《契丹国志》卷23《国土风俗》的记载与《北史》相同，这说明契丹的传统习俗相当稳定。南宋使臣楼钥在金大定九年（1169）出使金国途中，路过中原地区时，还看到契丹遗民尸木上的现象，其时已经距离辽朝覆亡有44年之久了。[2]这种古老的习俗直到今天，在东北地区仍然能够见到。[3]契丹早期的中下层墓葬很少发现，当与这种"死不墓"的传统习俗有关。契丹人的汉化是自上而下进行的，与一般的契丹人固守传统的习俗相对比的是契丹贵族的日益汉化，这个变化在早期墓葬中就有所反映，而且随着辽代社会经济状况的不断变化，汉化问题在墓葬中的反映情况也是相应变化的。

目前发现的纪年辽墓，以位于赤峰市阿鲁科尔沁旗东沙日台乡的宝山1、2号辽墓为最早。[4]据1号墓题记，墓主人名勤德，系"大少君"次子，年仅14岁，下葬于辽太祖天赞二年（923）。墓葬所在的茔区平面为长方形，方向略偏东，由夯筑的墙体围合，开东、南两门。茔区内原系北高南低的缓坡，墓葬均分布于中部以北，南北至少有三排，"其中似以居中或偏南位置的墓葬规模较大，年代偏早"，地表散存的砖瓦等建筑构件，表明墓地中原来应当有祭殿或享堂建筑。这种大规模的辽代贵族家族茔域，较完整的还见之于阿鲁科尔沁旗耶律羽之家族墓地[5]、耶律祺家族墓地[6]、水泉沟墓地[7]、辽宁北票莲花山耶律仁先家族墓地[8]。这些墓地的茔区有严格的规划，早晚排列有序，它们正是辽代贵族汉化在墓葬营建中的具体反映。坟垄的本身，就是契丹贵族放弃故俗而逐渐汉化的一个见证。这些墓葬墓地都选择在风景佳美、背山面水的山阳，墓地选择注重风水，耶律娄国被景宗缢杀之后，"诏有司择绝后之地以葬"，可以作为契丹人注重墓葬风水的一个例证。[9]种种情况表明，契丹早期贵族的墓葬已经采用汉人的葬经，只是目前发现的考古材料尚无法知道辽代早期墓葬排列是按照哪种葬经，但从年代上讲，肯定应该是编于唐代。

宝山1号墓由墓道、门庭、墓门、甬道、墓室、石房组成。门庭平面长方形，墙体采用砖雕、影作仿木结构。墓门也为仿木结构。该墓的墓室构造特殊，墓室平面为抹角长方形，宽5.42米，进深5.84米，高5.3米，四角有彩绘半明柱，立柱与阑额顶部绘有8朵斗栱，其中柱头铺作4朵、补间铺作4朵。斗栱托影作撩檐枋一周，其上自下而上凸砌8条支架，逐渐呈八角并状收成穹隆顶。石房长方形，长3.7米，宽3.16米，建于墓室正中；石房之门正对甬道，亦做仿木结构。其余三面外表抹白灰，影作仿木结构，四壁及顶部磨光作画。在石房顶上四角竖有彩绘的石雕圆柱以支撑墓顶。又于四边角近顶两侧与墓室立壁间，分别横架8根条形石过梁，其中在石房正面两侧过梁下，各设一道墓门，将墓室与石房之间的空间分割开。显然在墓室的整体范围内，可以将石房正面的空间视为半封闭的前室，石房则为主室，两边为耳室，后面并有回廊式空间。壁画的分布也可以分成两大区域，一部分画在墓室内，一部分画于石房内外壁。墓室前壁绘吏仆图，左右壁分绘侍仆和牵马图，后壁绘宴桌、犬羊图。阑额和撩檐枋绘建筑彩画，穹隆顶上绘火焰宝珠；石房外壁门两旁各绘一个门吏，其余三面影作建筑。石房内部前壁绘侍仆，后壁绘厅堂，左右壁分别绘《高逸图》和《降真图》，顶部绘《云鹤图》。《高逸图》旁有墨书题记："天赞二年癸未岁大大少君次子勤德年十四五月廿日亡当年八月十一日于此殡故记。"《降真图》绘汉武帝见西王母的故事。

对《高逸图》，学者已经有所论述，"通过对画史流传序列和墓室壁画传承序列的考察，表明宝山辽墓《高逸图》与东晋以来汉地流行的《竹林七贤图》存在着图本样式上的逻辑联系……《高逸图》在人物组合和画面结构方式上是《竹林七贤图》的借用，对于研究《高逸图》序列由前期结构向后期结构的演变有着实际参考价值"[10]。至于《降真图》，则不见于以前的墓室壁画中。汉武帝见西王母事本出于《穆天子传》，《穆天子传》中有"天子宾于西王母……西王母为天子谣"的说法，《汉武故事》其书记西王母下降事，可与《汉武帝内传》文相参照，亦缘《穆天子传》而附会，神话演变为仙话，西王母事由此流传更加广泛。《汉武故事》记"王母遣使谓帝曰：'七月七日，我当暂来。'帝至日，扫宫内，燃九华灯。七月七日，上于承华殿，斋日正中，

忽见有青鸟从西方来，集殿前。上问东方朔，朔对曰：'西王母暮必降尊像，上宜洒扫以待之。'……是夜漏七刻，空中无云，隐如雷声，竟天紫色。有顷，王母至，乘紫车，玉女夹驭……下车，上迎拜，延母坐，请不死之药……留至五更，谈语世事，不肯言鬼神，肃然便去。"[11]宝山1号墓中所绘，正是汉武帝迎接西王母的场面。2号墓与1号墓结构类似，也由墓道、门庭、墓门、甬道、墓室、石房组成，宽4.45米，进深4.9米。所不同者是墓室平面为方形，四角没有柱子。另外，石房贴后壁而建，因此后部也没有回廊式空间。墓室四壁的人物彩画大部分脱落，但可以看出题材与1号墓所绘生活场景类似。墓室顶部绘宝相花。石房外壁门绘门吏，影作建筑绘侍仆；石房内东壁绘侍仆，西壁绘牡丹，南壁绘《寄锦图》，北壁绘《颂经图》。《寄锦图》和《颂经图》，犹如唐代侍女画的翻版。壁画中重要人物所佩带的饰件，都用纯金打制成薄片镶嵌。《寄锦图》旁有墨书诗歌一首："□□征辽岁月深，苏娘憔悴□难任；丁宁织寄回纹锦，表妾平生□□心。"可知墓主是一位名叫"苏娘"的贵妇，其身份是契丹"大少君夫人"，下葬年代略晚于1号墓。《颂经图》旁也有墨书诗歌一首："雪衣丹嘴陇山禽，每受宫闱指教深；不向人前出凡语，声声皆是念经音。"据此，内蒙古的文物考古工作者将其与杨贵妃教鹦鹉事相联是对的。[12]这个故事是杨贵妃传奇中引人注目的一个，唐代擅长绘贵族仕女画的周昉就绘制了《杨贵妃教鹦鹉图》。故事说"广南进白鹦鹉，洞晓言词，呼为雪衣女。一朝飞上妃镜台上，自语：'雪衣女'昨夜梦为鸷鸟所搏。上令妃授以《多心经》，记咏精熟。后上与妃游别殿，置雪衣女于步辇竿上同去，暂有鹰至，搏之而毙。上与妃叹息久之，遂瘗于苑中，呼为鹦鹉冢"。[13]《杨贵妃教鹦鹉图》高0.7米，宽2.3

米，用工笔重彩绘制，一望而知具有晚唐风格。看来周昉的画不仅享誉中原，而且流传到北边。[14]两座墓葬中的人物画明显有两种风格，颇具唐风的画应当是契丹人聘请成长于中原的画家按照中原画风绘制的。

1992年发掘的耶律羽之（890—941）墓，建造于太宗会同五年（942）。墓主是辽代早期的皇族宗亲，为创建辽王朝曾立下赫赫战功。其墓室规模宏大，是具有前后室的双室墓，前室为长方形甬道式，并附左右耳室；后室方形。前室面积为4.32×1.92米，后室面积为4.3×4.06米，主室全部用绿色琉璃砖装饰，在辽墓中尚属首见。具有前后室的砖室墓中，后室规模接近于耶律羽之墓的墓葬，8世纪可用于食邑五千户的郡王。[15]前室规模虽然略小，但左右耳室面积较大。这种形制的墓葬，可以与河北曲阳同光二年（924）北平王王处直墓相对比。王处直墓是砖砌方形前后室，前室附有左右小耳室的双室墓。耶律羽之墓仅前室的顶部残存流云、飞鹤壁画；王处直墓前室上部也画有云鹤，下部绘人物花鸟屏风和墓室内安排奉侍、伎乐画面等，皆为中晚唐两京地区流行的题材。[16]耶律羽之墓的墓志放置在前室之中，目前发现的辽代贵族使用墓志的以此为最早。早于此的墓葬中最多只是发现了墨书题记。这说明契丹人随着与汉族接触的日益增多，墓葬中的汉化倾向也逐渐加深。

1953年赤峰发掘的辽穆宗应历九年（959）"故驸马赠卫国王"墓，墓主为同中书门下平章事、开国公、食邑二千户、食实封二百户的萧屈列。[17]墓室分为前中后三室，前室附有南北侧室，各室平面皆为长方形，穹隆顶。前室长1.9米，宽1.58米；中室长4.1米，宽3.5米；后室较小（原报告遗漏尺寸）。该墓以中室为主室，后室放置随葬器物，而且尺寸

无法与前、中室相比，严格说来，只能视为具有两个主室的多室墓。墓中随葬品有明显的划分，南侧室出土的主要是马具，北侧室出土的为瓷器。前室中部放置墓志，墓志上刻出十二辰；左面放置生活用的铁器，右面放置两套马具。中室出土的主要是墓主的随身物品。后室在明台上放置了炊事器皿。这种墓葬形制，显然与王处直墓有更多的共同之处，乃是沿袭唐代以来的中原制度。[18]

位于内蒙古喀剌沁旗保宁十一年（979）的涿州刺史耶律琮墓，正前方树立了一通观世音，神道两侧树立石羊两对、石虎一对、文臣武将各一对，另有汉文撰写的神道碑。这种墓仪采用中原公侯卿相的制度，与碑铭中所称"埋车涂盏免夫君子之讥，闭隧悬棺方称诸侯之礼"相符[19]，这应当和他到过中原、力主与宋议和、熟悉中原礼仪制度有关，充分反映了契丹贵族在思想意识上已经完全接受了汉文化的事实。

从以上几座早期纪年辽代贵族墓葬可以看出，宝山1、2号辽墓虽然采取了仿木结构的墓室，但无论是墓室结构还是壁画内容，都与它之前和同期的中原墓葬不同。尤其是壁画，虽然题材均见之于中原地区的史籍甚至绘画之中，但有许多题材并不见于汉地的墓室壁画。很显然，辽代初期的贵族墓葬，反映的是观念上的对汉文化的向往，并不拘泥于完全照搬汉人已有的墓葬制度，而是有选择地加以吸收，表现出更多的契丹民族的开放心态。耶律羽之墓和"故驸马赠卫国王"墓，则在墓室结构上采用了汉地的墓制，并且"辽代早期仿效此构造和葬式之后，便成为固定的制度一直延续到晚期，再未见有改动"[20]，形成了一套严格的等级制度——皇帝陵墓有三个正室和四个侧室，以后室为主室；节度使及其以上的高官显贵与其眷属的墓，一般都有前后

两室，以后室为主室，有的还有侧室；一般贵族则只有一个墓室。这种情况，结合耶律琮墓墓仪所反映出来的问题，说明随着时间的推移，契丹贵族更多地吸收了汉人原有的葬制，在墓葬中表现出来的等级制度，正是契丹社会封建化逐步加深的具体反映。这种变化，应当结合辽代中期的政治局势的变化来考虑。其实辽代中期以后，契丹贵族墓葬的变化表现也是多方面的。例如汉人墓葬中使用石棺早已有之，而辽代墓葬中"都是圣宗及以后时期的"[21]；再如，辽代中期起，契丹人的墓葬内也照搬了一些汉人的墓葬壁画。这些内容，均是辽代早中期契丹贵族墓葬中汉化方面的重要变化。

**参考文献:**

[1] 徐苹芳《宋元明考古》，《中国大百科全书·考古卷》，中国大百科全书出版社1986年版。

[2] 宋·楼钥《北行日录》上："宿临洺镇 ……道中有一晒尸棚，其俗行有死者不埋，立四木高丈余，为棚其上，以荆棘覆其尸，以防鸱枭狗鼠之害，立一碑以记其姓名年月，有人认识则从便埋葬，否则任之。"《攻媿集》卷一百一十一，四部丛刊初编本。

[3] 徐秉琨、孙守道《东北文化——白山黑水中的农牧文明》，上海远东出版社、香港商务印书馆1998年版。

[4] 内蒙古文物考古研究所、阿鲁科尔沁旗文物管理所《内蒙古赤峰宝山辽壁画墓发掘简报》，《文物》1998年第1期。

[5] 齐晓光《近年来阿鲁科尔沁旗辽代墓葬的重要发现》，《内蒙古文物考古》1997年第1期。

[6] 同[5] 。

[7] 李逸友《阿鲁科尔沁旗水泉沟的辽代壁画墓》，《文物参考资料》1958年第4期。

[8] 冯永谦、韩宝兴《发掘北票莲花山辽耶律仁先族墓的收获》，《辽金契丹女真史动态》1984年第3－4期。

[9] 《辽史》卷一百二十《耶律娄国传》，中华书局标点本。

[10] 罗世平《辽墓壁画试读》，《文物》1999年第1期。

[11] 汉武故事，《鲁迅全集》第八卷《古小说钩沉》，人民文学出版社1973年版。

[12] 《〈杨贵妃教鹦鹉图〉熠熠生辉》，《文汇报》1999年10月18日第七版。

[13] 乐史《杨太真外传》，《鲁迅全集》第十卷《唐宋传奇集》，人民文学出版社1973年版。

[14] 周昉的画影响很大，郭若虚《图画见闻志》第五卷记："昉平生画墙壁卷轴甚多，贞元间，新罗人以善价收置数卷，持归本国。"

[15] 宿白《西安地区的唐墓形制》，《文物》1995年第12期。

[16] 河北省文物研究所等《河北曲阳五代壁画墓发掘简报》，《文物》1996年第9期。

[17] 热河省博物馆筹备组《赤峰县大营子辽墓发掘报告》，《考古学报》1956年第3期。

[18] 宿白《关于河北四处古墓的札记》，《文物》1996年第9期。

[19] 李逸友《辽耶律琮墓石刻及神道碑铭》，《东北考古与历史》第一辑，1982年。

[20] 李逸友《辽代契丹人墓葬制度概说》，《内蒙古东部区考古学文化研究文集》，海洋出版社1991年版。

[21] 李逸友《略论辽代契丹与汉人墓葬的特征和分期》，《中国考古学会第六次年会论文集》，文物出版社1990年版。

# 辽代早期贵族墓墓制所反映的汉化问题
## The Han Influence on the Aristocratic Tomb System in the Early Period of the Liao Dynasty

杭侃 （上海博物馆）
**Hang Kan** (Shanghai Museum)

Study and exploration of the historical relics from the early period of Qidan is the focus of many academic circles. By mainly studying the burial documents of the early periods of the Liao Dynasty, this article analyzes the relationship between the changes in tomb systems and the Han influence on the early periods of Qidan aristocracy with an emphasis on the changes in tomb structure and mural content.

Qidan nationality had its own unique burial customs. Their original burial was so-called tree burial; that is, no tomb mounds were made for the dead. Instead, the dead was carried to a big mountain on a horse-driven carriage and to be placed on a tree. Such traditional burial custom was remarkably rooted in Qidan culture. The fact that few middle and deep grave burials from the early period of Qidan have been discovered must be related to the traditional custom of "no graves for the dead". The Han culture influenced on the Qidan people from the higher rank to the lower. In contrast to the common Qidan people steadfastly clinging to their traditions, Qidan aristocrats were gradually influenced by Han customs. This change was reflected in the grave burials of the early period. With the constant changes in the social and economic conditions of the Liao Dynasty, Han influence reflected in the grave burials varied from time to time.

Aristocratic gravesites of the early period of the Liao Dynasty on a large scale have been discovered. They are strictly planned out in well-arranged order according to time of death and concretely reflect the Han influence on the construction of graves of the aristocracy in the Liao Dynasty. They ware usually located on slopes facing the sun, having beautiful scenery, overlooking water and leaning against mountains. The selection of gravesite is mostly based upon the direction of *fengshui* geomancy (wind and water), that was believed to determine the suitability of a particular site. The grave mound itself is a testimony to the fact that Qidan aristocracy gave up its traditions and gradually accepted Han culture.

Of the Liao Dynasty tombs discovered recently, No.1 and No.2 Liao tombs in Baoshan, Alukeerqin Banner are the earliest ones. The occupant of Tomb No.1 named Qin De was buried in AD 918. The intricately constructed tomb is made up of an entrance passage, a vestibule, tomb door, corridor leading into the tomb, a chamber and a stone house. Located in the very center of the tomb, the stone house has a number of stone columns at the four corners on its top to support the tomb ceiling. And it also has eight bar-shaped stone beams horizontally laid respectively between the two sides near the top of the four corners and the vertical walls of the chamber for the purpose to separate the space within the tomb. On the left and right inner walls of the stone house are painted respectively "*Gaoyi* painting" (Hermits) and "*Xiangzhen* painting." The painting Hermits is very similar to "*Zhulin Qixian* painting" (Seven Scholars in the Bamboo Grove). *Zhulin Qixian* painting is popular in the Han Kingdom since the Eastern Jin Dynasty (AD 317-420). The former borrows a lot from the latter in terms of figure and painting compositions. Not seen in the tomb murals before that time, "*Xiangzhen* painting" depicts Han Wu Di (an emperor of the Han Dynasty) welcoming Xi Wang Mu (the Queen Mother of the West). Tomb No.2 is similar to Tomb No.1 in structure. Its occupant is the wife of Qin De. She was buried a little later than her husband was. The "*Jijing* painting" (Shinu genre) and "*Songjing* painting" (a scene of reading the Buddhist scriptures) in the stone house are just as the reproduction of maidservant paintings of the Tang Dynasty. "*Songjing* painting" depicts a story in which Yang Guifei (one of the Tang emperor's favorite concubines) teaches a parrot to read the Buddhist scriptures. Paintings of this subject matter have never been seen in the tombs of the Central Plains area. These murals with apparent Tang Dynasty style were most likely done by painters, who were born and grown up in the Central Plains area and were invited by the Qidan people.

The Yelu Yuzhi Tomb was built in the fifth year of the Huitong reign of the Liao (AD 914) and the *Gu-Fuma-Zeng-Weiguowang* Tomb was built in the ninth year of the Yinli reign of Muzhong emperor (AD 959). Both were made of bricks with anterior and posterior chambers, which bear some similarity to the Wang Chuzhi Tomb in the second year of Tong Guang reign found at Quyang, Hebei Province. Tombs of such rank were used for prefecture governors who could rule five thousand families in the 8th century. The Yelu Yuzhi Tomb was the first discovered aristocratic tomb of the Liao Dynasty with epitaph. In tombs discovered earlier,

there were only ink inscriptions. This indicates that with the increasing contact between Qidan people and Han people, the Han culture was gaining in influence. The Tomb of Yelu Zong, a prefecture governor of Zhuzhou in the eleventh year of Baoning, who adopted the funeral rites of dukes and prime ministers of imperial China, reflects the fact that Qidan aristocracy had completely accepted the Han culture in ideology.

It can be seen from the aristocratic tombs mentioned above that though the Liao tombs No.1 and No.2 adopt the pseudo wooden structured chambers, they are different from Central Plains tombs of the same or earlier periods both in tomb structure and in mural subject matters, especially in terms of mural. Although the same subject matters are often seen in the historical books and even paintings in the Central Plains areas, quite a number of subject matters are not seen in tomb murals in the Han areas. It is apparent that aristocratic burials of the early Liao Dynasty reflect their yearning for the Han culture in ideology instead of copying the existing Han burial system. Yelu Yuzhi Tomb and *Gu-Fuma-Zeng-Weiguowang* Tomb only adopt the tomb structure of the Han burial systems. This, in combination with what is reflected in the funeral rites of the Yelu Zong Tomb, indicates that with time past, Qidan aristocracy absorbed more and more from the original Han burial system. The hierarchy as shown in the grave burial is a concrete reflection of the fact that feudalization was gradually deepening in the Qidan society.

# 耶律羽之墓出土陶瓷研究
## *Research on Ceramics Unearthed from the Tomb of Yelu Yuzhi*

**陈克伦** （上海博物馆）
**Chen Kelun** (Shanghai Museum)

内蒙古赤峰市的耶律羽之墓出土的一批制作精美的陶瓷，对于我国古陶瓷界来说，是近十年最重要的发现之一。对这批文物进行系统研究，有助于廓清10世纪中叶中国陶瓷生产的格局和早期辽地窑场的生产情况，同时对于了解契丹民族在北方地区建国以后与内地的关系也有裨益。

耶律羽之（890－941）是辽开国元勋之一，《辽史》有传。他与辽太祖阿保机同出一脉，系堂兄弟。早年参预军事，为阿保机所器重。辽灭渤海以后，历任东丹右平章事、太尉、太傅、左相、上柱国等要职，为东丹实际主政，是太宗朝的重要官员。根据墓志，耶律羽之死于会同4年（941）8月，次年3月"葬于裂峰之阳"。耶律羽之墓位于赤峰市阿鲁科尔沁旗罕苏木苏木朝克图山南坡，1992年8月发掘。随葬品包括金银器、佩饰、丝织物及陶瓷器等数百件，制作十分精美。其中瓷器器形繁多、制作精良，既有皮囊壶、穿带壶等充满北方草原风格的器物，也有碗、罐、盒等传统生活用品。器物胎质细腻、胎体轻薄，釉色有白、褐、酱、青等多种，釉层晶莹，是一批少见的精品。

耶律羽之墓出土的陶瓷器，在《辽耶律羽之墓发掘简报》[1]（以下简称"简报"）中共介绍了17件，其中陶器2件，白瓷8件，酱褐釉瓷器4件和青瓷3件。

## 一 陶器

两件陶器分别是灰陶喇叭口瓜棱壶和绿釉穿带瓶（简报中称为"绿釉瓷瓶"）。

喇叭口壶的口部较深，形如一个无底的撇口碗，它与颈部相接处明显内凹，腹部有瓜棱。这种造型在内蒙古辽早期墓葬中并不鲜见，如时代下限为"契丹建国之初"的哲里木盟扎鲁特旗乌日根塔拉发现的土坑墓和荷叶哈达发现的石棺墓中都有相似陶壶随葬[2]；在科尔沁左翼后旗呼斯淖发现的早期契丹墓出土的两件黄釉陶盘口壶[3]，其基本造型也与喇叭口壶应属同类。克什克腾旗二八地[4]和巴林右旗巴彦琥绍[5]的早期辽墓中也有类似发现。辽宁阜新海力板一座辽中期墓葬中出土的"绿釉盘口壶"[6]虽然腹部以弦纹替代瓜棱，圈足又比较高，但其口部及腹部的形制与上述器物完全一致。这类陶器在内地同时期墓葬中未见，因此应属当地窑场的产品。

穿带瓶是一件残器，其颈部以上缺损。器物通体施绿釉，圈足上还用低温黄釉点缀。绿釉和黄釉均属低温铅釉，通常施于陶胎之上。根据现有的资料，在瓷器上施加低温釉或彩的装饰要到金代以后才出现，因此这件瓶可判断为陶胎。器身上的花纹运用模印、贴塑等辽三彩中常用的装饰技法，黄、绿两种彩色釉兼施是辽三彩的特征之一，因此简报中将它看作为"辽三彩之雏形"是合适的。判断辽三彩的始烧年代以纪年墓的资料最为可靠，1958年在辽宁锦西清理辽大安5年（1089）萧孝忠墓时发现三彩印花方碟和海棠盘[7]，此为随葬有辽三彩的最早纪年墓，许多学者据此认为辽三彩出现于辽中晚期。耶律羽之墓穿带瓶与辽三彩之间的发展关系比较清晰，但是它与真正的辽三彩相比还有距离，不能因此得出辽三彩开始于10世纪中期的结论。笔者查阅了耶律羽之墓之后至1081年二十余座辽代纪年墓资料，在长达近一个半世纪的时间内，辽墓中只有单色釉和白地彩绘陶随葬而不见辽三彩；而在萧孝忠墓以后的1090年至辽王朝灭亡前夕的1119年之间，14座纪年辽墓中就有3座出土了辽三彩；如果加上其他虽无纪年但时代明确的晚期辽墓，出土三彩器的墓葬资料就更多了。因此，早期辽墓资料的偶然性因素可以排除。那么，这是否揭示了辽三彩发展的缓慢性，目前发现的考古资料还不足以证明这一点。关于辽三彩的出现及其发展的情况，还有待于进一步的研究和考古发现。

## 二 白瓷

白瓷是耶律羽之墓陶瓷中的大宗，简报中介绍了8件。其中，一件"盈"字款白瓷大碗被认为是定窑产品，其余7件虽然没有明确产地，但简报结语部分还是倾向于认为是"辽白瓷"。

关于"盈"字款白瓷，50年代在西安唐代大明宫遗址曾发现底部刻有"盈"字的玉璧底碗[8]，上海博物馆也收藏有"盈"字款盖盒。[9]1984年在河北内丘邢窑遗址中采集到刻有"盈"字款的唐晚期细白瓷标本[10]，由此解决了这类白瓷的产地问题。耶律羽之墓出土的"盈"字款白瓷碗，胎釉均十分精细，与邢窑细白瓷的特点一致；其造型与窑址调查报告中所列唐代中晚期的平底碗相同。因此，这件碗无疑应是晚唐邢窑的产品。

耶律羽之墓出土的白瓷皮囊壶，其造型在皮囊壶序列中属矮身横梁式，它的渊源可追溯到唐代。西安何家村唐代窖藏中出土的鎏金舞马纹仿皮囊银壶[11]就是一例，西安郊区唐开元、天宝时期墓葬中出土的瓷皮囊壶[12]也属此类。1973年南通出土的青釉提梁式皮囊壶，除一侧有錾提梁下端作兽头状并内折于壶身上部之外，其造型及仿皮囊缝线等装饰均与矮身横梁式一致，该壶被认为是越窑产品。[13]众所周知，唐代文化具有海纳百川的气度，当时的中外交往和民族融合也是空前的，因此唐文化中包含了诸多汉文化以外的因素，仿皮囊器物的出现就是对游牧文化的认同和吸纳。但是，同样是草原游牧民族，同样都使用皮囊壶作便携式容器，不同地区不同民族，其造型存在差别，这种差别也反映到仿皮囊造型的器物上。除耶律羽之墓之外，尽管在一些辽代墓葬也出土有此类矮身横梁式皮囊壶，如辽宁阜新海力板[14]、白玉都[15]和康平后刘东屯[16]等地的辽墓，但它们的时代都是辽代中期以后，比耶律羽之墓要晚。而在其他早期辽墓中出土的皮囊壶基本上都是单孔扁身式。1979年赤峰城郊城子一处辽代窖藏中出土的一件辽早期"鎏金鹿纹鸡冠式银壶"[17]也是单孔式。由此可以认为，早期辽墓中的矮身横梁式与单孔扁身式皮囊壶时代相当而造型相去甚远，正是反映了上述差别。矮身横梁式由唐代皮囊壶发展而来，早期辽墓出土的此类器物应是引入了外地的产品，而中期以后辽墓出土的此类皮囊壶或是当地窑场借鉴了外族的造型风格，其文化当与契丹无关；单孔扁身式则完全是仿契丹族流行的皮囊形式制作，属契丹民族文化。从胎釉特点看，耶律羽之墓白瓷皮囊壶胎质细白、釉色洁白而莹润，而早期辽墓中出土的其他皮囊壶的胎、釉质地则要逊色得多，制作工艺也不相同。就是中期辽墓出土的矮身横梁式皮囊壶，虽然造型相仿，其制作也嫌粗糙。辽宁省博物馆早年收藏的一件白瓷提梁式皮囊壶，由于"胎质坚致细密、釉色温润"，与其他辽瓷区别明显而被认为"极似定窑产品"。[18]80年代初对河北邢窑窑址进行调查时，在临城祈村窑址发现矮身横梁式皮囊壶标本[19]，胎质细腻、胎色洁白、釉色晶莹光亮，属邢窑细白瓷。耶律羽之墓白瓷皮囊壶无论器形还是胎釉特点，均与该标本相同，因此，当属邢窑无疑。

穿带壶（简报中称为"盘口瓶"）的造型与上海博物馆收藏的邢窑穿带壶[20]相近，胎釉及制作又十分精致，也应是邢窑产品。瓜棱形盖罐造型规整、精巧，胎体甚薄，胎质洁白细腻，釉薄而润泽，盖罐上的宝珠钮平盖可在邢窑找到相同的标本，其基本特点亦与邢窑一致。其他白瓷如钵、罐、粉盒、葵口碗等，从简报上看，胎体都甚为轻薄，应该不属于早期辽瓷，而是邢窑或定窑的产品。

### 三　酱褐釉

褐釉皮囊壶与白瓷皮囊壶不仅大小相仿，而且造型完全相同；其胎质洁白细密，釉层均匀，釉面光亮，凸起的仿皮囊缝线部分由于釉薄而现出胎色，体现了较高的制作水平。尽管在邢窑窑址没有发现类似的褐釉皮囊壶，但酱褐色釉却是邢窑的传统品种[21]，而且胎釉特点与邢窑标本也十分接近。

浅褐釉喇叭口壶造型与同墓出土的喇叭口灰陶壶相似，应是当地的产品。

### 四　青瓷

耶律羽之墓出土青瓷中比较瞩目的是一件盖罐，其盖两侧各有一圆系，盖上时恰与罐肩部两侧的圆形双系相配。若将绳从三系中穿过，可固定罐盖，肩部的另两侧各竖有一个单孔板耳，系绳带后便于提携。与此功用相同、造型相似的青瓷盖罐还有两件，一件是1954年在广州石马村五代南汉墓出土的"青釉夹耳盖罐"[22]，除以方形板耳代替圆系之外，其造型、大小均与耶律羽之墓盖罐相当；另一件是1978年在浙江海盐出土[23]，器形略小，造型与上述广州一件相似。海盐盖罐被认为是越窑产品，广州南汉墓青瓷罐虽然窑口尚未确定，但学术界一般认为是南方的产品。耶律羽之墓出土的这件青瓷盖罐亦在1993年的文物精华展展出过。从其规整的造型、青中闪灰泛黄的釉色、器身上清晰的旋削痕来看，与晚唐五代越窑青瓷十分接近，特别是盖沿和圈足足端排列整齐而密集的支烧痕，完全符合越窑的装烧工艺特点。此盖罐应不是"系当地烧造的青瓷器"，而是越窑的产品。

另两件青瓷碗，从造型上看与南方青瓷比较接近,联系辽墓出土青瓷不多且大都为越窑或耀州窑产品[24]以及在内蒙古、辽宁辽代窑址中未见青瓷标本[25]的事实,判断可能也属越窑。

## 五 几点认识

根据以上初步的比较研究,耶律羽之墓的随葬陶瓷器中有相当部分是辽地以外的产品。结合其他考古资料,我们至少可以得出如下认识:

1. 辽建国之初当地已经有窑场生产陶瓷,陶器包括无釉和有釉两类。辽代早期已经出现在同一件釉陶器上以两种彩色釉进行装饰,并且有模印、贴花等为以后辽三彩常用的装饰技法。但是,如果就此认为辽代早期已经有了真正意义上的辽三彩,则尚嫌证据不够充分。

2. 早期辽瓷尚处于起步阶段,其制作还比较粗糙,器物上往往用白色化妆土遮盖淘炼不精的胎质,而且烧制不充分,瓷化程度不高。当时契丹贵族需要制作精美的瓷器还须由外地引进。

3. 瓷质皮囊壶应与当地流行的皮质囊壶造型一致。矮身横梁式皮囊壶源于唐代,它与早期辽墓中绝大多数的单孔扁身式不仅分属不同的器物序列,而且属于不同的游牧文化。对于契丹民族来说,前者是外来的器形,早期连器物都是引进的;中期以后当地才有仿制品,但质地要粗糙一些;后者才是本族文化的产物。

4. 辽代早期墓葬多见邢窑、定窑白瓷和越窑、耀州窑青瓷,晚期墓葬多见定窑白瓷和景德镇窑青白瓷这一现象,一方面说明在当时的历史条件下,封建政权之间的割据和战争还不至于构筑起阻隔相互交流的藩篱,辽地和内地之间的交往不仅没有中断,在某些领域内还十分频繁;另一方面,也反映了终辽一代,辽瓷窑场的生产无论在质量还是在数量方面都不能满足当地的需要,因此还要从政权管辖范围以外引进。在辽代高官、王族墓中发现邢窑"盈"字款和定窑"官"字款瓷器[26],说明辽代官府与内地也保持了一定的联系。而越窑、景德镇窑产品在遥远北方的出现,反映了这两个窑场在当时中国瓷业中所占据的突出地位。

**参考文献:**

[1] 内蒙古文物考古研究所等《辽耶律羽之墓发掘简报》,《文物》1996年第1期。

[2] 哲里木盟博物馆《内蒙古哲里木盟发现的几座契丹墓》,《考古》1984年第2期。

[3] 张柏忠《科左后旗呼斯淖契丹墓》,《文物》1983年第9期。

[4] 项春松《克什克腾旗二八地一、二号辽墓》,《内蒙古文物考古》第3期。

[5] 苗润华《巴林右旗巴彦琥绍辽墓和元代遗址》,《内蒙古文物考古》1994年第1期。

[6] 辽宁省文物考古研究所等《阜新海力板辽墓》,《辽海文物学刊》1991年第1期。

[7] 雁羽《锦西西孤山辽萧孝忠墓清理简报》,《考古》1960年第2期。

[8] 冯先铭《谈邢窑有关诸问题》,《故宫博物院院刊》1981年第4期。

[9] 汪庆正等《上海博物馆——中国·美の名宝2》,日本放送出版协会1991年。

[10] 内丘县文物保管所《河北省内丘县邢窑调查报告》,《文物》1987年第9期。

[11] 陕西省博物馆等《西安南郊何家村发现唐代窖藏文物》,《文物》1972年第1期。

[12] 李知宴《唐代瓷窑概况与唐瓷的分期》,《文物》1972年第3期。

[13] 国家文物局《中国文物精华大辞典》(陶瓷卷),上海辞书出版社等1995年版。

[14] 同[6]。

[15] 阜新蒙古族自治县文化馆《辽宁阜新白玉都辽墓》,《考古》1985年第10期。

[16] 康平县文化馆文物组《辽宁康平县后刘东屯辽墓》,《考古》1986年第10期。

[17] 朱天舒《辽代金银器》,文物出版社1998年版。

[18] 辽宁省博物馆《辽宁省博物馆藏辽瓷选集》,文物出版社1962年版。

[19] 河北省临城邢瓷研制小组《唐代邢窑遗址调查报告》,《文物》1981年第9期。

[20] 同[9]。

[21] 同[10]。

[22] 商承祚《广州番禺石马村南汉墓发掘简报》,《考古》1964年第6期。

[23] 同[13]。

[24] 冯永谦《叶茂台辽墓出土的陶瓷器》,《文物》1975年第12期;内蒙古文物考古研究所等《辽陈国公主墓》,文物出版社1993年版。

[25] 冯永谦《辽代陶瓷的成就与特点》,《辽海文物学刊》1992年第二期。

[26] 除耶律羽之墓出土"盈"字款白瓷外,哲里木盟陈国公主墓(内蒙古文物考古研究所等《辽陈国公主墓》,文物出版社1993年版)、赤峰大营子辽驸马赠卫国王墓(前热河省博物馆筹备处《赤峰县大营子辽墓发掘简报》,《考古学报》1956年第3期),也分别出土了"官"字款白瓷。这些瓷器都是唐、五代时期专门为朝廷和官府生产的定烧器。

# 耶律羽之墓出土陶瓷研究
## *Research on Ceramics Unearthed from the Tomb of Yelu Yuzhi*

**陈克伦**　（上海博物馆）
**Chen Kelun**　　(Shanghai Museum)

In 1992, a group of well-made ceramic wares was unearthed from the Tomb (AD 942) of Yelu Yuzhi in city of Chifeng, Inner Mongolia Autonomous Region. To those in the ceramics research circle, this was one of the most important discoveries in the past decade. The author has made systematic research on these wares by some related archaeological materials from tombs and kiln sites. The article concluded that the pottery wares from the tomb should be the products of local kilns, for they have local characteristics, which have only been seen on the wares from Liao tombs. Two kinds of color glazes, mold printed decorations and applied designs are seen on the glazed pottery, which suggest that three-color glaze of the Liao Dynasty had appeared in a primitive form in that period. Based on the Tang original shapes, the white glazed and brown glazed bottles in the shape of leather bags belong to a different nomadic culture than that of the bottles of the same kind often found in the early Liao tombs. Their shape, body and glaze are the same as those of Xing wares. Most of the white porcelains including the bowl with the *"Ying"* mark are products of the Xing kiln. The body, glaze and technique of the green glaze covered jar are considerably similar with those of Yue wares. Some of the ceramic wares from Yelu Yuzhi's tomb are produced outside Liao area. This, on one hand, suggests that the products of Liao kilns could not meet the needs of local people. On the other hand, it proves that there are still a lot of exchanges between the Liao area and the rest of China even though several feudal rulers divided China at that time.

# 草原帝国的繁荣—从蒙古汗国到大元一统
## *Prosperity of the Steppe Empire*
### *— From the Mongol Khan Empire to the Unification by the Yuan Dynasty*

黄雪寅 （内蒙古博物馆）
Huang Xueyin (Museum of Inner Mongolian Autonomous Region)

公元13世纪，蒙古高原上崛起了一个优秀的民族——蒙古族。这个民族集中国历代北方游牧民族之大成，在成吉思汗的率领下，发挥骑马民族的优势，在广阔的北方草原上纵横驰骋，不断壮大。他们南下中原，西征欧亚，创造了震惊世界的历史业绩，对中国历史和世界历史产生了深远的影响。

### 蒙古族的起源和早期墓葬

蒙古族源于古老的东胡系室韦部，公元7世纪蒙兀室韦的名字已出现于唐代文献。室韦在蒙古语的意思是茂密的森林——蒙古人最早生息于森林之中。他们在森林中不断发展，繁衍到人多地狭时，为了开拓更广阔的生存空间，毅然将所有的生活物品堆积在山上点燃，化铁出山，奔向广阔的草原。

在呼伦贝尔草原上，考古学家发现了蒙兀室韦的武士墓[1]，其时代是公元7世纪。放置遗体的独木棺用一段天然树木挖成，随葬品有马头等，武士的身边放着大弓，弓囊是用桦树皮制成的。武士的盆骨下面还有马鞍的鞍桥痕迹。独木棺葬法，流行于早期蒙古部落，相传成吉思汗死后，就沉睡在这种内侧镶金箔的独木棺中。

1997年考古学界在呼伦贝尔盟海拉尔市的谢尔塔拉1号墓地[2]又有一处重大的发现。墓地中所有墓葬均有木棺，有的棺盖板上铺盖一层齐整的桦树皮。6号墓是已发掘墓葬中规格最高的一座，木棺加工精细；墓内出土随葬品十分丰富，有木柄铁头的长矛，包裹一层桦树皮的木弓、马鞍子，底垫由桦树皮加工而成的木质鞍桥；还有陶罐、木盘和木筷子。墓主人的背部顺放有一件桦树皮制成的箭囊，里面装有数十枚木杆铁头的箭。此外，墓主人身上还穿有几层麻、丝织衣物。与蒙兀室韦武士墓的出土物十分相近。谢尔塔拉1号墓地的年代为公元7至10世纪左右。这一发现，填补了呼伦贝尔草原考古学研究方面关于7至10世纪民族历史的缺环。

### 成吉思汗时代的文化遗存

辽代，蒙古部已逐渐成长起来，13世纪初已经分衍出许多部落。12至13世纪的蒙古草原"天下扰攘互相攻劫，人不安生"[3]，铁木真的少年时代就是在饥饿和被追杀中度过的。由于父亲被杀，部众离散，他和母亲及弟妹们在血族复仇和饥饿中挣扎。铁木真长大后，利用他父亲生前的"安答"(伙伴)克烈部首领王罕的势力，聚集亡父的离散旧部，充实自己的力量，实力渐强。宋淳熙十六年（1189），乞颜部贵族推举27岁的铁木真为汗。从此，他率领部众开始了统一蒙古高原的艰苦战斗历程。

铁木真生活的时代，北方的统治权掌握在女真人建立的金王朝手中。当金朝发现铁木真的势力日益壮大时，在草原上构筑了总长度达6500公里不同走向的金界壕。今天的呼伦贝尔草原上，还留有金代长城的遗迹。但是，金界壕终于没有挡住强悍的蒙古军队，蒙古军队以势不可挡的力量给了金王朝以致命的打击。

铁木真统一蒙古高原的战争主要是在呼伦贝尔草原上展开的。铁木真把呼伦贝尔草原变成他日后发展壮大的"练兵场、粮仓和后援基地"[4]。著名的帖尼河之战和十三翼之战，就发生在这里。在呼伦湖上，至今还保留着相传铁木真打仗时用过的饮马石和拴马桩。

公元1206年，铁木真完成了历时18年的统一战争，在斡难河(鄂嫩河)源召开大会，树起九旄白旗，被各部推举为大汗，号"成吉思汗"，创立了蒙古汗国。蒙古高原从此结束了"星空团团旋转，各部纷纷作乱"、"人们相杀相残"的部落争战局面。[5]在登基大典时，萨满作了全套的法术，与长生天相通，奉天呈运，确立了成吉思汗是受命于天的神圣地位。成吉思汗成功地利用了草原宗教——萨满教，但他并不迷信宗教，在他的眼里，王权是至高无上的。

成吉思汗颁发了"大札撒"法典[6][7]，制订了汗国的军事、政治等各项管理制度，从此结束了草原牧民一盘散沙的局面。大汗的权力和威望是空前的，他发行的圣旨牌和腰牌，是其权力地位的最好见证。在内蒙古呼和浩特市清水河县，出土了一件八思巴文金字银牌，上刻有"借助长生天的力量，皇帝的名字是神圣不可侵犯的，不尊敬服从的人将会被定罪致死"等字样，是迄今发现的圣旨牌中之上品。

成吉思汗并不仅仅只识弯弓射大雕，他从未放弃对蒙古族自身文化素质的培养。他任用畏兀儿人塔塔统阿创制了畏兀儿体蒙古文。他在《大札撒》法典中指出："读书的糊涂人，终究要超过生来的聪明人。"在内蒙古伊盟鄂托克旗的百眼窑石窟中发现有畏兀儿体蒙古文题记共计百余条，写于石窟壁画的空栏处，内容为佛颂、菩萨颂等，文字古朴，时代属于13世纪，是研究蒙古文发展史的珍贵文物。

蒙古马善于长途跋涉、吃苦耐劳，蒙古骑兵常常可以"屯数十万之师不举烟火"[8]，成吉思汗利用蒙古马的快捷和骑兵的优势建立驿站制度。日行2000公里的传令兵，使前线与后方取得了紧密联系。后来，窝阔台进一步扩建驿站，加强了汗国军事、政治的信息传递速度。出土于兴安盟科右中旗的五体文夜巡铜牌，其正面中心部位铸"元"字，右侧铸"天字拾一号夜巡牌"，牌面阳铸八思巴文、回鹘蒙古文、察合台文、藏文和汉文。这是迄今发现的元代各种牌符中，使用文字最多的一件，它也是元代驿站管理方面的珍贵实物。

内蒙古博物馆馆藏的高足金杯、錾耳金杯、青花龙纹高足杯等文物，显示出牧人生活中酒的重要性。出土于锡盟正蓝旗的錾耳金杯，其做工精湛，为蒙古汗国宫廷用的饮酒器。成吉思汗教育他的人民，喝酒要适度，因为酒会影响战争。在《札萨法典》中曾明确规定："有酒瘾而不能禁饮者，每月只饮三次为限，如多于三次者，予以惩罚。"[9]

成吉思汗建立蒙古汗国后，将呼伦贝尔草原封给他的母亲和兄弟，建立起了草原城市。草原城市的建立，使草原呈现出一派前所未有的繁荣景象。耶律楚材在《西游录》一书中有这样的描写："在成吉思汗的行宫中，帐车如云，壮士如雨，牛马遍野，兵甲赫天，烟火互望，连营无尽，真是千古之盛，前所未有的伟容！"[10]山东道人邱处机应成吉思汗之邀晋见，旅途中他亲眼看见草原上有大片的"秋稼已成"[11]。

意大利旅行家马可·波罗在他的《马可·波罗游记》中，曾经记载过蒙古贵族用的金银制品和衣物，内蒙古博物馆馆藏品中有这样的文物。1988年内蒙古锡林郭勒盟镶黄旗乌兰沟古墓葬中[12]，出土的随葬品主要是一组属于13世纪时的金马鞍饰和其他生活用品。墓中出土有高足金杯、金手镯、金耳杯、铜镜、银马鞍具残件、木梳、黑釉长瓶、桦树残片等文物，还出土了蒙古贵族妇女戴的顾姑冠残片。

金马鞍饰通体用锤鎝法锤出精致的图案。它的主体图案为八曲海棠形框内半浮雕卧鹿纹。大角卧鹿体态丰满，神情安详。卧鹿前后间以花草纹，海棠形框之外饰缠枝牡丹花纹，饰件下部以双连弧纹为框，内饰忍冬纹。饰件的边为四圈栉齿纹间以莲瓣纹和草叶纹。这组金马鞍饰纹饰精美华丽，工艺十分精湛。其制作方法和纹饰具有中原文化的特点。此外，还出土有高足金杯一件，纯金质，重153.3克，侈口，口沿边缘有凸棱一周，深腹、素面，高圈足。圈足呈倒置喇叭状，底边上卷为棱。口径10.5厘米，高14.5厘米，底径6.2厘米。这件高足金杯与乌兰察布盟兴和县五股泉乡五甲地村出土的元代高足金杯相似，黑釉长瓷瓶亦是金元时期流行的器物。该墓葬出土的桦皮碎片呈弧形，内侧附一层薄绢，又有清晰的针眼，很可能是墓主人随葬时戴的"顾姑冠"。而戴"顾姑冠"是蒙元时期蒙古贵族妇女头饰的特有风尚。

在内蒙古博物馆，有一枚"监国公主"铜印[13]。这枚铜印1974年征集于内蒙古武川县五家村，印文为阳刻篆体九叠文"监国公主行宣差河北都总管之印"，印的正中有畏兀儿蒙文两行，为"总管之印"。它所反映的是成吉思汗将三女儿阿剌海别乞下嫁给汪古部首领的事实。汪古部在辽代时已有一定势力，金朝时臣服于女真人，为金王朝守卫壕堑和边堡。成吉思汗崛起后，汪古部归附铁木真，在实现统一蒙古各部的战争中，起了重要作用。成吉思汗授予其首领以五千户，并约定世代保持婚姻关系。作为监国公主，成吉思汗的女儿管理黄河以北的广大地区，印文的"河北"指的范围应是现在的华北地区。在内蒙古包头市达茂旗有一座阿伦斯木古城，是汪古部故地——赵王城。自公元1309年始，先后有八位赵王受封于此，历代赵王都世居于此。汪古部信奉景教，在这里发现有景教的墓志铭和教堂遗址。

内蒙古包头市达茂旗大苏吉乡明水墓地，是成吉思汗建国前汪古部的一处墓地，1978年出土了一批13世纪蒙古汗国时期的文物。其中有一件纳石失辫线袍[14]，呈黄褐色，交领右衽，肥大拖地，窄袖口，束腰，衣料考究，做工精细，主要面料采用方胜联珠宝花织金锦，形制完全是蒙古式的。但在袍子的右衬底襟左下摆夹层及两袖口，织有头戴王冠的人面狮身图案，具有明显的中亚风格，反映出蒙古汗国时期草原与西方的经济文化交流的迹象。四大汗国建立后，草原与外界的交流十分方便快捷，各种用品源源不断地输入草原腹地；同时，草原上大批牛、马、皮毛和手工业产品，也从草原输往世界各地。这件长袍便是中西文化交流的典型产物，是迄今发现13世纪蒙古贵族唯一的纳石失辫线袍。

### 四大汗国和元王朝时期的中西合璧文化

从成吉思汗称汗开始，直到忽必烈统治期间，蒙古军队南下攻金和西夏，西征灭西辽和花剌子模。几次西征的结果，逐步形成了钦察汗国、察合台汗国、窝阔台汗国和伊儿汗国四大汗国，成为沟通欧亚大陆的重要枢纽，对于促进中西方的经济文化交流起着非常重要的作用。

公元1260年，成吉思汗的孙子忽必烈在开平(后称上都)，登上汗位，建元"中统"，是为元世祖，巩固了在中原的统治地位。1271年定国号"大元"，定都燕京（今北京市），称大都。1279年灭南宋，统一了全国。由此打破了各民族政权之间的疆域界限，结束了自唐以来持续数百年的汉族与北方游牧民族对峙的分裂局面，各少数民族之间的往来和交流也日益频繁。

在东西方贸易额大增的情况下，许多具有高度艺术眼光的商人根据贵族和皇帝的需求，引导着陶瓷、珠宝和金银加工业向更高的艺术境地发展。1970年出土于呼市东郊白塔村的钧窑"小宋自造"香炉等窖藏瓷器[15]，从造型特色及花纹来看，制作精致，反映了元朝钧窑、龙泉窑制瓷工艺的高度水平，是元朝瓷器中的珍品。其中钧窑香炉，颈部有三个雕贴的麒麟，正面中间有一方形题记，刻有"己酉年九月十五小宋自造香炉一个"的楷书铭文，己酉年是元武宗至大二年(1309)。炉的造型浑厚硕人，通体施天青色釉，因施釉厚重，纵横流于器表，形成堆积，显得格外有气势。这件钧窑大香炉体现了元代粗犷雄浑的精神面貌，被瓷器研究者誉为"国之瑰宝"。1976年出土于乌盟察右前旗土城子元代集宁路故城的"格力芬"丝织被面、绣花夹衫等文物[16]，"格力芬"的嘴部如鹰，卷云纹的翅膀，兽身，是欧洲神话中的神兽。"格力芬"的形象出现于北方草原，是中西文化交流的又一见证。

忽必烈即位后，创制一种统一使用的新文字，史称"八思巴文"。八思巴文主要用于官方文书或官方造发的印章、碑刻、钱钞等上面，同时，畏兀儿体蒙古字仍通行于民间。蒙古文字的创造，推动了蒙古族政治、经济、文化、科技的繁荣和发展，使蒙古族形成了一个具有共同语言的稳定的民族共同体。

蒙古统治者为了培养为其效力的统治人才，极注意贵族子弟的教育，成吉思汗曾命诸王子弟随塔塔统阿学习畏兀儿字蒙文。忽必烈时期立京师蒙古国子学，以蒙古子弟入学受教。内蒙古考古研究所收藏一件出土于锡盟钻子山的五子登科画像石，用剔地浅浮雕手法，雕刻出一幅风俗画，画面的主题是表现童子五人正在摘取挂在树梢上的风筝。古代棵与科通用，童子攀登树木，也可称为"登科"。因此，这幅画的寓意，就是"五子登科"。画像石的用意是祈求子孙后代登科及第、全家富贵繁昌之意。

成吉思汗以前，蒙古地区占支配地位的是萨满教。到了元朝，除了草原宗教萨满教外，忽必烈允许佛教(包括喇嘛教)、道教、基督教和伊斯兰教同时并存。内蒙古地区出土的伊斯兰教墓顶石、景教墓顶石、佛教石雕香炉等文物，证明了蒙古族对宗教的开放态度。忽必烈较偏重于佛教，元朝中后期，佛教逐渐凌驾于各种宗教之上，以至于明朝以后，草原上的宗教以佛教占统治地位。

成吉思汗统一蒙古草原各部以及元朝的建立，缔造了一个统一的多民族的国家。内蒙古地区出土13至15世纪大量的遗迹和遗物，充分证实了这一历史时期我国民族文化的融合以及中外文化的交流空前发展。元朝虽然只存在近一个世纪，却是我国自唐朝末年以来空前的大统一，其版图比汉朝唐朝时期大，人民比汉唐时期多；同时，与元宗室在西方建立的钦察、伊儿诸汗国在各方面联系密切，因而使元朝与西方的水陆交通也出现了空前繁荣，大大促进了中西文化的交流，使草原帝国发展到鼎盛时期，使蒙古民族走向辉煌!

**参考文献:**

[1] 《额尔古纳河——蒙古族的摇篮》，《草原文化》，商务印书馆(香港)有限公司1996年版，第211页。

[2] 乌恩等《谢尔塔拉1号墓地发掘获重大成果》，《中国文物报》1998年12月27日第1版。

[3] 《蒙古秘史》第254节，四部丛刊本。

[4] 翦伯赞《内蒙访问》，《翦伯赞历史论文选集》，人民出版社1980年版，第384页。

[5] 《元朝秘史》254节，译自原文。

[6] 《太宗本记》(一)，《元史》第11页。

[7] 李亚萨诺夫斯基著、青木太郎译《蒙古法基本原理》第29页。

[8] 赵珙《蒙鞑备录》，王国维笺证本，第25页。

[9] (台湾)哈勘楚伦《浅谈成吉思汗大雅萨法典》，《成吉思汗研究文集》(1949—1990)，内蒙古人民出版社1991年版。

[10] 《元史》卷146《耶律楚材传》。

[11] 王国维《长春真人西游记注》卷上，第22、23页。

[12] 内蒙古博物馆、锡林郭勒盟文物管理站《镶黄旗乌兰沟出土一批蒙元时期金器》，《内蒙古文物考古文集》第一辑，中国大百科全书出版社1994年版，第605页。

[13] 丁学芸《监国公主铜印与汪古部遗存》，《内蒙古文物考古》第3期。

[14] 夏荷秀、赵丰《达茂旗大苏吉乡明水墓地出土的丝织品》，《内蒙古文物考古》1992年1-2期，总第6-7期第113页。

[15] 李作智《呼和浩特市东郊出土的几件元代瓷器》，《内蒙古文物资料续辑》，1984年12月，第242页。

[16] 潘行荣《元集宁路故城出土的窖藏丝织物及其他》，《内蒙古文物资料续辑》，1984年12月，第237页。

# 草原帝国的繁荣—从蒙古汗国到大元一统
# *Prosperity of the Steppe Empire*
## *— From the Mongol Khan Empire to the Unification by the Yuan Dynasty*

黄雪寅 （内蒙古博物馆）
**Huang Xueyin** (Museum of Inner Mongolian Autonomous Region)

The Mongols date from the ancient Shiwei Tribe of the Donghu Family. "Shiwei" means dense forests in Mongolian. The Mongols lived in forests at that time and then spread to the broad steppe in order to explore a broader living space. Wooden coffins have been discovered both in the warrior tombs of Mongolian Shiwei of the 7th century in Hulunbeier Steppe, Inner Mongolia and in the No.1 graveyard of Xieertala in Hailaier, Inner Mongolia. Some coffins were covered with a layer of orderly birch barks. The burial objets include wooden bows, saddles, saddle-bridges and arrow sheaths made of birch barks. These discoveries fill in the missing link regarding the racial history from the 7th century to the 10th century in the archaeological study of Hulunbeier Steppe.

By the beginning of the 13th century, the Mongols had increased and diversified into great many tribes. In 1206, Tiemuzhen put an end to the 18-year Unification War and was made Great Khan by Mongol tribes at Han-nan River (Er-neng River) seminary and thus the Mongol Empire was created. Genghis Khan issued a code law named "*Da Zha Sa*" and formalized various administration systems with regard to military and politics for the Khan Empire, thus ended the state of steppe nomads without governance. The edict plaques and the waist plaques issued by him attest to his power. On a silver plaque with gilded Phaspa characters unearthed in Qingshuihe County, there are such inscriptions as "With the power of the ever-lasting sky, the Emperor has his inviolable name and all those who refuse to show respect and submission will be given the death punishment." This silver plaque is the best in quality of all the edict plaques that have been found up to now. The system of courier stations, established in the Mongolian reign stepped up transmittal of military and political messages in the Khan Empire. The copper plaque for night patrol inscribed in five different styled characters and unearthed in Keerqinyouyizhong Banner, Xing-an League has the character "*Yuan*" cast in the front center and "No.11 Night Patrol Plaque of *Tian Zi*" cast on the right side. With Phaspa characters, Uygur Mongolian characters, Chahetai (Arabian) characters, Tibetan characters and Chinese characters cast in relief on its surface, this plaque carries the largest number of different characters among all the unearthed plaques of the Yuan Dynasty. And it is one of the most precious relics reflecting the administration of courier stations in the Yuan Dynasty.

The rulers of Mongolian Yuan Dynasty accepted and assimilated Buddhism, Taoism, Christianity, Islam and other religions. The Islamic gravestone, Nestorian gravestone and Buddhist stone-carved incense burners unearthed in the Inner Mongolia region are the testimony to the free and acceptant attitudes of Mongolian rulers towards religions. Over one hundred topical letters written in Mongolian characters in the 13th century Uygur style which were discovered in the One-hundred-eye Grottoes in Zhungeer Banner, are precious relics for the study of the development of Mongolian characters. On a carved stone stele, unearthed from Ximengzhuanzi Mountain, is carved in low relief "*Wu Zi Deng Ke* painting" (five sons passed the imperial examination) expressing praise that their sons became imperial officials and thus allowing the whole family to become prosperous.

Due to the practice of secret burial, only a few graves of Mangolian nobles have been found. The gold stemcup, gold saddle and head dresses for female nobles, unearthed at the 13th century grave in Wulangou, Xianghuang Banner, Xilinguole League reflect the Mongolian lifestyles of that time. The *Nashi* robe unearthed from the grave in Minshuiwanggubu, Dasujie Township, Damao Banner, Baotou City is in a typical Mongolian style. However, the knitted patterns of a human head on a lion's body with an imperial crown on the head is unmistakably of the central Asian style and reflects the economic and cultural exchanges between the steppe and the West during the Mongolian reign. Another important artifact, namely the copper seal of the "Jian Kingdom Princess" who was related to Wanggu Tribe is a testimony to the fact that Alahaibieqi, Genghis Khan's third daughter, was married to the chieftain of Wanggu Tribe. Wanggu Tribe once played a crucial role in the war unifying various Mongolian tribes.

Genghis Khan granted him the power to rule five thousand families and also agreed with him that they should keep marriage alliances throughout generations.

After the unification by the Yuan Dynasty, the bounds between various tribal regimes were broken and the hostility and separation between the Han nationality and the northern nomadic peoples, which had lasted over hundreds of years since the Tang Dynasty, ended finally. Exchange and communication between various minority tribes became increasingly frequent. Along with the East-West trading volumes greatly increasing, a great many businessmen with fine artistic taste and foresight led the porcelain, jewelry, and gold & silver manufacturing industries to an imperial quality level. The incense burner with the "*Xiao Song Zi Zao*" (made by Xiao Song) mark unearthed at Baita Village in the eastern suburbs of Huhehaote features fine workmanship, reflects the superb artistic technique of the Jun wares and Longquan wares of the Yuan Dynasty. It is also ranked as one of the precious articles among the porcelains of the Yuan Dynasty.

Griffin is an animal in European mythology. A silk quilt cover woven with the pattern of griffin unearthed from the Yuan Dynasty's old city site at Jininglu, Tuchengzi, Wumengchayouqian Banner, testifies again to the cultural exchange between the East and West.

# 内蒙古文物考古精品

## Archaeological Finds from the Inner Mongolia Autonomous Region

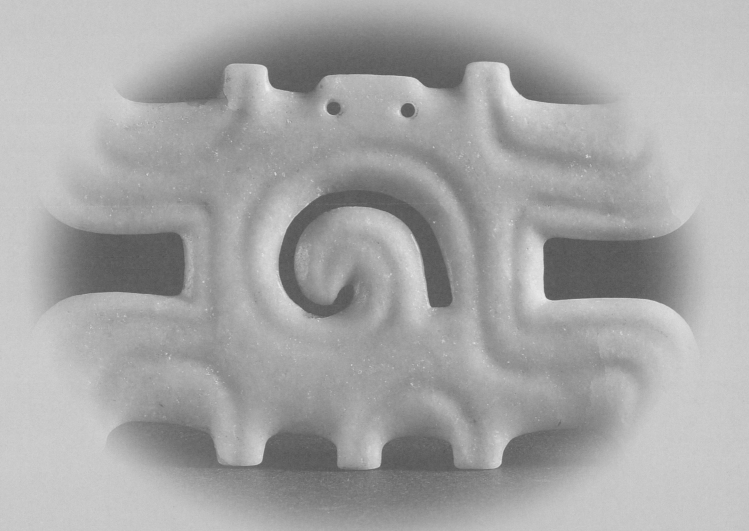

# 叩响草原文明的大门
## Ushering in the Era
## of the Steppe Civilization

内蒙古新石器时代的经济形态以原始农业为主，兼有采集、渔猎和家畜饲养业。其文化独立发展，相互影响，既保持自己的特色，又同周边地区尤其是中原地区有着密切的联系。

内蒙古境内发现的兴隆洼文化，是新石器时代早期的重要考古学文化，距今约八千年，其文化遗存中有我国目前年代最早的玉器；石雕女神像则开偶像崇拜之先河。红山文化发现的玉龙，是龙的最早造型，使"龙的传人"们追寻到了自己的根。先民们艰辛劳作，顽强生存，奏响了草原文明的序曲。

In the Neolithic age, the Inner Mongolian Autonomous Region was mainly an agricultural society combined with gathering, fishing, hunting and livestock raising. Its culture maintained its own characteristics, showing a tendency towards independent development, but also kept close contact with its neighbors, particularly the Central Plains, whom they mutually influenced.

Dating back to 8000 years ago, the Xinglongwa culture of Inner Mongolia was one of the archaeological cultures from the Neolithic age of ancient China, which had among others the oldest jade objects ever discovered in China and a stone carved goddess, the first example of idolatry. The jade dragon found from the Hongshan culture is the very first form of the dragon and is believed to be the root of descendants of the dragon. Through strenuous effort and perseverance, ancients finally stepped into the gate of steppe civilization.

## Jade *Jue*

Xinglongwa Culture, Neolithic Age (ca.6000 BC)

Diameter of one 2.9cm; diameter of the other 4.2 cm

Unearthed in 1989 from the ruins of Baiyinchanghan, Linxi County

Collection of the Archaeological Research Institute of Inner Mongolia

This green jade *jue*, with a soft and lustrous quality,
was made by drilling, carving and polishing.
These are the earliest jade pieces ever found
and are evidence of the beginning
of the jade reverence tradition.

## 玉玦

新石器时代兴隆洼文化（约公元前 6000 年）

直径 2.9 — 4.2 厘米

1989 年林西县白音长汗遗址出土

内蒙古文物考古研究所藏

青玉，材质莹润。

采用钻孔和切磋的加工方法制作。

是目前所见最早的玉器，

为崇玉风尚之先导。

## Jade Cicada

Xinglongwa Culture, Neolithic Age (ca.6000 BC)

Length 3.2 cm, width 1.8 cm

Unearthed in 1989 from the ruins of Baiyinchanghan, Linxi County

Collection of the Archaeological Research Institute of Inner Mongolia

Made by carving and polishing, this green jade cicada has a simple form. The front of the head protrudes out while two drilled round eyes are on the face. On the top portion of the tail there are three polished grooves. The back is semicircular and on the side there is a hole through the sides.

## 玉蝉

新石器时代兴隆洼文化（约公元前 6000 年）

长 3.2、宽 1.8 厘米

1989 年林西县白音长汗遗址出土

内蒙古文物考古研究所藏

青玉。采用琢磨工艺制作，造型古朴。

正面上端头部凸起，面部钻出两个圆眼，

尾部磨出三道凹槽，尾端微翘。

半圆形背部，侧面横穿一孔，可佩戴。

## Stone Pendant with Human Face Design

Xinglongwa Culture, Neolithic Age (ca.6000 BC)
Length 4 cm, width 3 cm
Unearthed in 1989 from the ruins of Baiyinchanghan, Linxi County
Collection of the Archaeological Research Institute of Inner Mongolia

This thin stone piece was carved and polished into
an oval shape from a reddish brown stone.
On the front, there are two carved eyes.
In the mouth, the teeth are inlaid with shells.
The ears have drilled holes.

## 人面形石佩饰

新石器时代兴隆洼文化（约公元前 6000 年）
长 4、宽 3 厘米
1989 年林西县白音长汗遗址出土
内蒙古文物考古研究所藏

红褐色石料磨制。
呈椭圆形片状。
正面上部磨刻出月牙形双眼，
嘴部镶嵌蚌壳制作的牙齿。
两侧耳部钻孔，可佩戴。

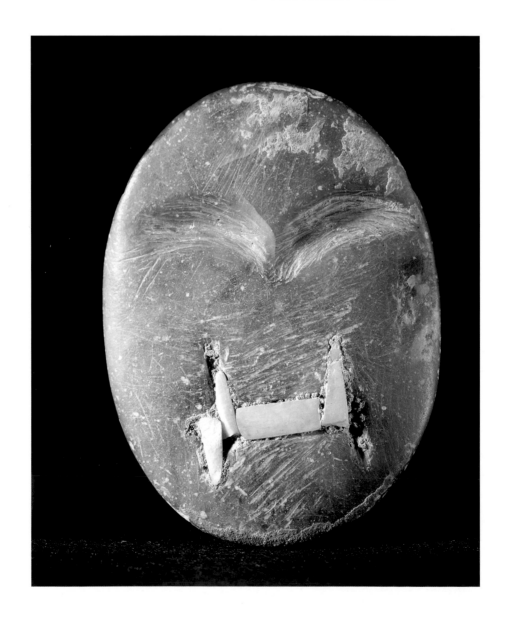

## Stone Carved Human Figure

Xinglongwa Culture, Neolithic Age (ca.6000 BC)

Length 16 cm, width 11.5 cm, height 35.5 cm

Unearthed in 1989 from the ruins of Baiyinchanghan, Linxi County

Collection of the Archaeological Research Institute of Inner Mongolia

This figure was made from a charcoal gray solid rock by hammering, chiseling and polishing. She has a pointed head with a protruding forehead and recessed eyes, a broad nose, prominent cheekbones and a jutting out mouth. She squats on her heels with her arms hang to the sides. The bottom was chiselled into a sharp point so it could stand in the ground. The swelling belly indicates the characteristics of a pregnant woman. This carving reflects the worship of goddesses in primitive society and was the beginning of primitive religion.

## 石雕人像

新石器时代兴隆洼文化（约公元前6000年）

长16、宽11.5、高35.5厘米

1989年林西县白音长汗遗址出土

内蒙古文物考古研究所藏

黑灰色硬质基岩制成。采用打、琢、磨制等加工技术。
颅顶尖削，前额突出，双眼深陷，鼻翼较宽，颧骨丰隆，
吻部略突，双臂下垂，作弓身蹲踞状。
下端打制加工成楔形。
微微隆起的腹部具备孕妇特征，
表现出原始氏族社会对裸体女像的崇拜，
即女神崇拜现象，开原始宗教之先河。

## Tubular-Shaped Pottery Jar

Xinglongwa Culture, Neolithic Age (ca.6000 BC)
Height 43 cm, diameter of mouth 43 cm, and of base 22 cm
Unearthed in 1989 from the ruins of Baiyinchanghan, Linxi County
Collection of the Archaeological Research Institute of Inner Mongolia

This sandy gray pottery jar has a mustard color outside and a charcoal color inside. The straight-flared wall connects to the flat bottom. The jar has three sections of decorative patterns. Nine bands of groove bow-string patterns decorate below the rim. One third of the body has a raised band with geometrical entwined patterns against vertically impressed lines. The zigzag patterns are impressed on the lower body of the jar.

## 筒形陶罐

新石器时代兴隆洼文化（约公元前 6000 年）
高 43、口径 43、底径 22 厘米
1989 年林西县白音长汗遗址出土
内蒙古文物考古研究所藏

夹砂灰陶，外壁黄褐色，内壁黑色。
外迭圆方唇，直壁外敞，平底。
三段式施纹方法，口沿下饰九道凹弦纹，
器壁三分之一处施一周附加堆纹带，在堆纹带上先压印平行折线，然后再压划交叉波折纹，
腹壁饰篦点式人字纹。

## Cloud-Shaped Jade Pendant

Hongshan Culture, Neolithic Age (ca.4000 BC)
Length 18.2 cm, width 10.9 cm, thickness 0.4 cm
Unearthed in 1981 from Narisitai, Bayanhansumu, Balinyou Banner
Collection of the Balinyou Banner Museum

This white jade pendant,
in a rectangular shape, was made by carving and polishing.
Four up-turned horns are on the four corners and an openwork design
of a curling cloud pattern in the center.
On the center of the upper rim there are two drilled holes. It is a fairly
large jade carving compared to similar objects found in the region.

## 勾云形玉佩

新石器时代红山文化（公元前 4000 年）
长 18.2、宽 10.9、厚 0.4 厘米
1981 年巴林右旗巴彦汉苏木那日斯台遗址出土
巴林右旗博物馆藏

黄白色玉，采用琢磨工艺制作。
略呈长方形，中心镂空，
作勾云形盘卷，外四角勾卷。
上缘中间有钻孔两个，可系绳佩戴。
是目前所见同类器中较大的一件。

## Jade Pig-dragon

Hongshan Culture, Neolithic Age (ca.4000 BC)
Height 16.8 cm, width 11.5 cm, thickness 2.8 cm
Collected in 1974 from E'ergenwusu at Yangchang Village, Balinyou Banner
Collection of the Balinyou Banner Museum

This dark green jade piece, made by carving and polishing,
is curled into a ball shape and has a head of pig, a dragon body,
a raised forehead and two upright ears.
The two round eyes are carved below the ears.
Grooved lines outline the lips and nose on the protruding jaw.
There is a drilled hole on the neck.

## 玉猪龙

新石器时代红山文化（公元前 4000 年）
通高 16.8、宽 11.5、厚 2.8 厘米
1974 年巴林右旗羊场乡额尔根勿苏村征集
巴林右旗博物馆藏

墨绿色玉，采用琢磨工艺制作。
整体呈卷屈状，首尾相接。
猪首，额头隆起，两个圆弧形耳直竖，
耳下雕出圆眼，下颌部前伸，
磨刻阴线勾出双唇、鼻子。颈部有一穿孔。

## Yellow Jade Dragon

Hongshan Culture, Neolithic Age (ca.4000 BC)
Length 17 cm
Collected in 1986 from Huanggutun at Guangdegong Village,
Wengniute Banner
Collection of the Wengniute Banner Museum

This dragon was carved and polished smoothly from a yellow jade.
The body is curved into a semcircular shape.
It has a jutting pig mouth, pretty eyes and curly hair on the neck,
which make this piece good for eyes. It is a symbol of totemism or
power of the primitive ancestors.

## 黄玉龙

新石器时代红山文化（公元前 4000 年）
长 17 厘米
1986 年翁牛特旗广德公乡黄谷屯征集
翁牛特旗博物馆藏

黄玉，龙身光洁，蜷曲如勾，
龙首作猪嘴形，长吻修目，
颈后鬃毛翻卷，
给人以飘逸的美感。
是原始先民们图腾或权利的象征。

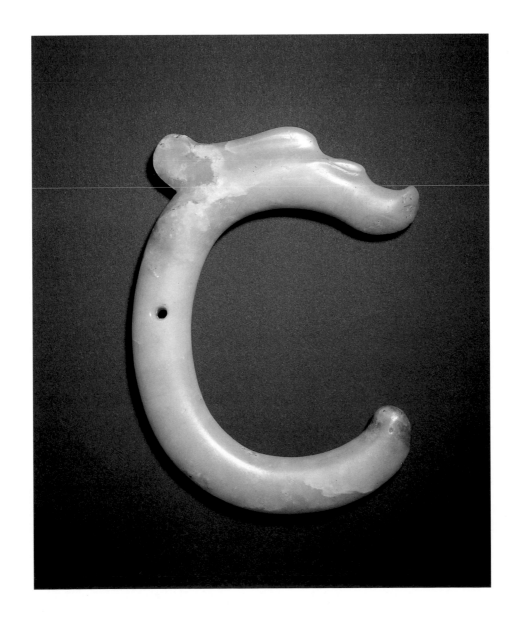

## Jade Owl

Hongshan Culture, Neolithic Age (ca.4000 BC)
Length 6.1 cm, diameter 6 cm, thickness 1.8 cm
Unearthed in 1981 from Narisitai, Bayanhansumu, Balinyou Banner
Collection of the Balinyou Banner Museum

This yellowish white jade owl,
made by carving and polishing,
has a pair of bulging eyes and a flat triangular mouth with its wings
spreading out. This bird is in the vertical climbing position.
It has a fat chest and bulging belly. On the flat back, spacing at the head
and under the wings, there are three pairs of holes.

## 玉鸮

新石器时代红山文化（公元前4000年）
通长6.1、直径6、厚1.8厘米
1981年巴林右旗巴彦汉苏木那日斯台遗址出土
巴林右旗博物馆藏

黄白色玉，采用琢磨工艺制作。

一对圆眼外凸，嘴呈扁三角形突起，

舒展双翅与肩齐平，展尾作攀附状，胸腹微鼓。

背面平直，在头部和两翼胁下

有交插钻孔三对，可佩挂。

## Painted Pottery Jar in the Shape of a Pig's Head

Xiaoheyan Culture, Neolithic Age (ca.3000 BC)
Height 18.6 cm, diameter of mouth 8.2 — 10.2 cm, and of Base 8.5 cm
Collected in 1985 from Sifendicun at Honghuagou Town,
Songshan District, Chifeng City
Collection of the Chifeng Municipal Antique Store

This red pottery jar has an oblate and bulging belly,
flat foot and a pair of loop ears on both sides.
Geometric patterns decorate the entire body,
outlined in dark brown and in between filled with red.
The jar is in the shape of a pig's head.
Its mouth is the opening of the jar.
It has two wide-open eyes.
Above the mouth are two flared nostrils and two ears.

## 猪首形彩陶罐

新石器时代小河沿文化（约公元前 3000 年）
高 18.6、口径 8.2 — 10.2、底径 8.5 厘米
1985 年赤峰市松山区红花沟镇四分地村征集
赤峰市文物店藏

泥质红陶。呈扁圆菱形、鼓腹、平足，
腹部有对称贯耳。通体以几何纹装饰，
黑褐色勾勒轮廓，红色填绘。
整体造型为猪首形，罐口作猪嘴状张开，
眼睛圆睁，口上部凸起处饰有两只鼻孔，
腹上部贴塑双耳。

# 大漠深处竞风流
## Competition for Leadership in the Depth of the Steppe

进入青铜器时代，畜牧经济已在农业的基础上发展起来，"马背上的民族"由此形成。这一变化过程大约发生于商周时期。兴盛于黄河两岸的早期鄂尔多斯青铜文化、发现于赤峰地区的夏家店上层文化是这种变化的杰出代表。

当时活动于这一地区主要是匈奴和东胡等系统的部族，他们逐鹿于北疆，并与中原地区保持着密切的交往。游牧民族的迅速壮大，丰富了古代中国的文化内涵，改变了中国和北方世界的历史格局。

By the Bronze Age, there was a separation between agriculture and animal husbandry. Those nationalities engaged in animal husbandry became nomadic and "the Nationality on the Horseback" came into being. This change happened approximately during the Shang and Zhou dynasties in the northern steppes. Both the early Ordus bronze culture which flourished along the banks of the Huanghe River and the Xiajiadian upper culture, discovered in Chifeng area, represent such remarkable changes.

Living and working around in this region were mainly the Xiongnu and Donghu tribes who fought for the supremacy in the northern border areas while keeping close contact with the Central Plains. The rapid rising of the nomadic nationalities enriched the cultural significance of ancient China and fundamentally changed the historical structure of China and the Northern world.

# 匈奴

　　匈奴是内蒙古西部地区最早见诸史籍的游牧民族,崛起于殷周时期,驰骋在大漠南北,汉初称雄草原,与中原王朝有密切的接触,"胡汉和亲,昭君出塞"成为千古佳话。其金属手工业以制作工艺的精美和表现动物生存竞争的主题著称于世。

# *Xiongnu*

The Xiongnu nationality, the earliest nomadic recorded in the historical documentation, emerged during the Shang and Zhou dynasties and resided in the western Inner Mongolia Autonomous Region. The Xiongnu dominated the vast steppe in the early Han and established a close relation with the imperial court of the Central Plains. "By marrying Wang Zhaojun, a beautiful daughter of the Han imperial family, to the Xiongnu prince, Hu (Xiongnu) and Han established good relations," that became a much-told tale through the age. The finely made metal works with meticulous animal patterns of the Xiongnu are world famous.

## Bronze Dagger

Early Shang Dynasty (16th — 15th centuries BC)

Length 24.6 cm

Unearthed in 1980 from the ruins of Zhukaigou, Yijinhuoluo Banner

Collection of the Archaeological Research Institute of Inner Mongolia

The end of the hilt is almost in a circular form.

The oblate hilt has grooves for binding hemp rope.

The cross guard stretches upward to sides.

The blade is straight and lozenge shape in cross-section.

This dagger is made in a simple and unsophisticated shape,
compact and light in weight.

This is one of the earlier bronze daggers of the Ordos.

## 环首青铜短剑

商代早期（公元前 16 世纪—前 15 世纪）

通长 24.6 厘米

1980 年伊金霍洛旗朱开沟墓葬出土

内蒙古文物考古研究所藏

剑柄首近似环状，扁柄中间有两道凹槽，外面缠绕麻绳。

剑格呈舌状向两侧斜突。

剑身两侧刃稍直，剖面呈菱形。

整体造型古朴，器形短小、轻薄。

时代相当于商代早期，

是目前发现的鄂尔多斯式青铜短剑中年代较早的一件。

## Bronze Knife with a Ring Pommel

Early Shang Dynasty (16th — 15th centuries BC)

Length of knife 34.1 cm, and of hilt 10.5 cm

Unearthed in 1980 from the ruins of Zhukaigou, Yijinhuoluo Banner

Collection of the Archaeological Research Institute of Inner Mongolia

The curved hilt ends with a ring.
The hilt is concave in the middle and divided in the center by a thin
engraved line. Between the blade and
the hilt there is a tooth-shaped cross guard.
The knife has a slightly concave back.
The tip of the sword is upturned. The blade is long and thin.
This is one of the earliest bronze knives ever found of the Ordos culture .

## 环首青铜刀

商代早期（公元前 16 世纪—前 15 世纪）

通长 34.1、柄长 10.5 厘米

1980 年伊金霍洛旗朱开沟墓葬出土

内蒙古文物考古研究所藏

环状首，扁柄向一侧稍弯曲，

中间凹，两侧起棱。

柄、刃间有突出的齿状阑，刀背微凹，

刀尖上翘。刀身细长轻薄。

是目前发现的鄂尔多斯式青铜刀中年代较早的一件。

## Bronze *Ge* with Tiger Design

Early Shang Dynasty (16th — 15th centuries BC)
Length 28.5 cm, length of blade 21 cm
Unearthed in 1980 from the ruins of Zhukaigou, Yijinhuoluo Banner
Collection of the Archaeological Research Institute of Inner Mongolia

This bronze has a long blade slightly raised in the middle. Between the straight tang and blade there is the cross guard. The end of the tang is decorated with curved nose and crescent-shaped-eye tiger disign. Between the cross guard and the tang some of the wood has rotted. It has a regular and standard shape with exquisite decorative designs.

## 虎纹青铜直内戈

商代早期（公元前 16 世纪—前 15 世纪）
通长 28.5、援长 21 厘米
1980 年伊金霍洛旗朱开沟墓葬出土
内蒙古文物考古研究所藏

长援，中脊稍凸，上下阑外突。

直内，尾端装饰虎头纹，卷鼻，月牙形眼。

阑和内之间遗有朽木。

整体造型规范，装饰讲究。

## Eagle Shaped Gold Crown

Late Warring States Period (ca.3rd century BC)
Height 7.1 cm, diameter 16.5 cm
Unearthed in 1972 from Aluchaideng, Amenqirige Village,
Hangjin Banner
Collection of the Inner Mongolia Museum

This crown was cast by molds in relief. The finial is in an eagle shape. The eagle stands on the dome with wings fully stretched. The head and neck, made of turquoise and gold leaves sewn together with gold thread, are movable. The hollow tail can be inserted with real feathers. The dome is carved with a design of four groups of wolves combating with sheep. The crown band, made up of gold bars with cord patterns, connects to each other with vertical tendons. On both ends of the band are animal patterns of reclined tigers, sheep and horses. This is the only complete crown of the Hu minority so it is a masterpiece of the Xiongnu.

## 鹰形金冠饰

战国晚期（约公元前 3 世纪）
通高 7.1、直径 16.5 厘米
1972 年杭锦旗阿门其日格乡阿鲁柴登出土
内蒙古博物馆藏

模铸浮雕。由冠顶和冠带两部分组成。
鹰形冠顶饰，一只展翅雄鹰立于半球形面上，
球面浅浮雕四组狼与羊咬斗的图案。
鹰的头、颈部由绿松石和金片串联构成，尾部中空可插羽毛，
并以一条金丝由头至尾穿连，头尾活动自如。
冠带由绳索状金条组成，前后上下有榫铆插合，带的两侧各装饰有卧虎、羊、马等动物纹。这是目前发现唯一完整的"胡冠"标本，属于匈奴王冠之精品。

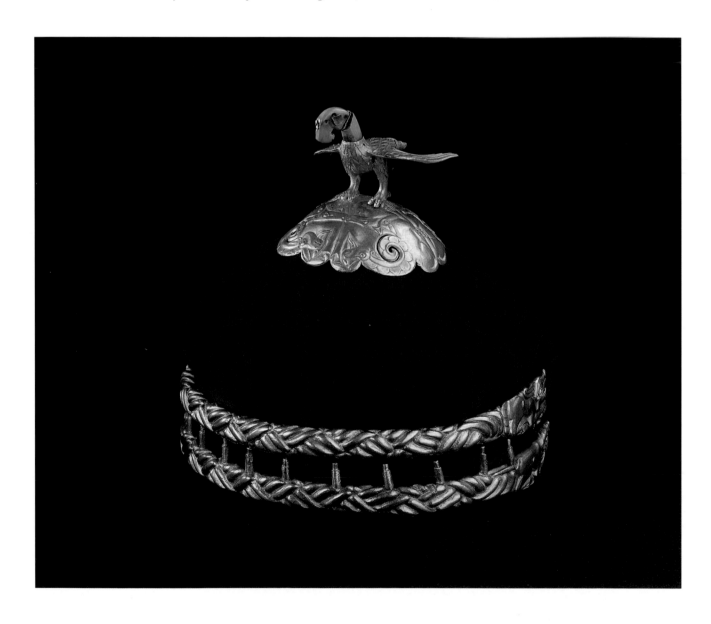

## Pair of Gold Belt Ornaments

Late Warring States Period (ca.3rd century BC)

Length 4.2 cm, width 3.4 cm

Unearthed in 1972 from Aluchaideng, Amenqirige Village, Hangjin Banner

Collection of the Inner Mongolia Museum

This pair of ornaments was made by casting in relief.
The motif of this piece is reclining tigers. The tiger has wide-open eyes,
perked ears and scrunched legs with hooked paws.
There are seven rubies and emeralds inlaid on the body.
There are eight birds over the tiger from its head to its tail.
On the back of the ornaments there are two arched knobs on both sides.
This is the decorative section of the Hu belt.

## 虎鸟纹金带饰

战国晚期（约公元前 3 世纪）

长 4.2、宽 3.4 厘米

1972 年杭锦旗阿门其日格乡阿鲁柴登出土

内蒙古博物馆藏

模铸浮雕。

主题图案为卧虎纹，四肢前屈、钩状爪。

虎瞪目露齿，耳前倾，虎身嵌红、绿宝石七块；

由头至尾排列八只鸟纹，鸟身呈"S"形。

背面两端各有一拱形钮，

为"胡带"之装饰构件。

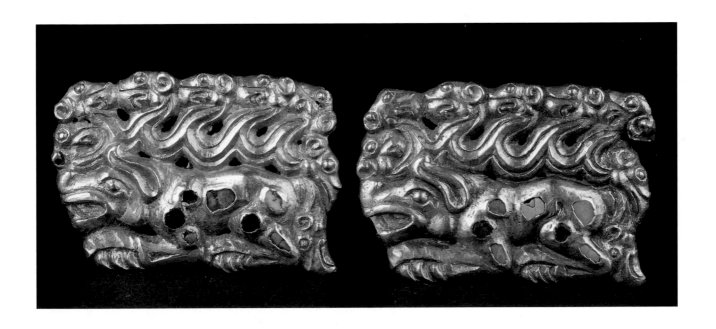

## Gold Plaque

Late Warring States Period (ca.3rd century BC)

Length 12.7 cm, width 7.4 cm, weight 203.8 g.

Unearthed in 1972 from Aluchaideng, Amenqirige Village, Hangjin Banner

Collection of the Inner Mongolia Museum

This is a cast rectangular plaque in relief.
The piece is bordered with string design. An ox is fighting off tigers.
Sitting in the center with four legs stretched out,
the ox is surrounded by four tigers looking at each other and biting at
the neck and belly of the ox. The ox stubbornly resists the attack
and has thrust its horn into the ears of the tiger biting its neck.
There are holes in each corner and raised knobs at each side of the back.
This piece is the main part of the center piece of a typical Hu belt.

## 虎咬牛纹金饰牌

战国晚期（约公元前 3 世纪）

长 12.7、宽 7.4 厘米 重 203.8 克

1972 年杭锦旗阿门其日格乡阿鲁柴登出土

内蒙古博物馆藏

模铸浮雕。长方形，边框饰绳索纹，
框内浮雕牛虎咬斗图案。牛居中，俯卧，四肢平伸，
两侧四只虎两两相对，分别咬住牛的颈部和腹部，
牛头微昂作奋力挣扎状，双角刺穿虎耳。
虎牛搏斗的场面难分难解。饰牌四角各有缀孔，
背面两端各有一拱形钮。出土时两件为一组，
一件有钩挂穿孔，为"胡带"之主要构件。

## Pair of Gold Earrings Inlaid with Turquoise

Late Warring States Period (ca.3rd century BC)

Length 8.2 cm

Unearthed in 1972 from Aluchaideng, Amenqirige Village, Hangjin Banner

Collection of the Inner Mongolia Museum

This pair of earrings is composed of rings and eardrops.
The thin gold thread mount to a ring connects
the oval turquoise.
Gold beads in a plum flower design are welded
on the top and bottom of the turquoise bead.
Three movable gold leaves hang at the end of the earrings.

## 镶绿松石金耳坠

战国晚期（约公元前 3 世纪）

长 8.2 厘米

1972 年杭锦旗阿门其日格乡阿鲁柴登出土

内蒙古博物馆藏

耳坠由环和坠两部分缀联而成。
细金丝盘绕成环，下连耳坠。
耳坠上部为椭圆形绿松石珠，
上下包金焊饰梅花珠，
下连三片金叶，活动自如。

## Group of Pendants
### (necklace, belt ornament and ring)

Late Spring and Autumn Period (ca. 5th century BC)
Bronze plaque with tiger design: length 10.7 cm, width 6.1 cm
Bronze plaque with double bird design: length 5 cm, width 3 cm
Unearthed in 1979 from a tomb at Maoqinggou, Liangcheng County
Collection of the Archaeological Research Institute of Inner Mongolia

This is a group of pendants: a necklace of assorted beads,
belt ornaments consisting of two bronze plaques with tiger designs
and double-bird design. The tiger design is clearly incised in an
unsophisticated shape. The double-bird plaque is engraved with a
deformed cloud and bird pattern. On the back of the plaque there is a
knob in the center. Burying daily garments, weapons and utensils
with the deceased was a feature of the northern nationalities and
represents the social status of the owner.

佩饰（项饰、腰带饰、链环）

春秋晚期（约公元前 5 世纪）
一组。虎纹铜饰牌长 10.7、宽 6.1 厘米
双鸟纹铜饰牌长 5、宽 3 厘米
1979 年凉城县毛庆沟墓地出土
内蒙古文物考古研究所藏

主要有各种料珠组成项饰，虎纹和双鸟纹铜饰牌所组成的
腰带饰及链环等。虎纹铜饰牌整体扁平，正面阴刻出虎的轮
廓。双鸟纹铜饰牌正面阴刻变形成云纹的鸟纹，背面中间有
穿钮。随葬生前佩戴的服饰品及兵器、工具等，是北方民族
特有的葬俗，特别是金、铜、铁动物纹饰牌组成的腰带饰更
独具特征，并具有身份标示作用。

## Bronze Chariot Fitting

Warring States Period (475 — 221 BC)

Length 19.5 cm, diameter of socket 5.8 cm

Collected in 1974 from Yulongtai, Zhungeer Banner

Collection of the Inner Mongolia Museum

This cast bronze ram-head has a pair of curved horns curling forward.

Its mouth is opened as if it were crying.

Its head is raised and eyes are wide opened.

The neck of the ram extends to become the socket for the chariot post.

Three holes in the socket were probably used to attach

the fitting to the post. The piece has an abrasive underside.

## 盘角羊首青铜辕饰

战国（公元前 475 年—前 221 年）

通长 19.5、銎内径 5.8 厘米

1974 年准格尔旗玉隆太征集

内蒙古博物馆藏

模铸浮雕。

盘羊首，双角向前盘卷至两颊，昂首远眺，口微张，

似鸣叫状；颈向后延伸成圆形銎，

銎上有钉孔三个，銎下侧有磨痕。

铸造精巧，形象逼真，

是一件融艺术与实用为一体的青铜珍品。

## Chariot Finial

Late Warring States Period (ca.3rd century BC)
Length 24 cm
Collected in 1962 from Waertugou, Zhungeer Banner
Collection of the Inner Mongolia Museum

This is a cast bronze chariot finial.

The crane has a long bill curved downward,
with eyes wide open.

Its neck has a hollow socket for chariot post.

Holes on the socket were used to attach it to the post.

## 鹤头形青铜竿头饰

战国晚期（约公元前 3 世纪）
通长 24 厘米
1962 年准格尔旗瓦尔吐沟征集
内蒙古博物馆藏

模铸浮雕。

鹤头长喙向下弯曲，双目圆睁。

长颈弯曲，中空成銎，

銎侧内有钉孔，用以固柲。

## Pair of Crouching Bronze Deer

Late Warring States Period (ca.3rd century BC)
The highest point 7.7 — 8 cm
Unearthed in 1962 from a hoard at Sujigou, Zhungeer Banner
Collection of the Inner Mongolia Museum

The cast bronze deer crouch with their heads raised high,
eyes looking into the distance and ears perked.
The male deer has a well-defined chest and legs.
The horns branch into several sections arched to the back.
This piece was cast by the piece-mold casting method.
It features the artistic characteristics of the Mongol nationalities.

## 蹲踞状青铜鹿

战国晚期（约公元前 3 世纪）
最高 7.7 — 8 厘米
1962 年准格尔旗速机沟窖藏出土
内蒙古博物馆藏

模铸浮雕。
均呈蹲踞状，四肢内屈，鹿昂首，
双目远眺，竖耳静听，胸、臀部肥硕，细腰、短尾。
雄鹿，双角分成数枝，后伸近臀。
采用分范合铸的铸造工艺，造型生动逼真，
具有浓郁的草原游牧民族艺术特征。

**Bronze *Fu* (food vessel)**

Western Han Dynasty (206 BC — AD 8)

Height 15.8 cm

Collected in 1974 from Yikezhao League Region

Collection of the Archaeological Research Institute of Inner Mongolia

This piece, piece-mold cast,
has a flared mouth and a ball-shaped belly supported
by an openwork trumpet-shaped circular foot.
The square handle was cast on the rim with a curved edge.
Prominent double straight lines decorate under
the handle and around the upper belly.
This is a typical daily utensil of the nomadic nationalities
of the Northern Steppe.

双耳圈足青铜镙

西汉（公元前 206 年—公元 8 年）

通高 15.8 厘米

1974 年伊克昭盟地区征集

内蒙古文物考古研究所藏

合范铸造。

敛口，球形腹，下接镂空喇叭形圈足，

口沿上铸扁平方形双耳。

耳部两侧边凸棱呈弧形下延，

双耳下和腹上部饰双道凸棱折线。

为北方草原民族特有的生活器皿。

## Flat-Back Bronze Pot

Qin — Western Han dynasties (221 BC — AD 8)
Height 48 cm
Unearthed in 1975 from the city ruins of Qinhan Guangyan,
Zhungeer Banner
Collection of the Inner Mongolia Museum

This piece has a straight mouth,
a square rim, a thin neck and round shoulders.
One side of the belly bulges out and the other side is flat.
It is supported by a semicircular foot.
On the shoulders and belly are two pairs of symmetrical belt loops.
This unique shaped piece is a suitable utensil for nomadic life.

## 穿带青铜背壶

秦—西汉（公元前 221 年—公元 8 年）
高 48 厘米
1975 年准格尔旗秦汉广衍故城出土
内蒙古博物馆藏

直口，方唇、细颈、溜肩，
圆腹一侧外凸，另一侧扁平，半圆形圈足。
肩、腹各有对称穿钮两对，便于穿系携带。
此壶造型独特，
是适用于游牧生活的器皿。

**Ivory Ruler**

Western Han Dynasty (206 BC — AD 8)

Length 22.9 cm, width 2.3 cm

Unearthed in 1992 from a tomb at Nalintaohai, Dengkou County

Collection of the Archaeological Research Institute of Inner Mongolia

This is a ground ivory ruler.

At one end there is a pierced hole.

On both faces there are ink painted scales with cloud,

saw tooth and net patterns in red and green colors.

Scales are even cut on both sides.

It is exquisitely made.

象牙尺

西汉（公元前206年—公元8年）

长22.9、宽2.3厘米

1992年磴口县纳林套海汉墓出土

内蒙古文物考古研究所藏

象牙磨制。

一端有穿孔。正反两面均用墨线绘出刻度。

尺间饰以云气纹、锯齿纹、网纹等，添以红、绿彩，

两侧面也标有刻度。

制作精巧，既实用又美观。

## Tomb Stele

The third year of the Jianning reign of the Eastern Han Dynasty (AD 170)
Length of the remain part 73 cm, width 48 cm, thickness 16 cm
Unearthed in 1993 from the tomb at Zhaowancun, Huanghe Ranch,
Southern Suburbs of Baotou City
Collection of the Archaeological Research Institute of Inner Mongolia

This stele was made from one piece of solid stone.
There are eighty-seven characters in nine lines carved
not only regularly and formally but also clearly and completely.
This is the first Han stele with dates ever found in Inner Mongolia.
The script style belongs to the official style of the Han,
which was the beginning of the tablet style.
This is a very rare masterpiece.

## 建宁三年墓碑

东汉建宁三年（公元170年）
残长73、宽48、厚16厘米
1993年包头市南郊黄河乳牛场召湾村墓葬出土
内蒙古文物考古研究所藏

青石制。
碑文阴刻隶书，现存9行87字，字体规整，端庄稳健。
此碑是内蒙古地区首次发现有明确纪年的汉代墓碑，
碑文基本完整，字迹清晰。
字体既具汉隶风格，又开魏碑之先河，
是一件难得的书法精品，为书法史研究提供了珍贵资料。

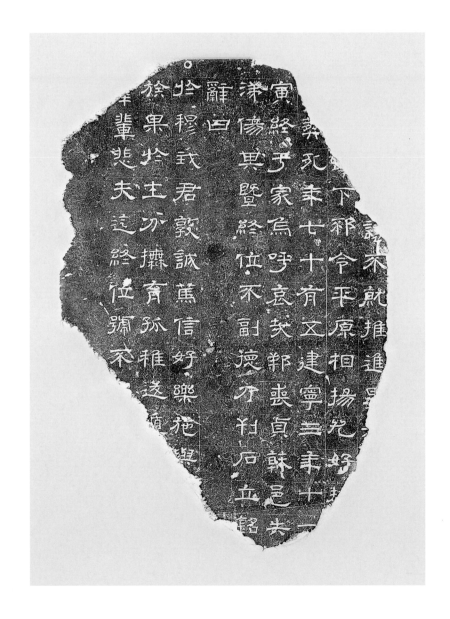

## Epitaph for the Prefecture Governor of Liang Zhou

The second year of the Longsheng reign, Xia (AD 408)

Length of edge 54 cm, thickness 5 cm

Unearthed in 1992 from a tomb at Guoliangcun, Nalinhe Village, Wushen Banner

Collection of the Archaeological Research Institute of Inner Mongolia

The inscriptions were carved on the dark gray brick in official script with fifty-three characters in six lines. The inscription records the occupant of the tomb, General Tianming's life and career. Tianming died in the second year of the Da Xia reign. Based on written documents, the Xiongnu chief, Helianbobo established the Xia State. He then changed the name of the state to Longsheng. Therefore, "the second year of the Da Xia" is the same as the second year of Longsheng, which is the year AD 408.

## 凉州剌史墓志

夏龙昇二年（公元 408 年）

边长 54、厚 5 厘米

1992 年乌审旗纳林河乡郭梁村墓葬出土

内蒙古文物考古研究所藏

志文镌刻于方形青砖之上。阴刻隶书，6 行 53 字，记述墓主人田哭将军的卒年及历任官职。

田哭卒于大夏二年。据史书记载，匈奴族首领赫连勃勃于 407 年建立大夏国，建号大夏，改元龙昇。"大夏二年"，即龙昇二年（公元 408 年）。大夏国史书记载甚少，此墓志为大夏国历史研究提供了珍贵资料。

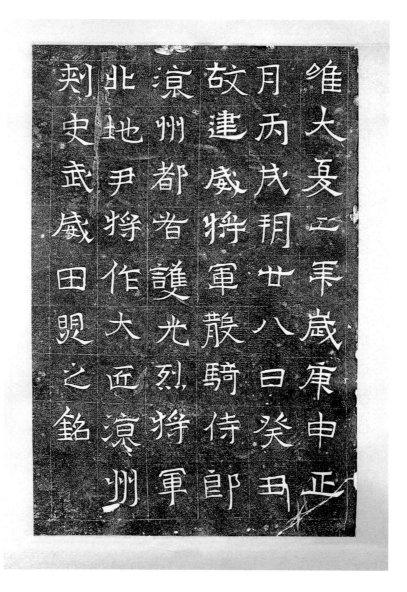

# 东胡

　　东胡是内蒙古东部地区最早见之于史籍的部族，出现于商周时期，春秋战国之际进入鼎盛时期。其独具鲜明民族特色的王权礼器、军事器械、生活器皿和车马行具等物件，将草原青铜文明推向了顶峰。

# *Donghu*

Donghu, active in the eastern area of Inner Mongolia Autonomous Region, rose to power in the Shang and Zhou dynasties and flourished during the Spring and Autumn period to the Warring States. They were the earliest tribe officially recorded in historical materials. Various imperial ritual vessels, weapons and armors, daily utensils, horse and chariot fittings, with distinguishing characteristics, raised the steppe bronze culture to its new height.

## Bronze Dagger with Deer Pattern Hilt

Spring and Autumn Period (770 — 476 BC)

Length 26 cm

Unearthed in 1993 from Xiaoheishigou Site, Ningcheng County

Collection of the Archaeological Research Institute of Inner Mongolia

The hilt is in a straight line with a hole at the end. There is a design of a reclined buck with horns on one side of the hilt and another design of three does without horns on the other side. On the cross guard is a rectangular spiral design. There is a recess part between the cross guard and blade. The straight blade has two grooves in the center.

## 鹿纹柄青铜短剑

春秋（公元前 770 年—前 476 年）

通长 26 厘米

1993 年宁城县小黑石沟遗址出土

内蒙古文物考古研究所藏

柄首近一字形，中间有穿孔。

扁平柄，一面饰枝状角雄性卧鹿三只，

另一面饰无角半蹲踞雌鹿三只。一字形格上饰回曲纹，

格与剑体间有凹缺，中间饰折线纹。

直刃，柱状脊上有两道细槽沟。

# Bronze Dagger with a Gold Ring

Spring and Autumn Period (770 — 476 BC)

Length 29 cm

Unearthed in 1998 from Xiaoheishigou Site, Ningcheng County

Collection of the Archaeological Research Institute of Inner Mongolia

The end of the hilt is almost in a straight line

with a hole and a gold ring.

The oblate and straight hilt has a cross guard.

Between the cross guard and the blade there is a recess part.

The gold ring on the dagger makes it precious and valuable.

## 金环饰青铜短剑

春秋（公元前 770 年—前 476 年）

通长 29 厘米

1998 年宁城县小黑石沟遗址出土

内蒙古文物考古研究所藏

柄首近一字形，

中间有穿孔，孔内穿套金环。

扁平直柄，一字形格，

格与剑体连接处有凹缺，直刃。

造型简洁规整，尤饰以金环弥足珍贵。

# Bronze Short Sword with Animal Pattern

Spring and Autumn Period (770 — 476 BC)

Length 28.5 cm

Unearthed in 1975 from Xiaoheishigou Site, Ningcheng County

Collection of the Chifeng Municipal Museum

The end of the sword hilt is decorated with a double-bird design. The two birds are joint together back to back. The oblate hilt is decorated with four groups of crouched lizard patterns. The animal has its four paws with curved claws stretched forward, its tail pointed downward and the whole body with a circle pattern. Both ends of the cross guard are cast with bird heads. The blade is straight and along its middle there are ten bear-like animals with long mouths, short tails and circle patterns on the bodies.

## 动物纹青铜短剑

春秋（公元前 770 年—前 476 年）

通长 28.5 厘米

1975 年宁城县小黑石沟遗址出土

赤峰市博物馆藏

剑柄端铸相背联结的双鸟头，
扁平柄部装饰四组相对呈蹲踞状似豹形的动物纹，
四肢前屈、环状爪、长尾下垂、身饰重圈纹。
剑格两端亦铸双鸟头，中间饰纹与柄部相似。
剑身两侧直刃，中间脊部饰十只呈伫立状似熊的动物纹，
长吻、短尾、身饰重圈纹。
此剑制作精细、造型别致，为同时期短剑中之珍品。

## Bronze Short Sword with T-Shaped Hilt

Spring and Autumn Period (770 — 476 BC)

Length 41.5cm

Unearthed in 1985 from Xiaoheishigou Site, Ningcheng County

Collection of the Ningcheng County Museum

The hilt and blade were cast together but clearly separated
by a trumpet cross guard.

The oval pommel cast for extra weight has three curved ridges.

The lute-shaped blade has a central ridge.

Turquoise stones are inlaid on the cross guard and pommel.

This is the most exquisitely cast piece among the similar swords.

## T 形柄曲刃青铜短剑

春秋（公元前 770 年—前 476 年）

通长 41.5 厘米

1985 年宁城县小黑石沟遗址出土

宁城县博物馆藏

剑柄和剑身联铸，柄筒分段明显，
下部喇叭状剑格与剑身相联。
上部椭圆形盘联铸半圆形加重器，上饰三道弧形脊棱。
剑身两侧刃弧曲，节尖明显。
柱状脊起棱，格与盘上镶嵌绿松石。
整体宽厚，铸造精良，为同类器中的精品。

# Bronze Short Sword with Human Figures

Spring and Autumn Period (770 — 476 BC)

Total length 31.6 cm, length of the hilt 10 cm

Unearthed in 1958 from Nanshangen Site, Ningcheng County

Collection of the Inner Mongolia Museum

The hilt was cast with two human figures one male and one female. The nude man figure has his hands on his belly. The reverse bears a nude woman with her arms crossed over her breasts. The lute shaped blade bears a central ridge with three incised lines. The cross guard is straight. This exquisitely made, thick and heavy bodied piece is the best sword with a curved blade.

## 立人柄曲刃青铜短剑

春秋（公元前 770 年—前 476 年）

通长 31.6、柄长 10 厘米

1958 年宁城县南山根遗址出土

内蒙古博物馆藏

剑柄铸成圆雕男女裸体立人像，男性两臂下垂，
双手护小腹；女性曲臂，双手交叉于胸前，
耳、肩下方两侧各有两长方形横穿。护手近似一字形。
剑身两侧刃弧曲，节尖位于中间，柱状脊上有三道棱线。
整体厚重，铸造精良，是曲刃剑中的珍品。
以裸体立人作装饰，说明使用者有特殊身份，
可能与部族信仰或宗教礼仪有关。

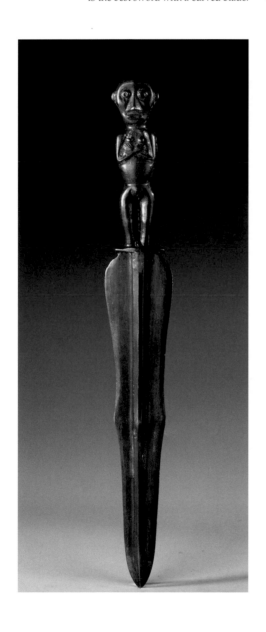

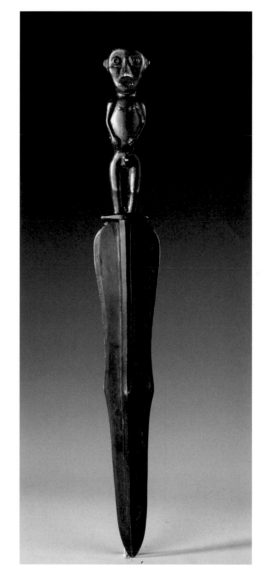

## Bronze Knife with Gold Animal Pommel

Spring and Autumn Period (770 — 476 BC)
Length 28.8 cm
Unearthed in 1998 from Xiaoheishigou Site, Ningcheng County
Collection of the Archaeological Research Institute of Inner Mongolia

The end of the hilt connects to a semicircular
gold decoration of two openwork animals.
There is a pierced hole at the end.
The blade is slightly curved.
Knives decorated with real gold
definitely indicate their value.

## 金饰兽首青铜刀

春秋（公元前 770 年—前 476 年）
通长 28.8 厘米
1998 年宁城县小黑石沟遗址出土
内蒙古文物考古研究所藏

刀柄端弯折联接一半圆形金饰，
金饰透雕两只对兽，顶端有一穿孔。
刀背略呈弧形，刀刃微凹。
以金质兽纹为装饰，
足见此物之珍贵。

# Bronze Knife with Tooth-Shaped Hilt

Spring and Autumn Period (770 — 476 BC)

Total length 37 cm, length of the blade 31.2 cm

Unearthed in 1985 from Xiaoheishigou Site, Ningcheng County

Collection of the Archaeological Research Institute of Inner Mongolia

The flat and short hilt has a tooth design on one side.

The blade and hilt bend sharply.

The straight blade has a thick back and is decorated

with double-lined triangle patterns.

This is the longest knife compared to similar ones with a tooth hilt.

## 齿柄青铜刀

春秋（公元前 770 年—前 476 年）

通长 37、刀长 31.2 厘米

1985 年宁城县小黑石沟遗址出土

内蒙古文物考古研究所藏

扁平短柄内侧铸一突齿，

柄与刀背间弯折。

直刃，刀背宽厚起棱，刀身装饰重三角纹带。

属于齿柄刀中最长的一件，

可能有特殊的功用。

## Bronze Knife with Standing Tiger Pommel

Spring and Autumn Period (770 — 476 BC)

Length 21.8 cm

Unearthed in 1992 from Xiaoheishigou Site, Ningcheng County

Collection of the Archaeological Research Institute of Inner Mongolia

The hilt has a standing tiger at the end.

The flat hilt is concave in the middle.

One side of the hilt is decorated with three standing tigers.

On the other side there is a thin line with triangle patterns.

The back of the blade is slightly curved and the tip of

the knife turned upward.

## 伫立虎首青铜刀

春秋（公元前 770 年—前 476 年）

通长 21.8 厘米

1992 年宁城县小黑石沟遗址出土

内蒙古文物考古研究所藏

柄首铸伫立状虎纹。

扁柄中间凹，

一面饰三只伫立状虎纹，

另一面饰细线、三角折线纹。

刀背稍弯，刀尖微翘。

# Bronze Knife with Ram's Head Hilt

Late Shang Dynasty (ca.11th century BC)

Length 37 cm, width 4.3 cm

Collected in 1987 from Tazigou Site at Fushandi Village, Balinzuo Banner

Collection of the Balinzuo Banner Museum

The hilt ends with a ram's head,
which has two horns curved to the front,
eyes wide open and mouth slightly open.
A circular loop is below the head.
The oblate hilt is slightly curved and decorated
with etched short lines. The blade is straight with an arched back.
Between the hilt and blade is a straight cross guard.

## 羊首青铜刀

商代晚期（约公元前 11 世纪）

长 37、宽 4.3 厘米

1987 年巴林左旗福山地乡塔子沟征集

巴林左旗博物馆藏

刀柄端铸羊首，双角盘曲，

双眼圆睁，口微张。颌下有环扣。

扁圆柄稍弯，饰短线纹。

直刃、弓背，柄刃间有突出的一字形阑。

整体厚重，制作精良。

## Bronze *Yue* (weapon) with Tube Socket

Spring and Autumn Period (770 — 476 BC)

Total length 13.5 cm, length of the tube 12 cm

Unearthed in 1985 from Xiaoheishigou Site, Ningcheng County

Collection of the Ningcheng County Museum

The fairly long tube socket is attached to the curved blade.
There is a hole in the center as decoration.
It has a contracted waist.
The tube socket is used for
fixing the piece onto a shaft.
Rotted wood still can be seen inside the socket.

## 管銎青铜钺

春秋（公元前 770 年—前 476 年）

通长 13.5、管銎长 12 厘米

1985 年宁城县小黑石沟遗址出土

宁城县博物馆藏

管状圆銎稍长，钺刃圆弧，

中间有圆形穿孔作装饰，亚腰。

銎下端有两个钉孔，

用作固柲，銎内残存朽木柄。

## Bronze Chest Shield

Spring and Autumn Period (770 — 476 BC)

Length 23 cm, width 8.3 cm

Unearthed in 1985 from Xiaoheishigou Site, Ningcheng County

Collection of the Ningcheng County Museum

The bronze shield is almost rectangular
in shape with convex obverse side and conave reverse.
Two bulgy eyes were cast on the upper part.
The raised diamond in the middle looks like a mouth or a nose.
The lower part of the shield is contracted into a narrower neck.
There are knobs at each corner of the back.
Other two shields with no decorative patterns were
found in the similar tombs.

## 人面纹护胸青铜牌饰

春秋（公元前 770 年—前 476 年）

长 23、宽 8.3 厘米

1985 年宁城县小黑石沟遗址出土

宁城县博物馆藏

整体造型近长方形，正面稍凸，上部铸出凸起的双眼，
中间有镂孔，鼻或口呈菱形凸起，下部两侧弧曲束颈。
背面凹，四角各附一竖穿钮。
同类墓葬内曾出土两件素面青铜牌，
出土时置于人骨胸部，
故推测此类器物应是征战时护胸的牌饰，类似盾牌。

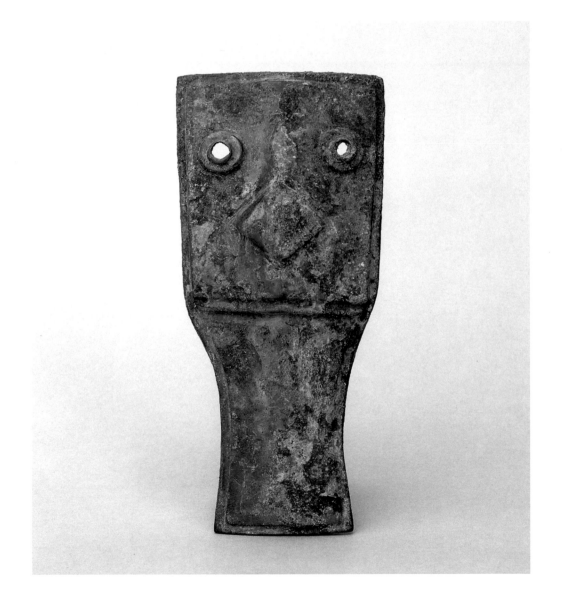

青铜马衔

春秋（公元前 770 年—前 476 年）

通长 23.5 厘米

1963 年宁城县南山根墓葬出土

赤峰市博物馆藏

y rings at each end.

r-shaped appendage.

he appendage is fixed

ne end of the appendage

is special structured bit is

que tool used to tame horses.

两节，中间由双环套联，两端各有一锚形附件，

抓钩向内，中间圆孔与节棍相套联，

可以转动，顶端联铸半圆套环，可以拴绳。

这种结构特殊的马衔，

为北方民族特有的驯马工具，极为少见。

## Bronze Chariot Pommel

Spring and Autumn Period (770 — 476 BC)

Length 48 cm, Height 18.6 cm

Unearthed in 1985 from Xiaoheishigou Site, Ningcheng County

Collection of the Ningcheng County Museum

The outer shape of the piece looks like the back of a bow.

There are two rings on its back.

On both ends there are vertical holes

for fixing rope to a chariot or animal.

This large and heavy piece might have been used

for an ox-driven chariot.

## 青铜车轭

春秋（公元前 770 年—前 476 年）

长 48、高 18.6 厘米

1985 年宁城县小黑石沟遗址出土

宁城县博物馆藏

外形似弓背，中空。

背部有突出双环中间穿孔，

两端亦各有竖向穿孔，可以系绳固定车衡或驾牲。

从器形之大而厚重，

推测驾车之牲可能为牛。

## Deer-Shaped Bronze Plaque

Western Zhou Dynasty (ca.11th century — 770 BC)

Height 20 cm, length 31.5 cm

Unearthed in 1988 from Longtoushan Site, Keshiketeng Banner

Collection of the Archaeological Research Institute of Inner Mongolia

The deer's horn is separated into several branches.
The deer is very strong and has a short tail.
Under the neck and at the bottom there are four pierced holes.
It is the largest animal-shaped bronze plaque ever discovered
from the northern area. It might be a totem of a tribe or a symbol of the
position and power of the tomb occupant.

## 鹿形铜饰

西周（约公元前 11 世纪—前 771 年）

高 20、长 31.5 厘米

1988 年克什克腾旗龙头山遗址出土

内蒙古文物考古研究所藏

铜鹿长角分作数枝，体肥硕，短尾。
颈下和后臀各有一对穿孔。
造型古朴，是北方地区发现的动物形牌饰中最大的一件，
估计非身上使用性饰物，
可能与部族图腾崇拜或墓主身份、权位有关。

### Horse-Shaped Gold Plaque

Spring and Autumn Period (770 — 476 BC)

Length 4.6 cm, width 4.5 cm

Unearthed in 1986 from Xiaochengzi Site, Ningcheng County

Collection of the Ningcheng County Museum

The gold horse is in a crouch position with

its head turned back, ears upright

and wide-open eyes.

There are two bridge knobs on its back.

This exquisitely made plaque is very vivid and lifelike.

### 马形金牌饰

春秋（公元前 770 年—前 476 年）

长 4.6、宽 4.5 厘米

1986 年宁城县小城子出土

宁城县博物馆藏

马呈蹲踞状，回首竖耳。

圆目、有孔。

背面有两桥形钮，可佩戴。

制作精巧，

形象生动传神。

## Boar-Shaped Bronze Plaques

Warring States Period (475 — 221 BC)
Length 5.2 — 6.1 cm, height 3.2 — 3.8 cm
Unearthed in 1990 from Tomb No 1 at Tiejianggou, Xinhui Village,
Aohan Banner
Collection of the Aohan Banner Museum

This group of seven pieces was made by mold casting in relief.
Among the seven, there is one in the form of a couple mating.
The boars have long protruding mouths,
sharp teeth, carved eyes and bristles.
There are two knobs on the back of each plaque.
These boar-shaped bronze plaques indicate that hunting played an
important role in the lives of the aborigines in the Yan State.

## 猪形青铜饰牌

战国（公元前 475 年—前 221 年）
一组七件。长 5.2 — 6.1、高 3.2 — 3.8 厘米
1990 年敖汉旗新惠乡铁匠沟 1 号墓出土
敖汉旗博物馆藏

模铸半浮雕。其中一件为双猪交媾形。
野猪嘴细长前伸，有獠牙、阴刻双眼、鬃毛。
背面有双钮，残存穿带痕。
以野猪形象作为青铜饰品，
反映出狩猎业仍是燕境土著民族的生产方式之一。

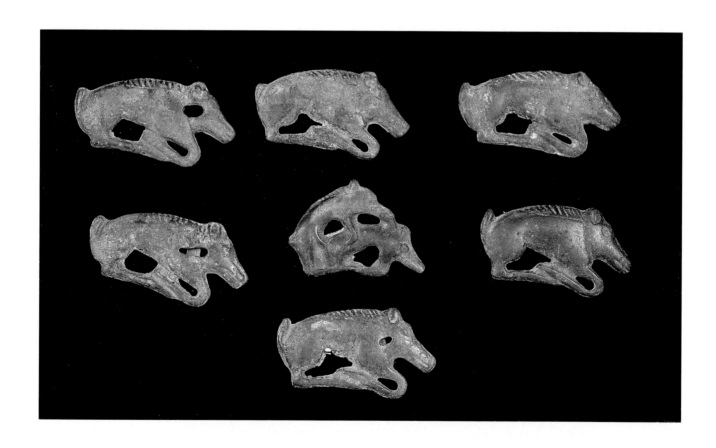

## Bronze Mirror with Double Knobs

Spring and Autumn Period (770 — 476 BC)

Diameter 17.3 cm, thickness 0.9 cm

Unearthed in 1998 from Xiaoheishigou Site, Ningcheng County

Collection of the Archaeological Research Institute of Inner Mongolia

This round mirror has two arch knobs
side by side on the back with short slating lines.
On the back, the broad zigzag patterns
resembling lightening, are the main decorations
over background of short lines.
This bronze mirror is very heavy. On the surface,
traces of silk fabrics (as wrapping) can be clearly seen.

## 几何纹双钮铜镜

春秋（公元前 770 年—前 476 年）

直径 17.3、厚 0.9 厘米

1998 年宁城县小黑石沟遗址出土

内蒙古文物考古研究所藏

圆形。

两个桥形钮并列于镜背之上部，钮上有斜线纹。

背面纹饰由地纹与主纹构成。

地纹为细密的平行短斜线，

主纹为宽条三角勾连雷纹，形如闪电。

镜体厚重，镜面残留丝织品包裹痕迹。

## "Shi Dao" *Gui* (food vessel)

Middle Western Zhou Dynasty (ca.11th — 10th centuries BC)
Height 23.4 cm, diameter of mouth 19.6 cm and of base 20.6 cm
Unearthed in 1996 from Xiaoheishigou Site, Ningcheng County
Collection of the Ningcheng County Museum

This *gui* has a descending drum belly and a wide ring foot.
There are three trunk-shaped flat legs decorated with animal mask
patterns. On both sides are animal-head handles
each holding a ring (now missing). A lid with a ring knob
cover the contracted mouth. The belly is decorated
with vertical string patterns, and rims of both the lid and the vessel are
decorated with stylized animal mask patterns. The base of
the interior bears an inscription of ninety-four characters in ten lines
recording that Shi Dao once received an award from the king.

## "师道"簋

西周中期（约公元前 11 世纪—前 10 世纪）
通高 23.4、口径 19.6、底径 20.6 厘米
1996 年宁城县小黑石沟遗址出土
宁城县博物馆藏

器腹鼓垂，圈足外撇，
圈足下置三个兽面象鼻形扁足；
双耳为兽头衔环式（环已佚）。
有盖，与器子母合口，盖捉手为圈状。
器腹装饰直条沟纹，器、盖口沿各饰变形兽面纹。
器内底有铭文 10 行 94 字，
记师道受王赏赐之事。

## "Xu Ji Jiang" *Gui* (food vessel)

Late Western Zhou Dynasty (ca. early 9th century — 771 BC)
Height 25 cm, diameter of mouth 21.4 cm and of base 21 cm
Unearthed in 1987 from a stone coffin at Xiaoheishigou Site,
Ningcheng County
Collection of the Inner Mongolia Museum

This piece has a wide flared mouth, a contracted neck,
a descending belly and a ring foot supported by a square base.
On both sides are animal-shaped handles with dragon-head-shaped
rings. On the other two sides, there are two handles
decorated with stylized animal mask patterns. The rim,
belly and base of the vessel are decorated with vertical string patterns.
Inside the *gui*, there are thirteen characters in three lines at the bottom.
The inscription tells that the *gui* was made by Ji Jiang of the Xu State.

## "许季姜"簋

西周晚期（约公元前9世纪上半叶—前771年）
高25、口径21.4、底径21厘米
1987年宁城县小黑石沟石椁墓出土
内蒙古博物馆藏

侈口束颈，宽垂腹。圈足下连方座。
腹两侧有兽形耳，环也作下垂卷扬的龙首。
腹前后各有一变形兽面纹。
器口沿、腹部和方座均饰直条沟纹。
器内底有铭文3行 16字。
记许国季姜所铸器。

## "Teng" *He* (wine vessel)

Early Spring and Autumn Period (ca. 770 — 7th century BC)

Height 21.3 cm, diameter of belly 18.5 cm

Unearthed in 1985 from Xiaoheishigou Site, Ningcheng County

Collection of the Ningcheng County Museum

The *he* has a short contracted neck, a wide sloped shoulder, a deep belly, a flat bottom and a lid. There is a spout on one side of the shoulder and an animal-head handle on the other side. A monkey connects the semicircular loops on both the lid and the handle. The vessel and the lid are decorated with horizontal groove patterns. On the knob of the lid there is the character "Teng".

## "滕"盉

春秋早期（约公元前 770 年—前 7 世纪上半叶）

通高 21.3、腹径 18.5 厘米

1985 年宁城县小黑石沟遗址出土

宁城县博物馆藏

短束颈，宽折肩，深腹、平底、有盖。

肩上一侧有直流，

另一侧有龙首形鋬。上半圆环与盖缘半圆环之间

由一猴形动物连接。

器、盖均饰横条沟纹。

盖顶捉手中间铸有一"滕"字。

# Bronze *Lei* (wine vessel)

Western Zhou Dynasty (ca.11th century — 771 BC)
Height 40 cm
Unearthed in 1985 from a stone coffin at Xiaoheishigou Site,
Ningcheng County
Collection of the Inner Mongolia Museum

This piece has a flared mouth, a contracted neck, slanting shoulders, a deep belly and a flat bottom with a wide ring foot. The shoulders are adorned with a band of stylized dragon patterns and two dragon handles with free moving rings. And the dragon handle is decorated with a stylized dragon pattern with head and horns. Around the belly there is a circle of double-ring patterns and six groups of double-dragon patterns in the form of triangles. The cloud pattern adorns the ring foot.

青铜罍

西周（约公元前 11 世纪—前 771 年）
高 40 厘米
1985 年宁城县小黑石沟石椁墓出土
内蒙古博物馆藏

侈口，束颈，斜肩，深腹斜收，平底，圈足外侈。
肩两侧附龙耳套环。
肩饰一周变形夔纹，折腹处饰重环纹一周，
腹部饰六组双夔组成的三角形图案，
圈足饰勾云纹。
龙耳身饰变形夔纹，龙头耳、角清晰。

## Bronze Square *Ding* (food vessel)

Western Zhou Dynasty (ca.11th century — 771 BC)

Height 19 cm, diameter of mouth 9.7 — 12.7 cm

Unearthed in 1985 from Xiaoheishigou Site, Ningcheng County

Collection of the Ningcheng County Museum

The upper part of the *ding* is rectangular in shape . Around the rim there are two-head dragon patterns. On both sides there are upright hanbdles. Four dragons with their up-turned tails are cast on the four corners of the vessel (two are missing). The lower part is the furnace. The four legs are cast into animals with owl beaks. At the front there are two doors which can open and close freely. The right doorknob is in the shape of a nude slave with one leg (right leg missing). The left doorknob is a tiger. For ventilation there are windows on both sides and an openwork whirl pattern at the back.

刖人守门青铜方鼎

西周（约公元前 11 世纪—前 771 年）

通高 19、口径 9.7 — 12.7 厘米

1985 年宁城县小黑石沟遗址出土

宁城县博物馆藏

上腹近长方椭圆形，口沿下饰双首夔龙纹，两侧有方形附耳，四角各铸回首卷尾伏龙一条（左侧两条已缺失）。下部为炉膛，四足各铸一鹰嘴兽；正面有两扇可闭启的方形门：右门压关铸一裸体刖刑（失右足）奴隶形象，左门压关为虎头形，原有门闩已失。两侧有窗户状通风孔，后面铸窃曲纹镂孔可通风，膛底有五个圆形通风口，亦可漏灰。1976 年周原庄白微氏家族窖藏出土一件与此器物极似，刖刑奴隶失左足，口沿下饰窃曲纹，时代定在西周懿王时期。

## Bronze *Dou* (food vessel)

Spring and Autumn Period (770 — 476 BC)

Height 24.6 cm, diameter 17.6 cm

Unearthed in 1996 from Xiaoheishigou Site, Ningcheng County

Collection of the Ningcheng County Museum

This is very shallow with eleven animals standing
on its flared mouth rim.  The thinly cast stem
is supported by a trumpet-shaped ring foot.
The bear-like animals have long protruding mouths
and short up-turned tails. Double circle patterns
decorate their bodies. This has a unique
shape particular in the style of the northern nationalities.

## 口缘饰兽青铜豆

春秋（公元前 770 年—前 476 年）

高 24.6、口径 17.6 厘米

1996 年宁城县小黑石沟墓地出土

宁城县博物馆藏

豆盘浅平，敞口，豆柄细高。
喇叭形圈足。
豆盘口沿上铸有 11 个立兽，长吻，
短尾上卷，身饰重圈纹，形似熊类。
造型独特，
具有浓郁的北方民族青铜器风格。

## Drum-Shaped Bronze Vessel

Spring and Autumn Period (770 — 476 BC)

Length 27.2 cm, diameter of mouth 12 cm

Unearthed in 1996 from Xiaoheishigou Site, Ningcheng County

Collection of the Ningcheng County Museum

This vessel is in the shape of a waist drum.

Both ends, in the trumpet shape,

hollow inside with no cover

are decorated with triangle patterns and bird designs.

Traces of cord can be seen on the vessel.

## 鼓形青铜器

春秋（公元前 770 年—前 476 年）

通长 27.2、口径 12 厘米

1996 年宁城县小黑石沟遗址出土

宁城县博物馆藏

整体呈腰鼓形，

两端喇叭口，

中空，不封口。

两端饰三角纹、鸟纹，

中间有系鼓绳索印痕。

## Pair of Bronze Ladles

Spring and Autumn Period (770 — 476 BC)
Length 20 cm, diameter of bowl 8.5 cm
Unearthed in 1963 from a tomb at Nanshangen, Ningcheng County
Collection of the Chifeng Municipal Museum

The ladle has a contracted mouth and a round belly.
The round straight handle is connected to the bowl
with a fork-shaped expansion.
The handle is in the shape of a phallus.
This is evidence of fertility worship
among the northern nationalities.

## 祖柄青铜勺

春秋（公元前 770 年—前 476 年）
通长 20、勺径 8.5 厘米
1963 年宁城具南山根墓葬出土
赤峰市博物馆藏

勺敛口，
圆腹圆底，圆柄斜直，
柄与勺腹相接处作双叉形，
柄首如祖，形象逼真。
是北方民族性崇拜观念的实证物。

## Painted Pottery Jar

Xia Dynasty (ca.21st — 16th centuries BC)

Height 22 cm, diameter of mouth 11.2 cm and of base 12.5 cm

Unearthed in 1974 from Dadianzi Site, Aohan Banner

Collection of the Chifeng Municipal Museum

This brown pottery jar has a flared mouth and a flat bottom. The surface is finely polished and painted. On the shoulder and lower belly there are symmetrical handles with holes. Three raised broad lines separate the painting decorations into four sections. The first and the third sections have the same cloud patterns, which are outlined in black ink and filled with orange paint over the white background. The second section of cloud patterns has white outline and filled with orange paint over the black background.

## 筒形彩绘陶罐

夏（约公元前 21 世纪—前 16 世纪）

高 22、口径 11.2、底径 12.5 厘米

1974 年敖汉旗大甸子墓地出土

赤峰市博物馆藏

泥质褐陶。器表磨光，绘彩。侈口，筒形斜直腹，平底。
肩与下腹两侧各有对称扳耳，中间有穿孔。
腹间有凸起的三道弦纹，将彩绘纹饰分为四段。
第一段和第三段纹饰相同，墨线勾勒轮廓，
内填橘红色，底饰白色；
第二段，白线勾边，内填橘红色，黑底。
彩绘图案为卷云纹。

# Painted Pottery Jar with Cloud Design

Xia Dynasty (ca.21st — 16th centuries BC)

Height 20 cm, diameter of mouth 18.5 cm and of base 9.7 cm

Unearthed in 1974 from Dadianzi Site, Aohan Banner

Collection of the Chifeng Municipal Museum

This has a contracted mouth, a straight neck, a drum belly and a flat bottom. Between the neck and shoulder, there is a band of embossed decoration. The shoulder is decorated with two lines of bow-string patterns in red and black. The >-shaped patterns in red and white are orderly arranged on the belly. The neck and body are adorned with cloud designs. Around the jar there are seventeen bosses.

## 勾云纹彩绘陶罐

夏（约公元前 21 世纪—前 16 世纪）

高 20、口径 18.5、底径 9.7 厘米

1974 年敖汉旗大甸子墓地出土

赤峰市博物馆藏

侈口，直领，鼓腹，平底。

领与肩结合处有附加堆纹。

肩部有红、黑彩勾勒的两道弦纹。

腹部是地上用红、白两彩勾画出排列整齐的“>”折线纹。

颈腹部饰勾云纹。

绕罐腹一周有 17 个乳钉。

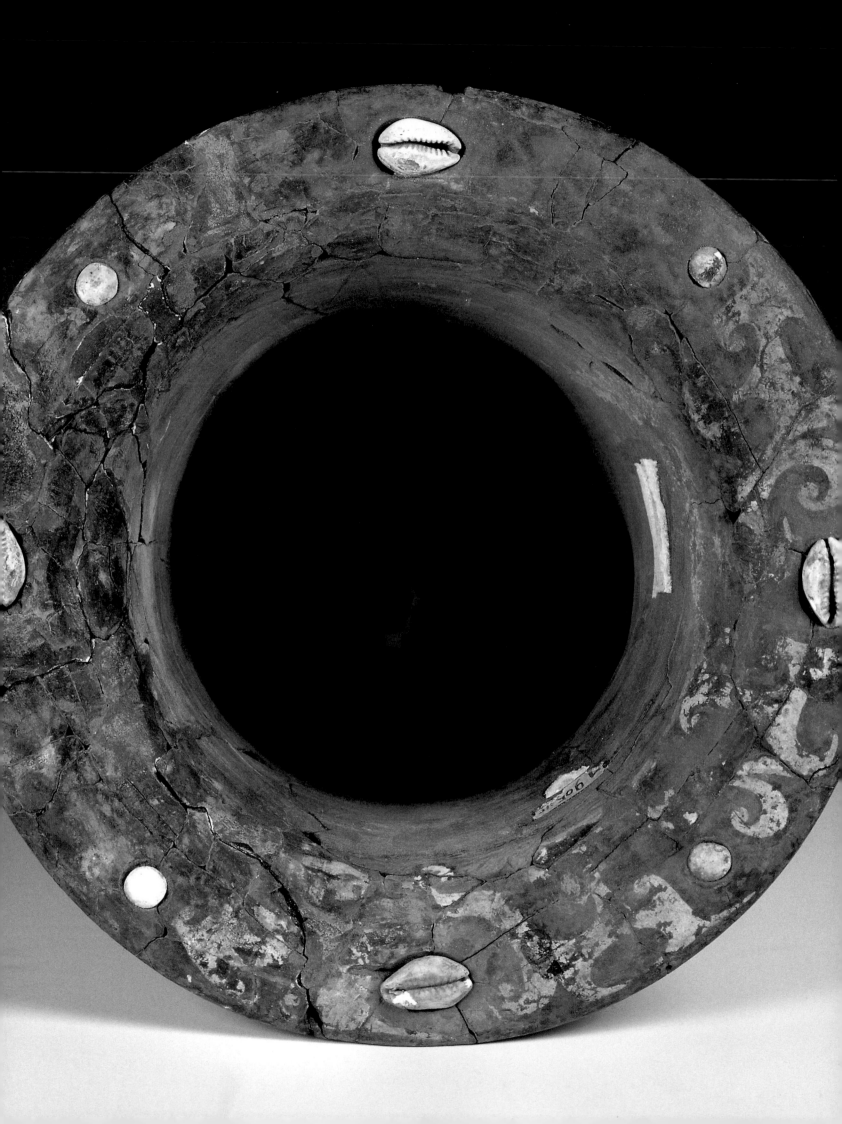

## Painted Pottery *Li* (food vessel)

Xia Dynasty (ca.21st — 16th centuries BC)

Height 29.5 cm, diameter of mouth 22 cm

Unearthed in 1974 from Dadianzi Site, Aohan Banner

Collection of the Chifeng Municipal Museum

This earthen piece has a wide flared mouth and straight bucket-shaped body supported by three pouched legs. There are four shells inlaid on the rim with four round shell beads in between. Cloud patterns are painted on the belly in red and white.

## 嵌贝彩绘陶鬲

夏（约公元前 21 世纪—前 16 世纪）

高 29.5、口径 22 厘米

1974 年敖汉旗大甸子墓地出土

赤峰市博物馆藏

泥质褐陶。

敞口卷沿，筒状腹，筒状空足，柱状足尖。

口沿上镶嵌四个贝壳，

贝壳间还粘贴四个圆形蚌泡。

器壁用红、白两色绘制勾云形图案。

装饰精美、别致。

## Pottery *Dou* (food vessel)

Warring States Period (475 — 221 BC)

Height 42.2 cm, diameter of mouth 8 cm and of base 11cm

Unearthed in 1998 from a tomb at Xiaoheishigou Site, Ningcheng County

Collection of the Archaeological Research Institute of Inner Mongolia

This grayish brown pottery was wheel-made and fired at a high temperature. The clay was mixed with shell powder so the surface is a lustrous silvery gray color. The lid is made in the shape of a long neck bird. It has a pot-like body, a straight mouth, a bamboo-joint stem and a trumpet base. Around the neck and shoulder of the piece are decorated cross designs, wave patterns and horizontal cloud patterns separated by groove lines.

陶豆

战国（公元前475年—前221年）

通高42.4、口径8、底径11厘米

1998年宁城县小黑石沟墓葬出土

内蒙古文物考古研究所藏

泥质灰褐陶，轮制，火候较高，

陶土内掺有蚌壳粉呈器表磨光，银灰色。

盖顶塑长颈鸟首。

豆身呈罐状，直口，喇叭形座。

颈部刻划三角折线纹，肩部刻划竖行水波纹、

横向卷云纹，间以凹弦纹。豆柄呈竹节状。

## Pottery Pot

陶壶

Warring States Period (475 — 221 BC)

Height 35.6 cm, diameter of mouth 12 cm and of base 9 cm

Unearthed in 1998 from a tomb at Xiaoheishigou Site, Ningcheng County

Collection of the Archaeological Research Institute of Inner Mongolia

战国（公元前 475 年—前 221 年）

通高 35.6、口径 12、底径 9 厘米

1998 年宁城县小黑石沟墓葬出土

内蒙古文物考古研究所藏

This grayish brown pottery was wheel-made and fired at a high temperature. The clay was mixed with shell powder so the surface is a lustrous silvery gray color. The tall convex lid has three stylized bird heads. It has a contracted mouth, a long neck, a drum belly and a flat bottom. There are symmetrical semicircle ears on the shoulder. Several bands of lines decorate around the shoulders and belly.

泥质灰褐陶，轮制，火候较高，

陶土内掺有蚌壳粉，器表磨光呈银灰色，

盖面隆起，顶塑三个变形鸟首。

壶，侈口，长颈，溜肩，鼓腹，平底，

肩部有对称的半圆形双扳耳。

肩部、腹部饰数道凹弦纹。

# 金戈铁马创辉煌
# Achieving Greatness with Shining Spears
# and Armored Horses

中国北方历代游牧民族，自幼在马背上成长，因而成为天生的骑士。鲜卑拓跋部建立的北魏王朝，是中国历史上少数民族在中原建立的第一个封建政权；契丹族建立的辽王朝，与两宋王朝对峙，兼容并蓄，不断壮大；蒙古族在成吉思汗的统帅下，建立了横跨欧亚大陆的蒙古帝国，其孙忽必烈建立的大元王朝，则将草原文化与汉文化融为一体。这一切，促进了草原经济的发展与封建王朝的更迭以及整个中华民族的大融合，对世界历史也产生了巨大影响。

Growing up on horseback from childhood, people of the northern nomadic nationalities in the past dynasties of China were natural equestrians. The Northern Wei dynasty, founded by the Tuoba tribe of the Xianbei nationality, became the first feudal empire established by a minority nationality in the Central Plains. Constantly clashing with the Northern Song dynasty, the Liao dynasty founded by the Qidan nationality, continued to build up its unprecedented strength. The great empire of Mongolia, spanning from Europe to Asia, was established by Mongolian nationality under the command of Genghis Khan. Kubilai Khan, grandson of Genghis Khan, set up the Great Yuan dynasty, which merged the native Han culture and steppe culture into one unit. This resulted in a strong push in the development of the steppe economy, integration of the Chinese nation and change of feudal dynasties that ultimately created tremendous influence on the world's history.

# 鲜卑族

　　鲜卑系东胡后裔，继战国后期东胡衰落之后而兴起，自汉代起南徙与西迁，势力逐渐强大，魏晋南北朝时成为统治大漠南北的主要民族。鲜卑拓跋部建立的北魏王朝（后分裂为东魏、西魏）曾统一了北方，之后相继有北齐、北周。其文化既有鲜明的草原民族风格，更有受汉文化影响的深深印记。

# *Xianbei*

The Xianbei nationality, the descendant of the Donghu, rose to power in the late Warring States after the fall of the Donghu. The Xianbei built up its forces and became the dominant ruling nationality of the steppe during the Wei, Jin and Southern and Northern Dynasties. The Northern Wei empire, founded by the Tuoba tribe of the Xianbei, once unified the northern region but later it separated into the Eastern Wei, Western Wei, Northern Qi and Northern Zhou Kingdoms. Therefore its culture shows distinguishing characteristics of the steppe nationalities and traces of the far-reaching influence of the Han culture.

# Bone Plaque with Hunting Scene

Eastern Han Dynasty (AD 25 — 220)
Length 15 cm, width 2.5 cm, thickness 0.3 cm
Unearthed in 1960 from a Xianbei tomb at Zhalainuoer,
Xinbaerhuyou Banner
Collection of the Inner Mongolia Museum

This plaque, made from an animal
leg bone, was polished with a thin slip.
Thin lines outline a scene of hunters shooting
at a deer by bow and arrow.
The lines of the painting are fine and simple.
Around the edge of the plaque there
are round or rectangular holes to attach other objects.

# 狩猎纹骨板

东汉（公元 25 年—220 年）
长 15、宽 2.5、厚 0.3 厘米
1960 年新巴尔虎右旗扎赉诺尔鲜卑墓出土
内蒙古博物馆藏

用动物肢骨加工成细长片状，表面磨光，
用细线刻划出猎人持弓箭射鹿的图案。
线条纤细、简洁明快。
骨板边缘有圆形和长方形穿孔，
用以系绳和固定在其他物件上。

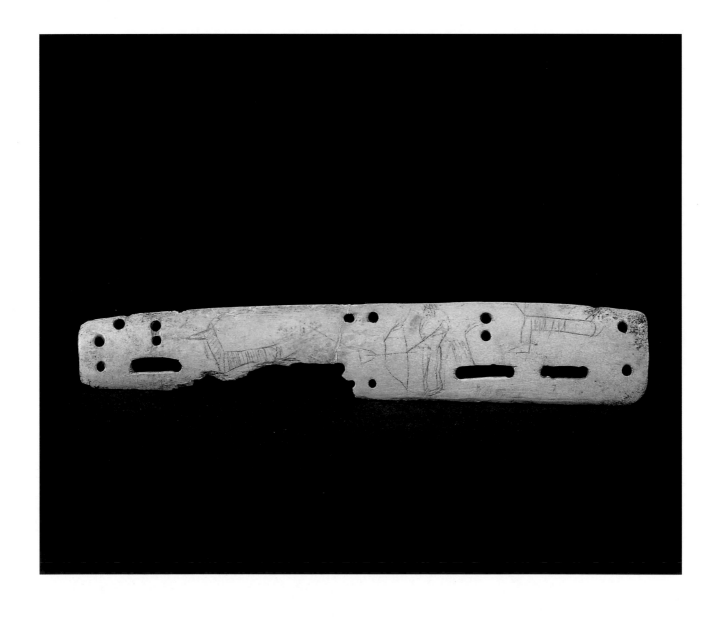

## Headdress in Cattle Design

Northern Dynasties (AD 386 — 581)
Height 18.5 cm, weight 70 g.
Unearthed in 1981 from Xihezicun,
Da'erhan Maoming'an United Banner
Collection of the Inner Mongolia Museum

This headdress was made in the shape of a cattle head with a large
rack of antlers over head with peach leaves.
The head, ears and main branches of the antlers
are all inlaid with red or white semiprecious stones edged
with fishroe marks. All the leaves would have rustled to produce a
very pleasant sound while wearing it on the head and walking.
This was a special headdress of the Xianbei women.

## 牛首金步摇冠饰

北朝（公元 386 年—581 年）
高 18.5 厘米、重 70 克
1981 年达尔罕茂明安联合旗西河子村出土
内蒙古博物馆藏

牛首，头顶连接细枝鹿角，
枝梢及双耳以环穿联桃形叶片。
牛首之面部及双耳镶嵌红、白石料，
边缘饰鱼子纹。
工艺精细，装饰华丽。
为鲜卑贵妇所特有的头上装饰物。

## Headddress in Red Deer Design

Northern Dynasties (AD 386 — 581)
Height 19.5 cm, weight 92 g.
Unearthed in 1981 from Xihezicun,
Da'erhan Maoming'an United Banner
Collection of the Inner Mongolia Museum

This headdress is made in the shape of a red deer's head.
The deer has upright ears and large branches
of antlers with peach leaves.
Its eyes, ears and main branches of the antlers are all inlaid
with red or white semiprecious stones edged with fishroe marks.
All the leaves would have jangled to produce
a very melodic sound while walking.
This is a special headdress of the Xianbei women.

## 马鹿首金步摇冠饰

北朝（公元 386 年—581 年）
高 19.5 厘米　重 92 克
1981 年达尔罕茂明安联合旗西河子村出土
内蒙古博物馆藏

马鹿首、竖耳、头顶联接枝状大角，
枝梢以环穿联桃形叶片。
鹿首之双眼、耳及角干等部位镶嵌红、白石料，
边缘饰鱼子纹。
动之则叶片摇摆声响，谓之"步摇"。
步摇冠为鲜卑贵妇所特有的头上装饰，弥足珍贵。

## Gold Dragon Necklace

Northern Dynasties (AD 386 — 581)
Length 128 cm, weight 213.8 g.
Unearthed in 1981 from Xihezicun,
Da'erhan Maoming'an United Banner
Collection of the Inner Mongolia Museum

This piece was made by gold thread woven into a dragon. Both of its ends are hooked with a dragon head made of hammered and rolled gold sheets. The eyes, ears and noses are decorated with thin gold thread. The mouths respectively have a hook and ring to lock into each other. On the body, there are seven pendants including a shield, spear, halberd and comb. The dragon heads and weapons are all decorated with semiprecious stones. This piece was made with exquisite workmanship particularly for the Xianbei nobility.

## 金龙项饰

北朝（公元 386 年—581 年）
长 128 厘米 重 213.8 克
1981 年达尔罕茂明安联合旗西河子村出土
内蒙古博物馆藏

用金丝编缀成长索状龙身，两端套接金片锤卷成的龙首，
用细金丝装饰出龙的双眼、耳、鼻，口中分含串钉及环，
用以相钩挂。龙身盘曲自如，
以环联缀盾、戟、钺、梳等七件饰物。
龙首和兵器上镶嵌有宝石。工艺精细，装饰特殊，
为鲜卑贵族所特有的腰或颈部佩戴物。

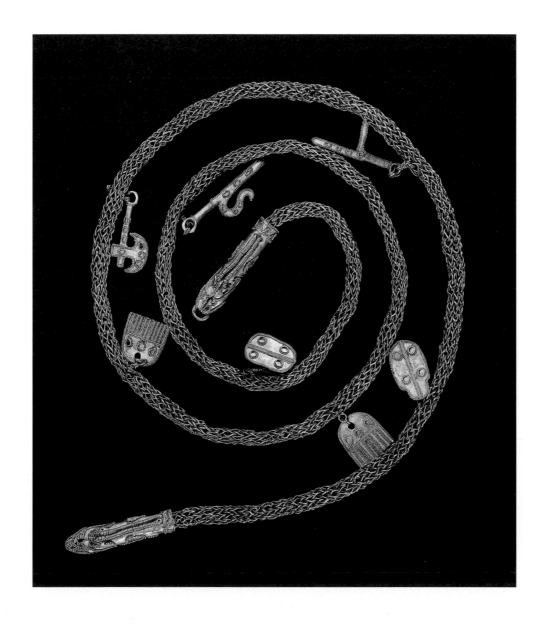

## Pair of Gold Plaques

Northern Dynasties (AD 386 — 581)
Length 9 cm, width 6 cm, weight 91.5 — 99.2 g.
Unearthed in 1990 from Beihalatu, Yaolinmaodusumu,
Keerqinzuoyizhong Banner
Collection of the Tongliao Municipal Museum

These are cast gold plaques in relief with openwork designs
on the front surface. The human face designs have large eyes,
high cheekbones and broad noses.
On the chest there are six bosses.
Stylized cloud patterns decorate the edge of the plaque.

## 人面形金饰牌

北朝（公元 386 年—581 年）
长 9、宽 6 厘米 重 91.5—99.2 克
1990 年科尔沁左翼中旗腰林毛都苏木北哈拉吐出土
通辽市博物馆藏

模铸。
正面凸起，浮雕出人面，大眼睛，高颧骨，阔鼻。
胸部有六个乳钉状凸起，
头部周边饰变形勾云纹。
背凹，镂孔，可以系挂作为佩戴装饰物。

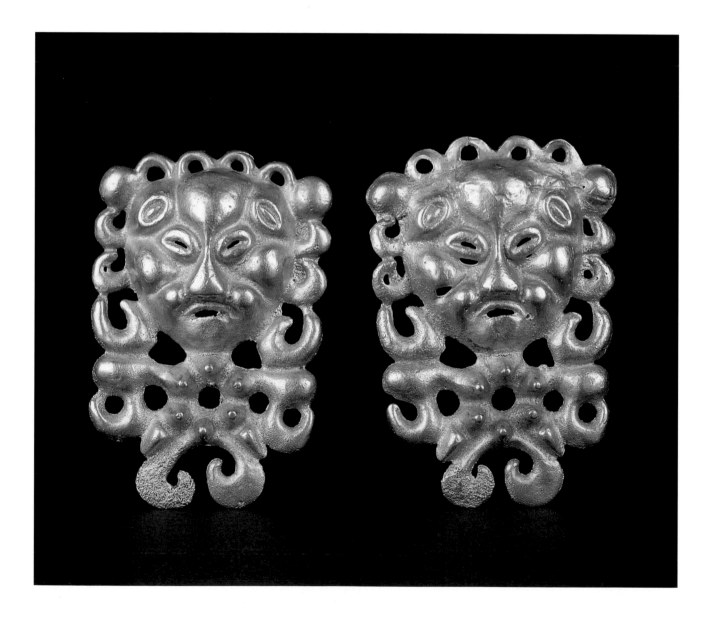

## Gold Plaque with a Human Figure and Lions

Northern Dynasties (AD 386 — 581)
Length 10 cm, width 5.8 cm, weight 130.8 g.
Unearthed in 1990 from Beihalatu, Yaolinmaodusumu,
Keerqinzuoyizhong Banner
Collection of the Tongliao Municipal Museum

This gold plaque, cast in relief is of a warrior
with deep-set eyes and a high nose standing with two lions
on either side. Stylized cloud patterns decorate the edge of the plaque.
This type of human features and the unique shape of double lions
definitely is the influence of Western Asian cultures. This plaque was
used as an amulet by the Xianbei nobility.

## 人物双狮纹金饰牌

北朝（公元 386 年— 581 年）
长 10、宽 5.8 厘米 重 130.8 克
1990 年科尔沁左翼中旗腰林毛都苏木北哈拉吐出土
通辽市博物馆藏

模铸。
正面凸起，浮雕一高鼻深目武士，
两侧各依偎着一只雄狮，周边饰以变形勾云纹。
背凹，镂孔。这种高鼻深目的人物和双狮形象造型独特，
显然受到西亚文化的影响。
是鲜卑贵族用以护身的佩饰。

## Bone Arrowhead

Eastern Han Dynasty (AD 25 — 220)

Length 6.4 — 12.9 cm

Unearthed in 1960 from a Xianbei tomb at Zhalainuoer,
Xinbaerhuyou Banner

Collection of the Inner Mongolia Museum

One of the three pieces

is in a spearhead shape with lozenge cross section

and the other two are diamond shaped

with triangular cross sections.

All of them have conical ends.

## 骨镞

东汉（公元 25 年—220 年）

长 6.4 — 12.9 厘米

1960 年新巴尔虎右旗扎赉诺尔鲜卑墓出土

内蒙古博物馆藏

一件为矛头式，

箭头剖面呈菱形，锥形铤；

另两件为三棱式，

箭头剖面为三角形，

铤为锥形。

## Pottery Musicians and Dancers

Northern Wei Dynasty (AD 386 — 534)
A group. Height cm15.5 — 19.8 cm
Unearthed in 1975 from a Northern Wei tomb at Daxue Road,
Huhehaote City
Collection of the Inner Mongolia Museum

The figures are wearing hats and floor-length robes.
The one standing with outstretched arms seems to be conducting the
band. The other seven, while crouching or kneeling,
display various positions related to playing musical instruments.
This is evidence that the Xianbei people
were found of singing and dancing.

## 舞乐陶俑

北魏（公元 386 年—534 年）
一组。高 15.5 — 19.8 厘米
1975 年呼和浩特市大学路北魏墓出土
内蒙古博物馆藏

陶俑头戴凤帽，着曳地长袍。
其中一俑直立，双臂抬起呈指挥状。
其余七件陶俑双膝跪坐或一腿跪一腿蹲，
做出各种弹奏的姿势，
是鲜卑族能歌善舞的形象实物。

# Pair of Tomb Guardian Figures

Northern Wei Dynasty (AD 386 — 534)
Height 39.5 cm, 43.5 cm
Unearthed in 1975 from a Northern Wei Dynasty tomb at Daxue Road,
Huhehaote City
Collection of the Inner Mongolia Museum

The pottery figures wear helmets,
armor and high boots. In both figures, one arm is stretched out
and the other is bent as if he was carrying something in his hand.
The head, arms and body were made separately and assembled
afterwards. They are roughly shaped and full of power
and grandeur. They were used to guard the tomb.

镇墓陶俑

北魏（公元 386 年—534 年）
高 39.5 厘米、43.5 厘米
1975 年呼和浩特市大学路北魏墓出土
内蒙古博物馆藏

陶俑头带盔，身着甲，足着靴，
一臂伸展，一臂弯曲，
作手中执物形象。
俑头、手、身分制，后组合而成。
造型粗犷、形象威武，司职镇墓。

## Necklace with Agate and Crystal Tassel

The fourth year of the Huitong reign of the Liao Dynasty (AD 941)

Length 78 cm

Unearthed in 1992 from the tomb of YeluYuzhi, Alukeerqin Banner

Collection of the Archaeological Research Institute of Inner Mongolia

This necklace was made of highly polished carnelian tubes and crystal beads. Two gold pendants one heart-shaped and one tube-like are attached to the chain. The carnelian tubes, varying in size and thickness, are highly polished with a pierced hole in the center. The length of the tube differs from 1.7 cm to 8.3 cm and the diameter from 0.5 cm to 0.9 cm. The crystal beads are also of different sizes from 0.6 cm to 1.4 cm in diameter.

## 玛瑙、水晶璎珞

辽会同四年（公元 941 年）

周长 78 厘米

1992 年阿鲁科尔沁旗辽耶律羽之墓出土

内蒙古文物考古研究所藏

用红玛瑙管与水晶珠间隔串联呈链状，

另外再连缀心形、长管形的金坠。

圆柱形玛瑙管表面抛光，中间对钻穿孔，

长短、粗细略有不同，

长 1.7—8.3、管径 0.5—0.9 厘米。

圆球形水晶珠大小略有不同，直径 0.6—1.4 厘米。

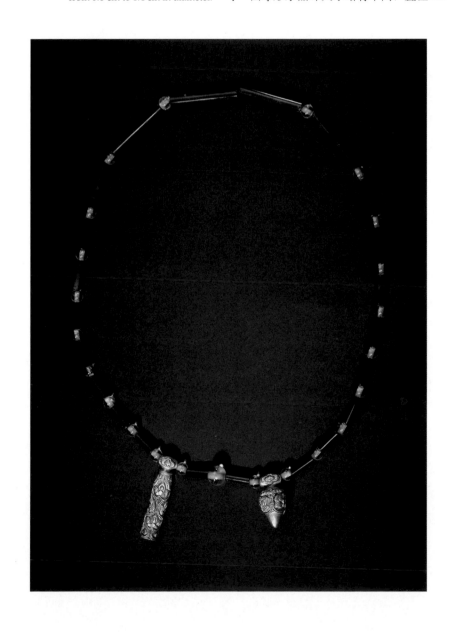

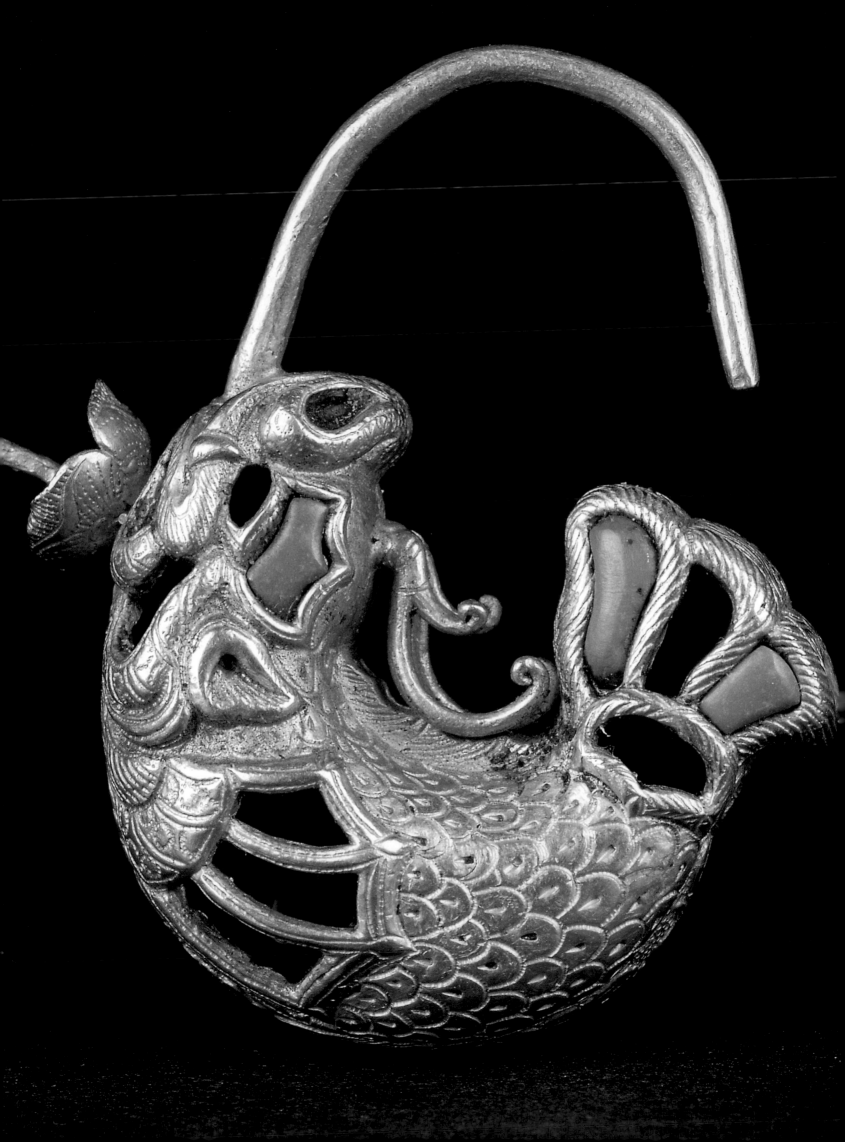

## Gold Earrings

The fourth year of the Huitong reign of the Liao Dynasty (AD 941)
Length 4.4 cm, Width 4.4 cm
Unearthed in 1992 from the tomb of YeluYuzhi, Alukeerqin Banner
Collection of the Archaeological Research Institute of Inner Mongolia

This exquisite earring,
in the shape of a dragon head with curved fish body,
was made by hammering, welding, chiseling and polishing.
There are antlers on the head and its head,
body and tail are inlaid with turquoise.
These earrings skillfully combine
the Indian and Chinese cultures together.

## 摩羯形金耳坠

辽会同四年（公元941年）
通长4.4、宽4.4厘米
1992年阿鲁科尔沁旗辽耶律羽之墓出土
内蒙古文物考古研究所藏

耳坠采用锤镍、焊接、錾刻、
打磨等技法加工而成。
摩羯造形为龙首鱼身，头部有鹿形双角，
鱼身蜷曲，头、腹、尾部镶嵌绿松石。
此件耳坠将印度文化和中国的传统文化巧妙地融为一体，
可谓匠心独运，技艺高超。

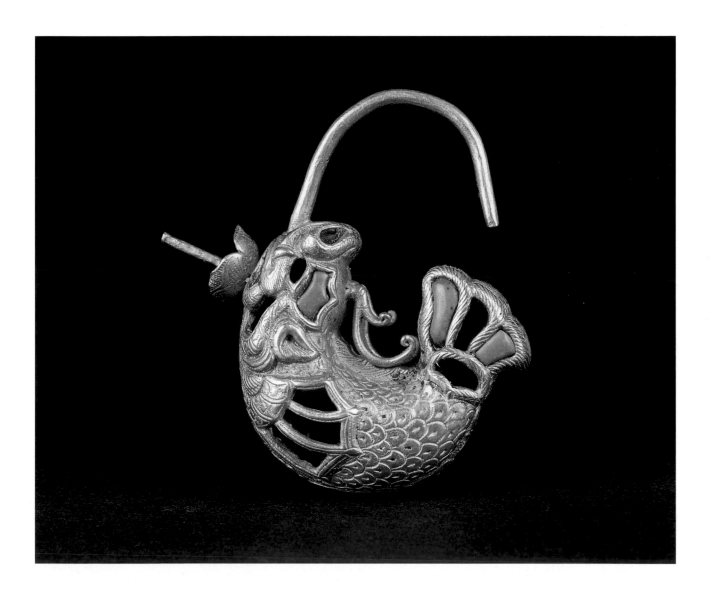

## Jade Bear 玉熊

Liao Dynasty (AD 916 — 1125)
Length 6.8 cm, width 3.8 cm
Unearthed in 1978 from a hoard at Youaicun, Bayanhansumu,
Balinyou Banner
Collection of the Balinyou Banner Museum

辽（公元916年—1125年）
长6.8、宽3.8厘米
1978年巴林右旗巴彦汉苏木友爱村窖藏出土
巴林右旗博物馆藏

This reclining bear is carved of white jade
and has small ears and a protruding mouth,
a short tail and bristles.
Its head is turned to the left and rests on the front paws.
Its eyes are wide open in a lovely expression.

白玉，圆雕。
熊小耳尖嘴，短尾长鬃，呈伏卧状，
头左向紧贴于前爪，
双目圆睁，
神态温顺可爱。

## Crystal Fish

Liao Dynasty (AD 916 — 1125)
Length 4 cm, width 1.7 cm
Unearthed from the Jiwangyingzi tomb at Gongjiayingzi Village,
Kalaqin Banner
Collection of the Chifeng Municipal Museum

This carved crystal fish has a slightly opened mouth
as if taking a breath. The drilled eyes are looking ahead
and its tail is waving.
The hatch marks on the body are the fish scales.
The fin on the back is standing up.
It is vivid and of high quality.

## 水晶鱼

辽（公元916年—1125年）
长4、宽1.7厘米
喀喇沁旗宫家营子乡吉旺营子辽墓出土
赤峰市博物馆藏

水晶，圆雕。
鱼张嘴呈呼吸状，钻孔鱼眼凝视前方，
鱼尾下摆，
鱼鳞用交叉斜线刻划，鱼鳍耸立。
形象逼真，质地上乘。

## Bronze Mirror with Dragon Design

The fourth year of the Huitong reign of the Liao Dynasty (AD 941)

Diameter 28 cm

Unearthed in 1992 from the Tomb of Yelu Yuzhi, Alukeerqin Banner

Collection of the Archaeological Research Institute of Inner Mongolia

This mirror has a broad rim and a round knob. The surface is highly polished and the dragon in relief is gold plated. The long horned dragon is raising his head and has its mouth wide open swallowing a pearl. The claws are powerful and the tail and hind legs are twisted together. The whole body is covered with scales from head to tail. The dragon pattern is a common pattern from the Liao dynasty, mostly used in stone carvings, murals, daily utensils and silk fabrics. This is evidence that the Qidan people learned from the Central Plains culture.

## 盘龙纹铜镜

辽会同四年（公元941年）

直径28厘米

1992年阿鲁科尔沁旗辽耶律羽之墓出土

内蒙古文物考古研究所藏

宽平沿，圆形钮。镜面抛光，浮雕龙纹通体鎏金。镜背浮雕一盘龙，龙首昂起，双角耸立，张口吐舌，欲吞一珠，龙爪雄健有力，尾与一后腿相扭结，通体饰鳞纹。龙纹是辽代常见的主要纹饰，多用于石刻、壁画、生活用品以及丝绸织物上。辽代的龙纹与唐代的龙纹基本相同，多表现为头长口深，梳状上唇，鹿形角，鹰形爪，蛇形尾常缠绕于一后腿上，通体饰有鳞纹。这是契丹族学习吸收中原汉文化的形象实物。

## Crystal Rat

Liao Dynasty (AD 916 — 1125)
Length 3.6 cm, width 2.3 cm
Unearthed from the Jiwangyingzi tomb at Gongjiayingzi Village,
Kalaqin Banner
Collection of the Chifeng Municipal Museum

This carved crystal rat has a sharp protruding mouth,

two wide-open eyes looking straight ahead.

It is crouched as if terrified.

This vivid piece

is crystal clear and skillfully carved.

## 水晶鼠

辽（公元916年—1125年）
长3.6、宽2.3厘米
喀喇沁旗宫家营子乡吉旺营子辽墓出土
赤峰市博物馆藏

水晶，圆雕。
尖嘴前突，双眼圆睁，直视前方，缩臀收腹，
似突感惊恐状。
晶莹剔透，圆润光洁，
刀法娴熟，形象逼真。

## Gold Ornaments in Human Figure Shape

Liao Dynasty (AD 916 — 1125)
Height 9.2 cm
Unearthed in 1993 from Huagentala at Zhagasitaisumu,
Alukeerqin Banner
Collection of the Alukeerqin Banner Museum

These male and female standing ornaments were made
from hammered gold sheets laid over an iron mold.
They have round eyes and broad nose.
Each wears a headdress on the head, a narrow sleeve jacket with
straight collars, trousers and a pair of high boots.
The garments are decorated with entwined flower designs.
The male has an engraved mustache.
There are pierced holes in the neck, sleeves and boots.

## 人形金饰件

辽（公元 916 年—1125 年）
高 9.2 厘米
1993 年阿鲁科尔沁旗扎嘎斯台苏木花根塔拉辽墓出土
阿鲁科尔沁旗博物馆藏

薄金板锤鍱而成。
男女直立人形，圆眼，阔鼻。
头戴冠饰，上身穿直领左衽窄袖衫，下身着裤，
两足穿高靿靴，腰部系带。
衣服錾饰缠枝花纹，男子上唇錾刻胡须。
颈部、双手、双脚部位有穿孔。

## Gilded Eagle Pendant

The fourth year of the Huitong reign of the Liao Dynasty (AD 941)

Height 24.3 cm, width 30.5 cm, thickness 0.03 cm

Unearthed in 1992 from the Tomb of Yelu Yuzhi in Alukeerqin Banner

Collection of the Archaeological Research Institute of Inner Mongolia

This pendant is made from a bronze sheet engraved
with an eagle with a sharp beak and claws.
It spreads its wings out as if it were flying in the air and ready to hunt.
This is a lifelike piece with flowing lines.
There are nail holes scattered around the edge of the pendant. It might
have been used as a decorative piece for the net of the coffin bed.
It was a custom for the Qidan people to raise eagles for hunting.

## 海东青鎏金铜饰件

辽会同四年（公元 941 年）

高 24.3、宽 30.5、厚 0.03 厘米

1992 年阿鲁科尔沁旗辽耶律羽之墓出土

内蒙古文物考古研究所藏

薄铜片制成。正面鎏金。

錾刻一只海东青，双翅张开，尖嘴利爪，
似乎正翱翔于空中，随时准备捕捉猎物。
形象生动，线条流畅。
铜饰周边有钉孔，可能为棺床小帐上的装饰物。
契丹人驾鹰出猎，为其民族风尚。

## Gilded Bronze Door-Guardian

The fourth year of the Huitong reign of the Liao Dynasty (AD 941)
Height 40.8 cm, width 23.6 cm, thickness 0.03 cm
Unearthed in 1992 from the Tomb of YeluYuzhi in Alukeerqin Banner
Collection of the Archaeological Research Institute of Inner Mongolia

Made of bronze leaf with the front surface gilded,
the standing warrior wears armor and a helmet,
carries a sword in hand
and has a very serious looking expression on his face.
There are nail holes around the edge of the pendant.
It might have been a decorative piece for the net of the coffin bed.

## 鎏金门神铜饰件

辽会同四年（公元 941 年）
高 40.8、宽 23.6、厚 0.03 厘米
1992 年阿鲁科尔沁旗辽耶律羽之墓出土
内蒙古文物考古研究所藏

薄铜片制成。
正面鎏金。整体裁制成一站立的人形，
錾刻出一身披铠甲、头戴盔、手持利剑，
肃目含威的武士。
周边有钉孔，
应为棺床小帐上的装饰物。

## Pair of Painted Wooden Doors

The fourth year of the Huitong reign of the Liao Dynasty (AD 941)
Each door: length 28 cm, width 20.8 cm, thickness 1.7 cm
Unearthed in 1992 from the Tomb of YeluYuzhi in Alukeerqin Banner
Collection of the Archaeological Research Institute of Inner Mongolia

The painted doors, with bolts on both ends,
can be opened from both sides.
On the corners of the joints are T or L-shaped bronze bindings for
reinforcement with engraved decorative patterns.
The frame is painted with tung paint and the upper frame around the
bars is painted red. The lower part of the door is painted with
symmetrical crouched lions facing each other.

## 彩绘双扇木门

辽会同四年（公元 941 年）
（单扇门)长 28、宽 20.8、厚 1.7 厘米
1992 年阿鲁科尔沁旗辽耶律羽之墓出土
内蒙古文物考古研究所藏

双扇门对开，两端各有插轴，
边角榫卯接合部位以直角
或丁字形鎏金錾花铜构件加固。
门框施桐漆，上部竖栏施彩，
下部门板彩绘相对称呈蹲踞状的雄狮。

## Gilded Silver Vase

Tang Dynasty (AD 618 — 907)

Height 28.5 cm, diameter of mouth 5 cm, of belly 20.4 cm and of Base 15 cm

Unearthed in 1976 from a hoard at Jinshan Town, Kalaqin Banner

Collection of the Culture Relics Office of Kalaqin Banner

This is an oblate vase in the shape
of two standing fish, face to face.
The mouths of the two fish are the spout of the vase
and the fish tails spread out to form the base of the vase.
This piece is beautifully engraved.

## 双鱼形鎏金银壶

唐（公元 618 年—907 年）

高 28.5、口径 5、腹径 20.4、底径 15 厘米

1976 年喀喇沁旗锦山镇窖藏出土

喀喇沁旗文管所藏

直立形双鱼合抱呈扁圆形壶体，
双鱼嘴相合为壶嘴，
鱼尾展开围成为壶底。
鱼鳃、鳍和鳞錾刻精细，
造型优美。

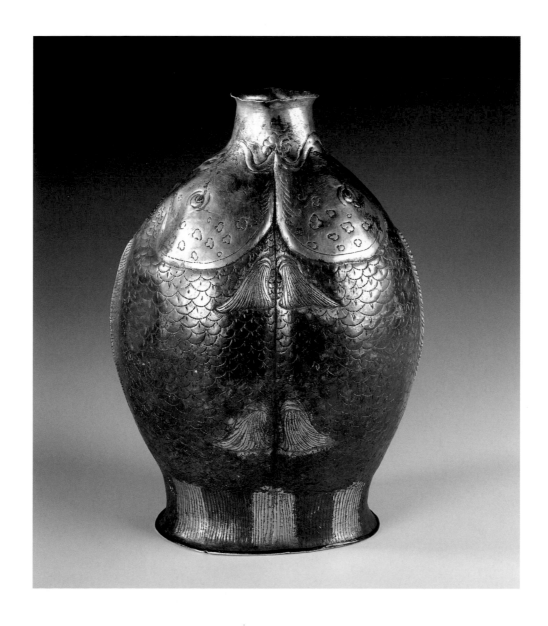

## Gold Lobed Cup

The fourth year of the Huitong reign of the Liao Dynasty (AD 941)

Height 3 cm, diameter of mouth 7.7 cm and of base 4.2 cm, weight 61.2 g.

Unearthed in 1992 from the tomb of Yelu Yuzhi, Alukeerqin Banner

Collection of the Archaeological Research Institute of Inner Mongolia

This is a five-lobed cup with a ring foot.
Inside and outside the cup designs are engraved
over the background of fishroe marks.
Inside and on the edge of the ring foot,
there is a band of lotus pedal design.
On the bottom of the cup,
there is an engraved design of two fish playing in the water.
Five groups of double geese with flowers decorate the belly.

## 花式口金杯

辽会同四年（公元 941 年）

高 3、口径 7.7、底径 4.2 厘米　重 61.2 克

1992 年阿鲁科尔沁旗辽耶律羽之墓出土

内蒙古文物考古研究所藏

花式口，

弧腹分为五瓣，圈足，

内外壁鱼子纹地上錾刻花纹。

内沿及圈足底边各錾刻一周宝相莲瓣纹，

内底錾刻双鱼戏水纹，

腹外壁錾刻五组双雁衔花纹。

## Silver Bowl

The fourth year of the Huitong reign of the Liao Dynasty (AD 941)

Height 6.5 cm, diameter of mouth 20 cm and of base 10.2 cm

Unearthed in 1992 from the tomb of Yelu Yuzhi, Alukeerqin Banner

Collection of the Archaeological Research Institute of Inner Mongolia

The silver bowl, made by hammering with gilded engraved designs, has a wide flared rim and contracted belly supported by a ring foot. Around the inner rim and the bottom, there are two circles of bead patterns and lotus petal designs. The center of the bowl is engraved with a capricornus. The capricornus is a peculiar creature in Indian myth. It was first introduced into China in the 4th century. Influenced by traditional Chinese culture during the Sui and Tang dynasties, the capricornus gradually transformed into a strange creature with a dragon head and fish body.

## 摩羯纹金花银碗

辽会同四年（公元 941 年）

高 6.5、口径 20、底径 10.2 厘米

1992 年阿鲁科尔沁旗辽耶律羽之墓出土

内蒙古文物考古研究所藏

银质。锤制，花纹鎏金。敞口，腹部弧收，圈足。
碗口内沿及内底一周錾刻联珠纹和莲瓣纹，
碗内錾刻一龙首鱼身的摩羯纹。摩羯是印度神话中的异兽，
公元 4 世纪传入中国，隋唐之后受中国传统文化的影响，
摩羯纹逐渐演变成龙首鱼身的鱼龙形怪兽。
契丹人喜爱摩羯纹，不仅在金银器上，
在其他诸如石刻、陶瓷器、铜器上也常用摩羯纹装饰。

## Engraved Gilded Silver Plate

The fourth year of the Huitong reign of the Liao Dynasty (AD 941)
Height 3.5 cm, diameter of mouth 18.4 cm and of base 11.5 cm
Unearthed in 1992 from the tomb of Yelu Yuzhi, Alukeerqin Banner
Collection of the Archaeological Research Institute of Inner Mongolia

This oval gilded silver plate has a broad rim with five lobes.
The flower and bird patterns are engraved on the rim
within its raised edges.
The straight wall slants to the flat bottom
and is supported by a flared ring foot.
In the center of the interior, there is an engraved interlocking curling
grass design. Around the base and on the ring foot,
there are lotus rossette designs.

## 鎏金錾花银盘

辽会同四年（公元 941 年）
高 3.5、口径 18.4、底径 11.5 厘米
1992 年阿鲁科尔沁旗辽耶律羽之墓出土
内蒙古文物考古研究所藏

银质，鎏金。
五曲形宽平沿，沿内外缘起棱，
腹壁斜直，平底，圈足外撇。
沿面錾刻一周花鸟纹，
盘底中心錾刻缠枝卷草纹，
内底外缘及圈足底边刻宝相莲瓣纹。

# Gilded Silver Loop-Handled Pot

Liao Dynasty (AD 916 — 1125)
Height 33 cm, diameter of mouth 5.4 cm and of base 15.3 cm
Unearthed in 1979 from a hoard at Dongshancun,
Chengzi Village, Chifeng City
Collection of the Chifeng Municipal Museum

This piece has an oval body and a straight mouth
with a hat-shaped cover, on the top of which
there is a pearl-shaped knob. The flat silver bar was hammered
to be a handle and welded to its shoulder. On both sides
of the body are two engraved standing capricornuses.
Their mouths are wide open and long, tough tails stretch down
to the bottom. They face each other clinging up on the vessel.
Their heads rise out to form the broad shoulder of the piece.

## 双摩羯形鎏金银提梁壶

辽（公元 916 年—1125 年）
通高 33、口径 5.4、底径 15.3 厘米
1979 年赤峰市城子乡洞山村窖藏出土
赤峰市博物馆藏

椭圆形壶身，直口，圆帽形盖，顶端饰宝珠形钮，
扁平银条打制的提梁焊接于肩部。
腹壁两面錾刻两尾直立状摩羯鱼。
龙首，鱼身，昂首张口，口吐长舌，双尾着地，
相对攀附于器腹，作相向戏珠状。
头部突起，形成宽平的壶肩。

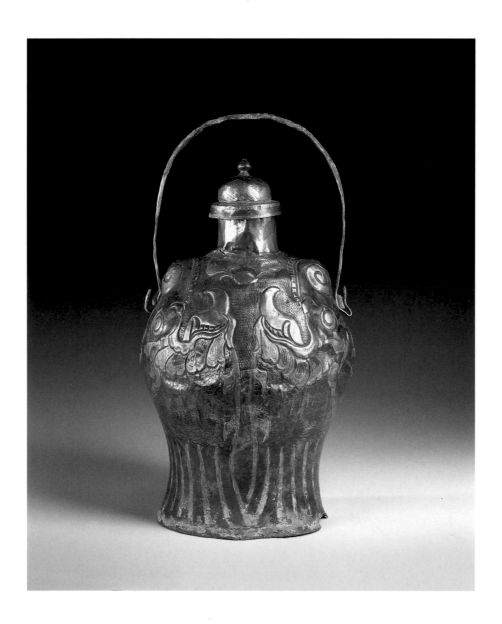

# Gilded Silver Plate with Engraved Lion Design

Tang Dynasty (AD 618 — 907)

Height 2.4 cm, diameter of mouth 46.6 cm

Unearthed in 1976 from a hoard at Jinshan Town, Kalaqin Banner

Collection of the Culture Relics Office of Kalaqin Banner

This gilded silver plate was made by hammering, but the detailed parts were made by engraving. The plate has a broad rim with six-lobed mallow-petal and a shallow bottom. A crouched lion in relief adorns the center of the plate. The lion is turning its head with a fierce expression and its mouth is wide open. Around the lion there are posy designs separated by rossette lotus-petal patterns. The rim is adorned with posy sprays with broad leaves.

## 狮纹鎏金錾花银盘

唐（公元 618 年—907 年）

高 2.4、口径 46.6 厘米

1976 年喀喇沁旗锦山镇窖藏出土

喀喇沁旗文管所藏

锤击成型，细部錾刻，纹饰鎏金。

六曲葵式口，宽平折沿，浅腹。

盘心浮雕一蹲狮，回首张大口，

作奋蹄嘶鸣状，神态威猛。

周围绕以折枝团花，间以宝相仰莲瓣。

口沿饰阔叶折枝扁团花。

## Silver Spittoon with Gold Pattern

The fourth year of the Huitong reign of the Liao Dynasty (AD 941)
Height 12 cm, diameter of mouth 15.4 cm, of belly 10.5 cm and of base 8.3 cm
Unearthed in 1992 from the tomb of Yelu Yuzhi, Alukeerqin Banner
Collection of the Archaeological Research Institute of Inner Mongolia

This is a silver piece gilded with floral patterns.
It has a dish-shaped mouth, a straight collar,
a drum belly and a flared ring foot. Around the rim,
the bottom and the ring foot is engraved with a band of rossette
lotus-petal designs. There are three peony and posy designs and
three groups of flowers and bird patterns on the body.
The interior is adorned with double lotus-petal designs.

## 金花银渣斗

辽会同四年（公元941年）
高12、口径15.4、腹径10.5、底径8.3厘米
1992年阿鲁科尔沁旗辽耶律羽之墓出土
内蒙古文物考古研究所藏

银质，花纹鎏金。
盘口，直领，鼓腹，圈足略外撇。
盘口和盘底边缘及圈足底边各錾刻一周宝相莲瓣纹，
盘面刻三组牡丹团花纹。
腹部刻三组鸿雁衔授团窠图案，
腹底刻一周双重仰莲纹。

## Silver Incense Burner

The seventh year of the Dakang reign of the Liao Dynasty (AD 1081)
Length 36.5 cm
Unearthed in 1993 from Maiwanggou, Toudaoyingzi Village,
Ningcheng County
Collection of the Archaeological Research Institute of Inner Mongolia

The incense burner was made in the shape
of a bunch of lotus flowers.
The lotus stem is the handle
and the full bloom lotus is the body of the incense burner,
which is supported by the lotus leaf as a base.
It has a unique and ingenious design
and excellent workmanship.

## 莲花鹊尾银香炉

辽大康七年（公元1081年）
通长36.5厘米
1993年宁城县头道营子乡埋王沟墓葬出土
内蒙古文物考古研究所藏

外形似一束莲花，
莲茎为手柄，
盛开的莲花为炉身，莲叶为炉座。
设计和制作堪称巧夺天工，
匠心独运。
莲花型香炉是礼佛者行进时手持的小香炉。

# 契丹族

契丹为鲜卑族的一支，唐初逐渐强盛，公元907 年建立辽王朝。陈国公主墓、耶律羽之墓及庆州白塔中的精美文物，代表了灿烂的契丹文明，也是北方草原文明发展史上的一个新高峰。

# *Qidan*

Qidan, a nationality originating from the Xianbei, came into force in the early Tang period and established the Liao dynasty in AD 907. The magnificent cultural relics found in the Tomb of the Princess of Chen, the Tomb of Yelu Yuzhi and from the white pagoda in Qingzhou clearly represent the glory of the Qidan civilization, which was a new height in the development of steppe civilization in the north.

## Incised White Glazed Vase

Liao Dynasty (AD 916 — 1125)
Height 52.8 cm, diameter of mouth 13.8 cm and of base 10 cm
Unearthed in 1985 from a Liao tomb at Buhetehada,
Bayanerdengsumu, Balinyou Banner
Collection of the Balinyou Banner Museum

The vase has a cup-shaped mouth, a long neck,
a slanting shoulder and a contracted belly supported by a ring foot.
A bow string pattern adorns the neck and a pair of carved peony
patterns is on the body. The vase is made from rough clay
and white glaze and is a treasured white glazed
ware of the Liao dynasty.

## 刻花长颈白瓷瓶

辽（公元 916 年—1125 年）
通高 52.8、口径 13.8、足径 10 厘米
1985 年巴林右旗巴彦尔灯苏木布和特哈达辽墓出土
巴林右旗博物馆藏

杯形口，长颈，溜肩，腹部斜收，圈足。
颈部饰一道弦纹，
腹部采用剔地法刻出一对牡丹图案。
粗胎，施白釉，
是辽白瓷中之珍品。

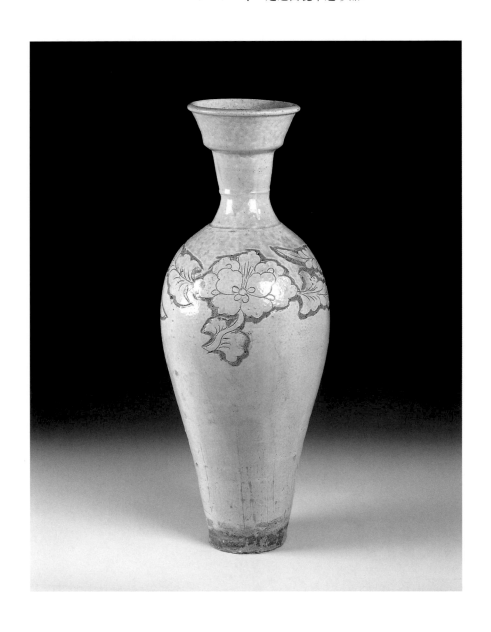

## White Glazed Bowl

The fourth year of the Huitong reign of the Liao Dynasty (AD 941)

Height 8.4 cm, diameter of mouth 23.6 cm and of base 10.8 cm

Unearthed in 1992 from the Tomb of Yelu Yuzhi, Alukeerqin Banner

Collection of the Archaeological Research Institute of Inner Mongolia

This bowl has an unglazed round rim,

a contracted belly and a false foot ring.

It has a refined body and well glazed.

In the center of the base there is the Chinese

character *"Ying"* in cursive script.

This bowl should be the product of the Xing Wares.

## "盈"字款白瓷碗

辽会同四年（公元 941 年）

高 8.4、口径 23.6、足径 10.8 厘米

1992 年阿鲁科尔沁旗辽耶律羽之墓出土

内蒙古文物考古研究所藏

圆唇，芒口，

腹壁弧收，假圈足。

胎质细腻，

施釉均匀，釉质清亮。

器底正中刻行书"盈"字款。

属邢窑产品。

# White Glazed Double-Gourd Ewer

Liao Dynasty (AD 916 — 1125)

Height 23.2 cm, diameter of mouth 2.8 cm and of base 8.2 cm

Unearthed in 1988 from a Liao tomb at Yangchang Village,
Balinyou Banner

Collection of the Balinyou Banner Museum

The ewer, in the shape of a double gourd,

has a small mouth, a dragon-head short spout,

a curved handle and a ring foot.

The neck and belly are decorated with stylized lotus leaf patterns.

The clay is fairly rough.

This white glazed ewer belongs to the Liao porcelain.

## 葫芦形白瓷执壶

辽（公元916年—1125年）

通高23.2、口径2.8、底径8.2厘米

1988年巴林右旗羊场乡辽墓出土

巴林右旗博物馆藏

葫芦形造型，

小口，龙首形短流，

曲柄，圈足。

颈部及腹部刻变形莲叶纹。

胎质较粗，施白釉，属辽瓷。

## White Glazed Kasyapa Figure

Liao Dynasty (AD 916 — 1125)
Height 26.5 cm
Collected in 1986 from Qianwulibugecun,
Nailingaosumu, Kulun Banner
Collection of the Tongliao Municipal Museum

Kasyapa is seated on a wooden stool with his left hand resting on his knee
and his right hand raised as if he were lecturing.
He is dressed in monk's robe with loose sleeves and covered with a Kasaya.
He is in deep thought wearing an air of solemn expression,
which makes him appear wise.
Its lustrous glazing and refined clay indicates
that this piece was a Ding ware masterpiece .

## 迦叶白瓷像

辽（公元916年—1125年）
高26.5厘米
1986年库伦旗奈林稿苏木前勿力布格村征集
通辽市博物馆藏

迦叶端坐于木凳之上，
左手扶膝，右手作演讲姿势。
身穿右衽斜领长衫，外披袈裟，
神情似凝思静想，俨然一位饱经风霜、
满腹经纶之士。瓷像胎质细腻、釉色光亮、
造型栩栩如生，是定窑中的精品。

## White Glazed Anada Figure

阿难白瓷像

Liao Dynasty (AD 916 — 1125)
Height 27 cm
Collected in 1986 from Qianwulibugecun,
Nailingaosumu, Kulun Banner
Collection of the Tongliao Municipal Museum.

辽（公元 916 年—1125 年）
高 27 厘米
1986 年库伦旗奈林稿苏木前勿力布格村征集
通辽市博物馆藏

Anada is seated on a wooden stool with his left hand resting
on his knee and right hand turning his rosary beads.
Wearing a smile on his face,
Anada looks sympathetic and peaceful.
This figurine is completely glazed and has a beautiful and
lustrous soft color. This piece is a Ding ware.

阿难端坐于木凳之上，
左手扶膝，右手捻佛珠。
脸庞丰满，面含微笑，深沉和善，神情自若。
瓷像通体施白釉，色泽光润。
属定窑产品。

## Pair of Brown Glazed Bowls

Liao Dynasty (AD 916 — 1125)
Height 5.2 - 5.6 cm, diameter of mouth 16.5 - 17.1 cm and of footring 5.4 cm
Collected in 1975 from Shibeicun, Baiyinchang Village,
Naiman Banner
Collection of the Tongliao Municipal Museum

The two pieces have unglazed rims,
slanting bodies and small foot rings. Molded designs of peony,
lotus flower, plum flower and morning glory
are adorned inside the bowls and molded chrysanthemum designs at
the bottom. These bowls of fine texture are thin-walled
and are completely glazed brown.
This is the rare treasure of the Ding wares.

## 印花紫定碗

辽（公元916年—1125年）

高5.2—5.6、口径16.5—17.1、底径5.4厘米

1975年奈曼旗白音昌乡石碑村征集

通辽市博物馆藏

两件形制基本相同。

芒口，斜直腹，小圈足。

碗内周壁印有牡丹、荷花、梅花、牵牛花等折枝花卉，
碗内底印一组菊花。

胎质细腻，胎壁轻薄，通体施褐紫色釉，釉面均匀、润亮。

为定窑珍稀品种，世称"紫定"。

## Black Glazed Double-Gourd Vase

Liao Dynasty (AD 916 — 1125)
Height 35.7 cm, diameter of mouth 3 cm and of base 9.4 cm
Unearthed in 1987 from Hurenbaohecun at Xinhui Village,
Aohan Banner
Collection of the Aohan Banner Museum

This double-gourd vase, made of grayish brown clay,
has a bright luster from the black glaze.
The veiled decoration covers over the mouth to the lower belly.
The upper part is painted with geometrical designs.
The lower part is a painting of a water-village scene.
This is a masterpiece of the Liao ceramics,
which indicates the high quality workmanship of ceramic making.

## 暗花黑釉葫芦瓶

辽（公元916年—1125年）
高35.7、口径3、底径9.4厘米
1987年敖汉旗新惠乡呼仁宝和村出土
敖汉旗博物馆藏

亚腰葫芦形，灰褐色瓷胎，黑釉光亮。
从口至下腹部绘暗花。
上腹部为几何形装饰图案，
下腹部绘一幅水乡景色画，
有盛开的荷花、摇曳的芦苇，水鸟飞翔于其间，
显示出辽代高超的制瓷工艺，为辽瓷中罕见之精品。

## Green Glazed Pottery Cockscomb Pot

Liao Dynasty (AD 916 — 1125)
Height 23.5 cm, diameter of base 7.5 cm
Unearthed in 1965 from a Liao tomb at Guangdegong Village,
Wengniute Banner
Collection of the Chifeng Municipal Museum

This pot has an oval body, a straight mouth,
large belly and a flat bottom.
Its loop handle is made of a dragon walking
on the pot with its head raised and back arched.
On the body of the pot there is a semicircle of leather-like stitches.
This is a typical daily utensil of the Qidan people.

## 龙首绿釉鸡冠壶

辽（公元 916 年—1125 年）
高 23.5、底径 7.5 厘米
1965 年翁牛特旗广德公乡辽墓出土
赤峰市博物馆藏

椭圆形壶体，
直口，垂腹，平底，
提梁是一昂首、曲颈、弓背的行龙。
腹部有半环形仿皮囊缝合线。
为契丹民族特有的生活器皿。
属辽地窑场产品。

# Green Glazed Pottery Cockscomb Pot

Liao Dynasty (AD 916 — 1125)

Length 16 cm, width 9 cm, height 27 cm

Unearthed in 1989 from a Liao tomb at Guangdegong Village,
Wengniute Banner

Collection of the Culture Relics Office of Wengniute Banner

This oblate squared pot has a descending belly, a straight mouth and a
tower-shaped lid with a pearl like finial. Two strap holes on the top lip
are decorated with sculptured monkeys on the outside corner. The
monkeys are in a riding posture with two hands holding the lip.
Beneath the top lip, there is a band of fish-shaped tassels in relief.
Incised curly grass patterns decorate the belly. Around the side
there is a raised leather-like stitch design.
The pottery clay is reddish in color and has a grass green glaze.

双猴绿釉鸡冠壶

辽（公元 916 年—1125 年）

长 16、宽 9、高 27 厘米

1989 年翁牛特旗广德公乡辽墓出土

翁牛特旗文物管理站藏

壶体呈扁体方形，垂腹，直口，上有塔形盖，
盖顶饰一宝珠形钮。两方形耳穿孔，耳间呈马鞍形，
外侧各堆塑一小猴，双手扶耳作骑跨状。
耳下饰一排凸起的鱼形璎珞纹，腹部刻卷草纹。侧边有凸起
的仿皮缝合线纹。胎质为陶胎，呈红褐色，施草绿色釉。
装饰趣味浓厚，作为实用器，
也是一件难得的艺术珍品。属辽地窑场产品。

## *Sancai* (tricolor) Glazed Capricornus Pot

Liao Dynasty (AD 916 — 1125)

Height 22.3 cm, length 30 cm, diameter of footring 9 cm

Collected in 1975 from Keerqinzuoyizhong Banner

Collection of the Tongliao Municipal Museum

This pot is in the shape of a capricornus reclining on a lotus flower.
It holds its head high with its tail waving.
The pearl in its mouth is the spout.
Behind the horn there is an opening for adding water.
The handle is connected between its wings and the tail.
It is covered with scales in relief. In a unique design and shape,
this pot is a gem of the Liao sancai glazed pieces.

## 摩羯形三彩壶

辽（公元916年—1125年）

高22.3、长30、足径9厘米

1975年科尔沁左翼中旗征集

通辽市博物馆藏

整体造型为龙首鱼身的摩羯，
卧于莲花之上，圈足底。
摩羯昂首摆尾，口含一珠，穿孔为流，
龙角后面有一注水口，翼与尾之间以梁相连成执手。
鱼身浮雕鱼鳞。造型奇特优美，
线条流畅，为辽三彩中的精品。

## Sancai (tricolor) Glazed Mandarin Duck Pot

Liao Dynasty (AD 916 — 1125)

Height 20 cm, diameter of mouth 8.2 cm and of base 9 cm

Collected in 1977 from Songshan District, Chifeng City

Collection of the Chifeng Municipal Museum

This pot is cast in the shape of a mandarin duck floating on the water.

On the back of the duck is a flower petal shaped mouth.

An arc handle with ripple patterns connects the opening to the tail.

The bill of the duck is the spout.

The piece has a false ring foot (the bottom is flat).

It is brightly colored with yellow and green glaze.

This pot is an example of the high artistic skills in design.

## 鸳鸯形三彩壶

辽（公元 916 年—1125 年）

高 20、口径 8.2、底径 9 厘米

1977 年赤峰市松山区征集

赤峰市博物馆藏

壶体造型为浮水鸳鸯。鸳鸯背上有喇叭状五瓣花形壶口，
壶口下部以一弧形水波纹握柄与尾部相接，
鸳鸯抬头部凝视前方，嘴部中空为流，腹下有假圈足。
釉色黄绿相间，色彩鲜艳。
运用三彩釉刻画鸳鸯的美丽羽毛，
在造型艺术上具有很高的造诣。

## *Sancai* (tricolor) Glazed Ewer with Dragon Design

Liao Dynasty (AD 916 — 1125)

Height 18.8 cm, diameter of mouth 3.5 cm and of base 7.8 cm

Collected in 1977 from Songshan District, Chifeng City

Collection of the Chifeng Municipal Antique Store

This piece has a straight mouth, a narrow long neck,
a ball-shaped belly, a false circular foot and a short slanting spout.
The flat handle connects the neck to the belly.
On the body there is a pair of dragons face to face
surrounded by waves and small fish jumping in the water.
A blooming lotus flower is in front of the dragon.
Around the neck and shoulder of the pot there are interlocking flower
patterns and rosette designs.
The pink clay was applied with yellow and green glaze.

龙纹三彩执壶

辽（公元916年—1125年）

高18.8、口径3.5、底径7.8厘米

1977年赤峰市松山区征集

赤峰市文物店藏

直口，细长颈，球形腹，假圈足，斜直短流。
颈与肩部连接扁体把手。
腹部刻画出昂首相对的蟠龙，四周衬以海水波浪纹，
小鱼翻跃其间。
龙首前盛开的莲花心上有一火焰宝珠。
壶颈和肩部印有缠枝花卉和宝相花。
胎呈粉红色，施黄、绿色釉。

## Octagonal Pottery Ink-Stone

The sixth year of the Xianyong reign of the Liao Dynasty (AD 1070)
Height 12.6 cm, diameter 22 cm
Unearthed in 1992 from Maiwanggou, Toudaoyingzi Village,
Ningcheng County
Collection of the Archaeological Research Institute of Inner Mongolia

This artifact, in octagonal shape, has two separate pieces;
when assembled the top serves as the inkstone and the reverse as a
brush-washer. The inkstone has a concave area,
around with scallop carved edge, for grinding ink.
The flower and grass patterns in relief decorate the eight sides. Orange
color is the main glaze with some green or white glaze filled in. The
brush washer has a bowl-shaped belly with yellow glaze.

## 八角形三彩砚

辽咸雍六年（公元 1070 年）
高 12.6、直径 22 厘米
1992 年宁城县头道营子乡埋王沟墓葬出土
内蒙古文物考古研究所藏

由砚台与笔洗对扣成盒形。平面作等边八角形。
砚面呈风字形，砚池斜凹，边缘作云角弧曲形，
八侧面浮雕花草纹，釉色以橘黄为主，
间隙补填绿、白釉，釉色鲜亮。
笔洗八角形宽平沿，腹凹弧如碗形，
施黄釉。使用砚时，可将砚台与笔洗分开，既美观又实用。

## Sancai (tricolor) Glazed Xun (a musical instrument)

The sixth year of the Xianyong reign of the Liao Dynasty (AD 1070)
Height 6.3 cm, diameter 8.3 cm
Unearthed in 1992 from Maiwanggou, Toudaoyingzi Village,
Ningcheng County
Collection of the Archaeological Research Institute of Inner Mongolia

The oblate spheroid piece, green and yellow glazed,
has a mouth-shaped opening and
a small round hole on top.
The upper belly has peony spray designs in relief and the
lower belly is adorned with lotus.

## 三彩埙

辽咸雍六年（公元 1070 年）
高 6.3、直径 8.3 厘米
1992 年宁城县头道营子乡埋王沟墓葬出土
内蒙古文物考古研究所藏

扁圆球形，
顶端有一嘴状扁孔和一圆形小孔，施绿釉。
上腹浮雕缠枝牡丹，施黄釉；
下腹浮雕仰莲纹，施绿釉。

## Yurt-Shaped Funerary Urn with Deer Pattern

Liao Dynasty (AD 916 — 1125)
Height 25.5 cm, diameter of base 31 cm
Unearthed in 1973 from Hadatucun, Hadayingge Village,
Balinzuo Banner
Collection of the Balinzuo Banner Museum

This gray pottery urn, wheel-made,
has embossed decoration and incised
designs of ten deer on top
and outside the urn with a single door,
two side windows and a round lid.
This urn is in the shape of a yurt,
which strongly reflects the nomadic lifestyle of the Qidan people.

## 鹿纹穹庐式骨灰罐

辽（公元 916 年—1125 年）
通高 25.5、底径 31 厘米
1973 年巴林左旗哈达英格乡哈达图村墓葬出土
巴林左旗博物馆藏

泥质灰陶，轮制。外壁有堆塑及刻划装饰。
圆壁穹顶，正中设带轴单扇门，两面各开一方窗。
顶部有圆形口，附圆饼形盖。
周壁及顶部共刻划有十只鹿。
整体造型类似蒙古包，具有浓郁的草原生活气息，
真实地折射出契丹民族的生活习俗。

## Gilded Bronze *Duo* (a hearse fitting)

Liao Dynasty (AD 916 — 1125)
Height 42 cm, length of the long end 30 cm and of the short end 20 cm
Unearthed in 1993 from the family burial site of Yelu Yuzhi,
Alukeerqin Banner
Collection of the Archaeological Research Institute of Inner Mongolia

On the top of the bronze there is an iron knob and was raised edges
encircling it. This gilded piece is covered with incised curling cloud
pattern. The hearse specially designed for the dead from Qidan noble
family and royal family. It is recorded in the book *History of the Liao,
Chapter Yiweizhi*: "The hearse for the dead is covered with silk and
silver, under the bottom hangs a *Duo*, and on the back a felt rug hangs
from above. The hearse is driven by buffalo."
From this, it is known that *Duo* is an object for the hearse.

鎏金铜铎

辽（公元 916 年—1125 年）
高 42、长径 30、短径 20 厘米
1993 年阿鲁科尔沁旗辽耶律羽之家族墓地出土
内蒙古文物考古研究所藏

顶部有铁质吊钮，四底边呈拱形。
通体鎏金，錾刻卷云纹。
契丹贵族和皇族死后有专用的送终车，
《辽史·仪卫志》记载："送终车，车楼纯饰以锦，
螭头以银，下悬铎，后垂大毡，驾以牛。"
据此可知，该铜铎应是送终车上的物件。

## Gold Plaque with Incantation of Dharani

The eighteenth year of the Chongxi reign of the Liao Dynasty (AD 1049)
Length 16.7 cm, width 9.6 cm, thickness 0.03 cm
Unearthed in 1989 from the laksta of the Sakyamuni pagoda
in Qingzhou, Balinyou Banner
Collection of the Balinyou Banner Museum

This rectangular plaque has an inscription,
engraved horizontally, of seventy-seven
Sanskrit characters in five lines. On the left side,
vertically engraved, are eight Chinese characters,
which read: Incantation of Dharani in the laksta.
This is a very precious relic.

## 陀罗尼咒金板

辽重熙十八年（公元 1049 年）
长 16.7、宽 9.6、厚 0.03 厘米
1989 年巴林右旗辽庆州释迦佛舍利塔塔刹出土
巴林右旗博物馆藏

长方形金板，
单面横书，
双勾镌刻梵文陀罗尼咒 5 行 77 字，
左侧竖行镌刻汉字"相轮樘中陀罗尼咒" 8 字。
字迹清楚，弥足珍贵。

## Sutra Container with Ten Painted Buddha Figures

The eighteenth year of the Chongxi reign of the Liao Dynasty (AD 1049)
Height 45.5 cm, diameter of base 13 cm
Unearthed in 1989 from the laksta of the Sakyamuni pagoda
in Qingzhou, Balinyou Banner
Collection of the Balinyou Banner Museum

This artifact, made of cypress wood,
stored a printed sutra in small script. The wrapping,
a piece of white silk, has words written in ink.
The outside of the container is incised with ten seated Buddha images.
The middle is carved with the characters "Ten Buddha."
Except for the Buddhas, the container is painted
with colors of orange, red, blue and gray.

## 十方佛彩绘舍利塔

辽重熙十八年（公元 1049 年）
通高 45.5、底径 13 厘米
1989 年巴林右旗辽庆州释迦佛舍利塔塔刹相轮樘出土
巴林右旗博物馆藏

柏木制作。
塔身内置小字雕版印经《妙法莲花经》一卷，
包裹佛经的白绢袱上有墨书"法华经一部全身舍利在此塔中"。
塔身外壁减地浅刻十尊坐佛，
正中刻"十方佛"三字，塔表除佛像为原木本色，
余皆平涂橙、红、蓝、灰等色彩。

# Sutra Container with Seven Gilded Buddha Figures

The eighteenth year of the Chongxi reign of the Liao Dynasty (AD 1049)
Height 23 cm, diameter of base 9.1 cm
Unearthed in 1989 from the laksta of the Sakyamuni pagoda
in Qingzhou, Balinyou Banner
Collection of the Balinyou Banner Museum

This sutra container is made of cypress wood.
Around the container is engraved seven standing Buddhas.
The snail-coiled hair of the
Buddha is painted in blue
and their bodies are covered with gold leaf.
The garments are depicted simply
and smoothly and show a forceful and experienced carving skill.

# 七佛贴金舍利塔

辽重熙十八年（公元 1049 年）
通高 23、底径 9.1 厘米
1989 年巴林右旗辽庆州释迦佛舍利塔塔刹相轮橖出土
巴林右旗博物馆藏

柏木制作。
塔身外壁雕刻七佛立像，
七佛螺发为蓝色，全身贴金。
衣着线条简练流畅，
刀法遒劲娴熟。
塔刹上系以悬鱼夹层锦塔幡。

# Gilded Silver Sutra Container Decorated with Phoenix

The eighteenth year of the Chongxi reign of the Liao Dynasty (AD 1049)
Height 40.5 cm, diameter of base 10.7 cm
Unearthed in 1989 from the laksta of the Sakyamuni pagoda
in Qingzhou, Balinyou Banner
Collection of the Balinyou Banner Museum

This hexagonal-tower-shaped artifact was made of hammered silver sheets. The whole piece was hammered separately, incised with patterns, nailed and then welded all together. Five side-doors are decorated with donors and guardians. The top of the piece is in the shape of a lotus flower and is covered with an upside-down monk's alms bowl and a pearl. A phoenix is standing on the top of the post with a tassel of twenty-four pearls in its beak. In front of the base, there is a standing gilded figure with a Buddhist monk's staff and an alms bowl in hand. A piece of incantation of Dharani was found within this container.

## 凤衔珠银鎏金舍利塔

辽重熙十八年（公元 1049 年）
通高 40.5、底径 10.7 厘米
1989 年巴林右旗辽庆州释迦佛舍利塔塔刹相轮樘出土
巴林右旗博物馆藏

塔座、塔身、塔檐、塔刹等部分，分别用薄银板分段锤鍱、
錾刻及铆固、焊接、然后插接并附加装饰组成。
覆莲座上有六边形勾栏。塔身正面辟门，
其余五面刻供养人和力士像。
塔顶以莲台作刹座，上置覆钵、宝珠，刹杆上装三重华盖，
顶端立一凤鸟，喙衔 24 颗珍珠编缀而成的璎珞。
塔檐、刹杆、华盖皆垂挂风铎。在塔座之前单独嵌一持仗、
托钵鎏金人物。塔内原藏银板陀罗尼咒一卷。

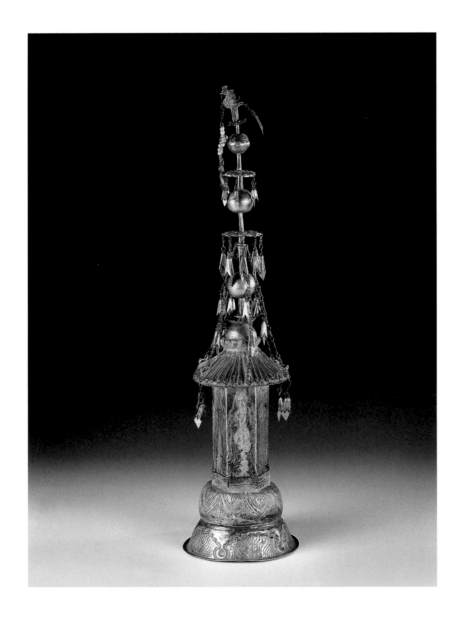

## Sutra Container with Seven Painted and Gilded Buddha Figures

The eighteenth year of the Chongxi reign of the Liao Dynasty (AD 1049)
Height 22.8 cm, diameter of base 22.8 cm
Unearthed in 1989 from the laksta of the Sakyamuni pagoda
in Qingzhou, Balinyou Banner
Collection of the Balinyou Banner Museum

This piece, made of cypress wood, is composed of a round base,
a tube body and a laksta-shaped top. They are joined together with
pegs. Seven standing Buddhas are engraved around the container.
The snail-coiled hair of the Buddhas is painted in blue and the bodies
are covered with gold leaf. Except for the Buddha, the container is
painted with colors of yellow, red and blue.

## 七佛彩绘贴金舍利塔

辽重熙十八年（公元 1049 年）
通高 22.8、底径 22.8 厘米
1989 年巴林右旗辽庆州释迦佛舍利塔塔刹相轮橖出土
巴林右旗博物馆藏

柏木制作。
由圆形塔座、筒形塔身、塔檐、塔刹对口插接而成。
塔身外壁雕刻七佛立像，七佛螺发为蓝色，全身贴金。
塔表除佛像以外，余皆平涂黄、红、蓝等色彩。
塔刹挂平首花绫幡。

## Embroidered Scarf with Plum Flowers, Bees and Butterflies

The eighteenth year of the Chongxi reign of the Liao Dynasty (AD 1049)
Length 65 cm, width 50 cm
Unearthed in 1989 from the laksta of the Sakyamuni pagoda
in Qingzhou, Balinyou Banner
Collection of the Balinyou Banner Museum

This embroidered scarf has blue silk gauze
as the top layer with grass green silk lining.
The motif of the embroidery is plums.
There are bamboo, bees and butterflies, over which mountains are
embroidered with yellow and blue silk threads.
The lower, left and right edges are embroidered with
a chain of beading of white silk thread.

## 梅花蜂蝶蓝色罗地绣巾

辽重熙十八年（公元 1049 年）
长 65、宽 50 厘米
1989 年巴林右旗辽庆州释迦佛舍利塔塔刹相轮橖出土
巴林右旗博物馆藏

刺绣，平针绣法。
正面为蓝色素罗，
背面用草绿色绢作夹层。
主题图案为梅、竹、蜂、蝶等。
上方用黄和蓝色丝线绣出山峰，
左右下三边缘用白色丝线绣联珠纹边饰。

# Embroidered Scarf with Dragon Design

The eighteenth year of the Chongxi reign of the Liao Dynasty (AD 1049)

Length 79.2 cm, width 58.5 cm

Unearthed in 1989 from the laksta of the Sakyamuni pagoda
in Qingzhou, Balinyou Banner

Collection of the Balinyou Banner Museum

This piece is embroidered with curved dragons playing with pearls.
Each foot of the dragons has three claws.
The tail is fairly round and thick. A flaming pearl is depicted
in front of the dragons' head. Near the lower edge there is a pair of
symmetrical walking dragons surrounded by clouds.
The yellow and white glazed cloud patterns cover
the whole piece. A chain of white beading is
embroidered along the lower, left and right edges.

# 联珠云龙纹橙色罗地绣巾

辽重熙十八年（公元 1049 年）

长 79.2、宽 58.5 厘米

1989 年巴林右旗辽庆州释迦佛舍利塔塔刹相轮樘出土

巴林右旗博物馆藏

平针刺绣。主题图案为云龙戏珠纹。
龙身蟠曲，龙背用浅黄色丝线绣出鳞纹，
龙足三爪，龙尾较粗圆，龙嘴前有一火焰宝珠。
底边处有对称的行龙，上下祥云环绕，
黄白相间的如意形云朵散布整个画面，
左右下三边缘用白色联珠纹勾边。

## Embroidered Red Gauze Sutra Bag

The eighteenth year of the Chongxi reign of the Liao Dynasty (AD 1049)
Length 27.5cm, width 27cm
Unearthed in 1989 from the laksta of the Sakyamuni pagoda
in Qingzhou, Balinyou Banner
Collection of the Balinyou Banner Museum

The front layer of the wrapping is red gauze lined with white silk.
On the lower right corner there is a silk ribbon for binding.
In the center of the bead-circled pattern is a Qidan horseman with two
eagles in hand on an armored galloping horse. In between there are
rhinoceros horns, double coins, bamboo-made music instrument,
Dharma wheels and other treasures.
Two bands of blue and white bead patterns are decorated
near the upper and lower edges.

## 联珠人物红罗地绣经袱

辽重熙十八年（公元 1049 年）
长 27.5、宽 27 厘米
1989 年巴林右旗辽庆州释迦佛舍利塔塔刹相轮樘出土
巴林右旗博物馆藏

平针刺绣。正面为红罗，背面用白绢作夹层，
右下角缀有打节用绢丝带。
正中联珠环内绣一骑马驾鹰的契丹人物，
戴皮棉帽，穿皮棉袍，着棕色皮靴，
两手高擎两只海冬青。马身上披挂铠甲，作奔跑状。
空隙处绣犀角、双钱、竹磬、法轮、珊瑚等杂宝，
上下各有两条蓝白色联珠边饰。

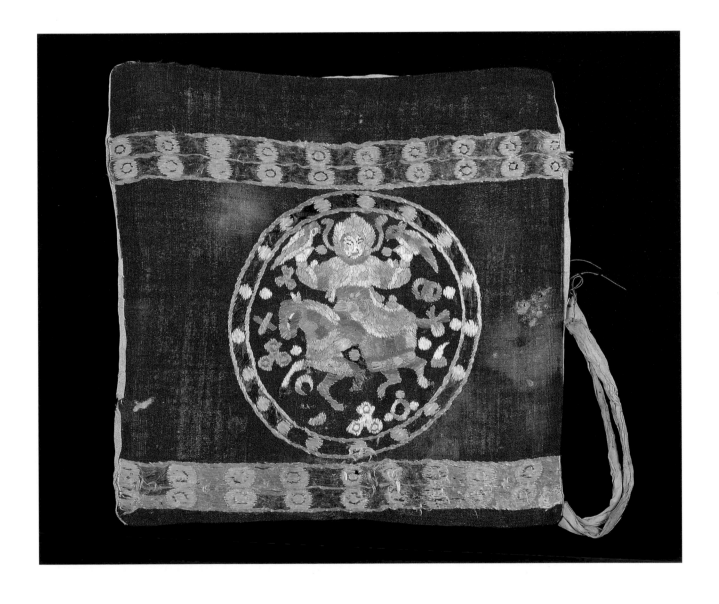

## Painted White Jade Sculpture of the Nirvana of Sakyamuni

The eighteenth year of the Chongxi reign of the Liao Dynasty (AD 1049)
Height 36 cm, length 60 cm, width 33 cm
Unearthed in 1989 from the Sakyamuni pagoda
in Qingzhou, Balinyou Banner
Collection of the Balinyou Banner Museum

This piece was sculpted from white jade.
Sakyamuni, wearing a calm expression,
is resting his head on a lotus pillow and reclining on his right side
with his right hand under his neck.
On the four sides of the stone bed there
are carved lions in relief in different poses.

## 释迦佛涅槃彩绘汉白玉雕像

辽重熙十八年（公元 1049 年）
通高 36、长 60、宽 33 厘米
1989年巴林右旗辽庆州释迦佛舍利塔内出土
巴林右旗博物馆藏

汉白玉圆雕。
释迦佛神态安详，头枕莲花枕，
面向右侧身而卧，右手托于颈下。
石床四侧门内各雕一小雄狮，
神态各异。

# Gold Mask and Silver Netted Clothes (head part)

The seventh year of the Kaitai reign of the Liao Dynasty (AD 1018)
Length 21.7 cm, width 18.8 cm, weight 293.5 g.
Unearthed in 1986 from the Tomb of the Princess of Chen,
Naiman Banner
Collection of the Archaeological Research Institute of Inner Mongolia.

The exquisite mask was made of a sheet of gold,
which was hammered to resemble the real face of the deceased.
The eyes and eyebrows are etched. The holes on the edge of the mask
tie it to the silver head part of the netted clothes.
This mask was on the face of the consort of the Chen State Princess.
Using metal masks and netted clothes is a particular custom
of the Qidan burial tradition.

金面具、银丝网络(部分)

辽开泰七年(公元 1018 年)
长 21.7、宽 18.8 厘米　重 293.5 克
1986 年奈曼旗辽陈国公主墓出土
内蒙古文物考古研究所藏

薄金片制作。依照死者真容用薄金片捶击成型，眉、
眼局部錾刻，制作精细。
面具周边有穿孔，与银丝头网连缀。
此件面具出土时覆盖于陈国公主之驸马面部。
在殡葬中采用金属面具和网络葬衣，
是辽代契丹贵族所特有的葬俗。

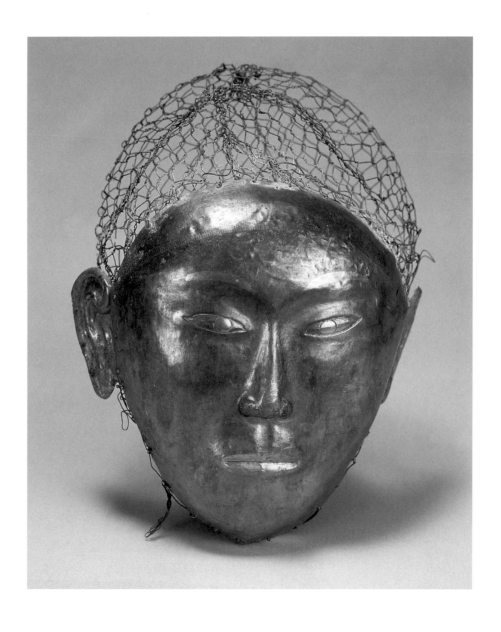

# Gilded Silver Crown

The seventh year of the Kaitai reign of the Liao Dynasty (AD 1018)
Height 31.5 cm, width 31.4 cm, diameter of mouth 19.5 cm, weight 587 g.
Unearthed in 1986 from the Tomb of the Princess of Chen,
Naiman Banner
Collection of the Archaeological Research Institute of Inner Mongolia

This crown was made of hammered and engraved thin sheets and then
assembled together with silver thread. At the front,
there are engraved phoenixes, flying cranes and Taoist figures.
Under the feet of the figure, there is a tortoise with its head upward.
This crown is also attached with twenty-four pendants of phoenixes,
birds, flowers and flaming pearls. This burial object indicates the
Qidan people's worship of Taoism.

## 鎏金银冠

辽开泰七年（公元 1018 年）
通高 31.5、宽 31.4、口径 19.5 厘米　重 587 克
1986 年奈曼旗辽陈国公主墓出土
内蒙古文物考古研究所藏

由鎏金薄银片重叠缀合而成。
薄银片先分片捶击成型，再镂雕錾刻花纹，
然后用细银丝缀合成冠体。
冠正面錾刻凤鸟、飞鹤和道教人物，人像脚下刻一仰首乌龟，
另钉缀 24 件凤、鸟、花卉、火焰宝珠等银饰件。
为陈国公主之驸马殡葬用具，反映出契丹贵族对道教的信仰。

## Pair of Silver Boots with Gilded Design

The seventh year of the Kaitai reign of the Liao Dynasty (AD 1018)
Height 34.6cm, length of sole 30.4cm
Unearthed in 1986 from the Tomb of the Princess of Chen,
Naiman Banner
Collection of the Archaeological Research Institute of Inner Mongolia

This pair of boots was made of thin silver sheets
of 0.05 centimeter in thickness.
The sheets were hammered into the upper part of the shoe.
The instep and sole were made according to the real size then
assembled with silver thread. On the upper part and instep there are
engraved and gilded designs of clouds and phoenixes.

## 金花银靴

辽开泰七年（公元1018年）
高34.6、底长30.4厘米
1986年奈曼旗辽陈国公主墓出土
内蒙古文物考古研究所藏

用0.05厘米厚的薄银片，
仿照实物分靴靿、靴面、
靴底各自打制成型，
然后用细银丝缀合。
靴靿、靴面錾刻云凤纹，花纹鎏金。

## Silver Pillow with Gilded Designs

The seventh year of the Kaitai reign of the Liao Dynasty (AD 1018)
Height 0.9-14 cm, length of surface 36 cm, width 49.6 cm, weight 1510 g.
Unearthed in 1986 from the Tomb of the Princess of Chen,
Naiman Banner
Collection of the Archaeological Research Institute of Inner Mongolia

This pillow was made of hammered
silver sheets welded together.
The surface of the pillow with gilded cloud
and phoenix designs is like the nimbus of the Buddha.
The surface of the pillow is welded to the base,
which is in the shape of a dustbin,
the front is higher and the back is lower.

金花银枕

辽开泰七年（公元 1018 年）
枕面长 36、宽 49.6、高 0.9 — 14 厘米　重 1510 克
1986 年奈曼旗辽陈国公主墓出土
内蒙古文物考古研究所藏

用薄银片打制焊接成形。
枕面呈半圆连弧形，形同佛像的背光；
枕座箕状，前高后低呈斜坡形，
焊于枕面底部。
枕面錾刻云凤纹，
花纹鎏金。

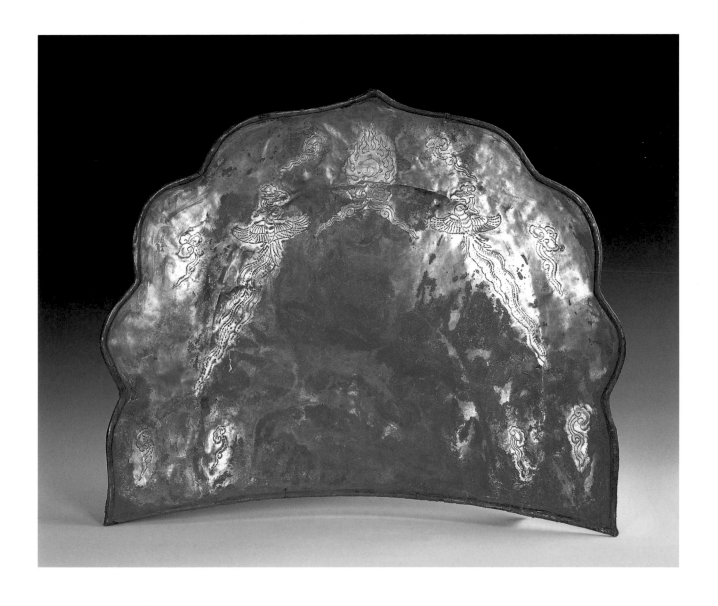

## Silver Belt with Inlaid Ornaments

The seventh year of the Kaitai reign of the Liao Dynasty (AD 1018)
Length 137.5 cm
Unearthed in 1986 from the Tomb of the Princess of Chen,
Naiman Banner
Collection of the Archaeological Research Institute of Inner Mongolia

This belt was made of silver sheets.

The belt head is riveted with an oval silver buckle.

Three bubble-shaped silver ornaments are fixed

to the belt with three short silver belts.

There are another three heart-shaped bronze ornaments

near the end of the belt.

## 银、铜铸银鞓鞢𫐌带

辽开泰七年（公元 1018 年）

通长 137.5 厘米

1986 年奈曼旗辽陈国公主墓出土

内蒙古文物考古研究所藏

带鞓用薄银片制作，
带具则分件打制或模铸，用铆钉固定于银带上。
银带前端铆接椭圆形银带扣，带上套银带箍；
中部钉缀三件圆泡形银带铐，
下垂三条长短不齐的小银带；
后部钉三件桃形铜带铐，尾端钉缀圭形银铊尾。

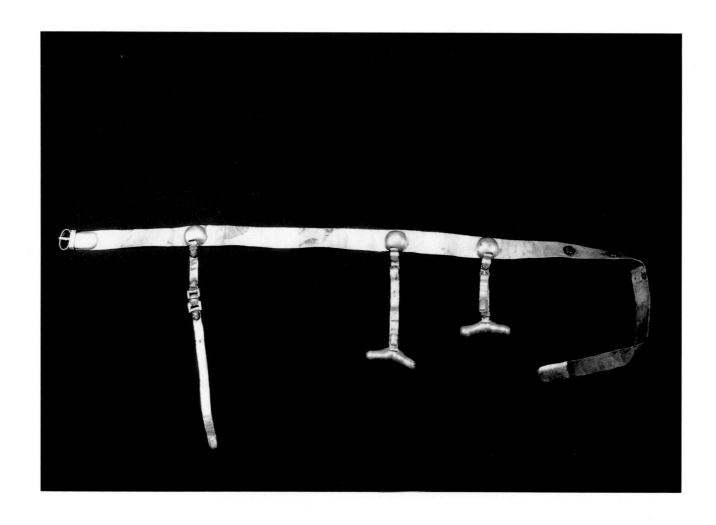

## Silver Belt with Jade Inlaid Decoration

The seventh year of the Kaitai reign of the Liao Dynasty (AD 1018)
Length 163.7 cm
Unearthed in 1986 from the Tomb of the Princess of Chen,
Naiman Banner
Collection of the Archaeological Research Institute of Inner Mongolia

This belt was made of hammered silver sheets. The head of the belt is jointed with a gold belt buckle. The belt is inlaid with fourteen square jade ornaments and a peach-shaped jade ware. The tail of the belt is threaded with an elongated pointed tablet of jade. There is another short silver belt, pierced with six holes attached to it. Both belts would have been used together.

## 玉銙银带

辽开泰七年（公元 1018 年）
通长 163.7 厘米
1986 年奈曼旗辽陈国公主墓出土
内蒙古文物考古研究所藏

薄银片制作。前端铆接金带扣，
银带上钉缀 14 件方形白玉銙，
一件桃形玉銙，带尾钉缀一件圭形玉铊尾。
另附短银带一条，带上有六个穿孔。
两条带配合使用。

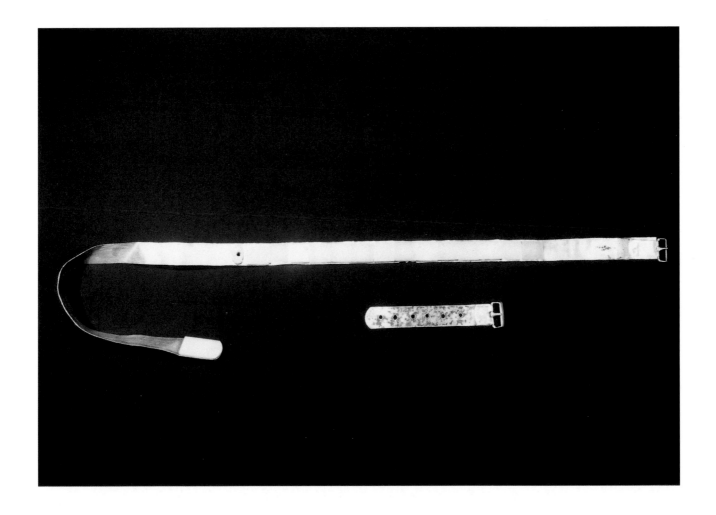

## Pair of Gold Bracelets with Dragon Design

The seventh year of the Kaitai reign of the Liao Dynasty (AD 1018)
Diameter 5.5 — 7.7 cm, weight 66.5 g. (one piece)
Unearthed in 1986 from the Tomb of the Princess of Chen,
Naiman Banner
Collection of the Archaeological Research Institute of Inner Mongolia

This piece is a pair of flat curved bracelets.
The designs of two twisted dragons are engraved
and etched on the surface.
The dragon head is engraved
as the end of the bracelet.

## 双龙纹金镯

辽开泰七年（公元1018年）
镯径5.5 — 7.7厘米 （单件）重66.5克
1986年奈曼旗辽陈国公主墓出土
内蒙古文物考古研究所藏

打制。细部花纹錾刻。
镯体宽扁弯成椭圆形，
镯面錾刻互相缠绕的双龙，
两端錾刻龙首，形象富有生趣。

## Silver Awl with Jade Handle

The seventh year of the Kaitai reign of the Liao Dynasty (AD 1018)
Length 17.8 cm, and of the silver scabbard 15 cm
Unearthed in 1986 from the Tomb of the Princess of Chen,
Naiman Banner
Collection of the Archaeological Research Institute of Inner Mongolia

This silver awl was made by hammering.
One end is fixed into the jade handle,
which was made of green jade. The silver scabbard
was made of a silver plate hammered into a roll
and welded. There is a silver chain on
the upper part of the scabbard.

## 玉柄银锥

辽开泰七年（公元 1018 年）
锥通长 17.8、银鞘长 15 厘米
1986 年内蒙古奈曼旗辽陈国公主墓出土
内蒙古文物考古研究所藏

银锥锻制，末端嵌入玉柄中。圆柱形柄青玉磨制。
银鞘用长条薄银片锤打卷曲成筒形，
合缝处焊接。鞘的上部系银链，可随身佩挂，
游猎时刺杀猎物。此锥即史书所载的辽代
贵族们春季"捺钵"时专用的刺鹅锥。

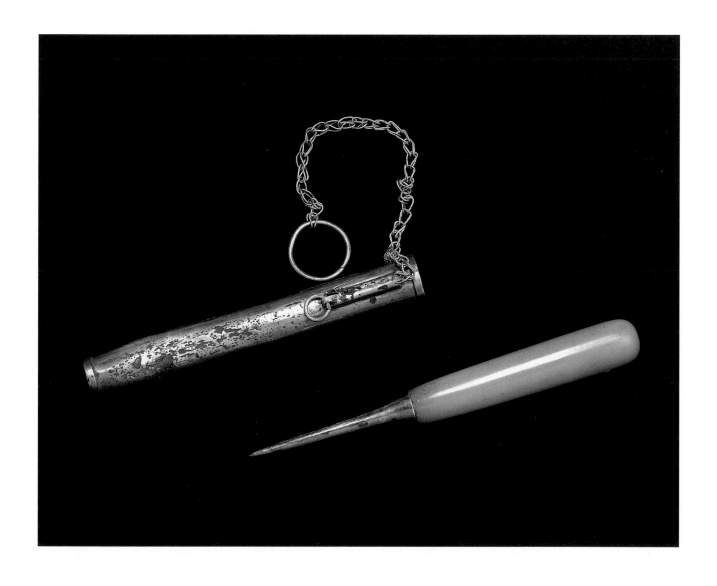

## Octagonal Gold Box

The seventh year of the Kaitai reign of the Liao Dynasty (AD 1018)
Height 1.7 cm diameter 5.5 cm, weight 85 g.
Unearthed in 1986 from the Tomb of the Princess of Chen,
Naiman Banner
Collection of the Archaeological Research Institute of Inner Mongolia

This oblate box was made of hammered and engraved gold sheets.
Two gold loops are welded to the upper part and lower part of the box.
The upper loop is for a gold chain to attach to a person and
the lower one chains a lock. One side of the box is engraved
with a picture of mandarin ducks playing in the water and the
other side is carved with the view of two cranes standing on the beach.
A circle of beaded patterns decorate the edge of the box.
The exterior side of the box is engraved with entwined leaf patterns.

## 八曲式金盒

辽开泰七年（公元 1018 年）
高 1.7、直径 5.5 厘米　重 85 克
1986 年奈曼旗辽陈国公主墓出土
内蒙古文物考古研究所藏

打制。细部纹饰錾刻。扁圆形，
以子母口相合。盒外两侧焊接两对金钮，
一侧穿系金链用于佩挂，一侧穿系插栓。
一面錾刻鸳鸯戏水纹，
一面錾刻立于沙汀之上的双鹤，
周边錾刻联珠纹，盒外侧錾刻缠枝卷叶纹。

# Mandarin Duck Jade Pendant

The seventh year of the Kaitai reign of the Liao Dynasty (AD 1018)
Length 6 cm, width 2 cm, height 2.8 cm
Unearthed in 1986 from the Tomb of the Princess of Chen,
Naiman Banner
Collection of the Archaeological Research Institute of Inner Mongolia

This lovely white jade is in the shape of two
mandarin ducks sitting face to face
with their necks crossed. They have plump bodies,
closed wings and descending short tails.
On the neck there is a pierced
hole for stringing a thread to wear around on the body.

交颈鸳鸯玉坠

辽开泰七年（公元 1018 年）
长 6、宽 2、高 2.8 厘米
1986 年奈曼旗辽陈国公主墓出土
内蒙古文物考古研究所藏

白玉圆雕。
两只鸳鸯相对交颈而卧，
充满情趣。鸳鸯体形肥硕，
双翅并拢，短尾下垂。
颈部斜穿一孔，可佩挂。

# Jade Fish-Shaped Box

The seventh year of the Kaitai reign of the Liao Dynasty (AD 1018)
Length 23.5 cm
Unearthed in 1986 from the Tomb of the Princess of Chen,
Naiman Banner
Collection of the Archaeological Research Institute of Inner Mongolia

This set of ornaments consists of a fish-shaped box,
a jade plaque, pearls, amber beads and turquoise beads,
assembled together by a thin gold thread.
The jade box is made of white jade
in a fish form and is hollow inside.

## 鱼形玉盒

辽开泰七年（公元1018年）
一组。通长23.5厘米
1986年奈曼旗辽陈国公主墓出土
内蒙古文物考古研究所藏

由鱼形玉盒、玉佩、珍珠、琥珀珠、
绿松石珠及水晶珠用细金丝穿系而成。
玉盒用白玉雕刻，整体呈鱼形，
腹内凿空，对开，以子母口相合。

## Jade Animal Pendants

The seventh year of the Kaitai reign of the Liao Dynasty (AD 1018)
Length 15 cm
Unearthed in 1986 from the Tomb of the Princess of Chen,
Naiman Banner
Collection of the Archaeological Research Institute of Inner Mongolia

This set of pendants consists of a jade disk and a gold-plated silver chain with five jade charms. The finely polished disk and charms are all made of white jade. The disk is bordered with a cloud designs. The front is carved with the twelve Chinese zodiac animals. The carved charms are in the shapes of a snake, monkey, scorpion, toad and lizard.

## 动物形玉佩

辽开泰七年（公元 1018 年）
通长 15 厘米
1986 年奈曼旗辽陈国公主墓出土
内蒙古文物考古研究所藏

玉佩由一件玉璧以鎏金银链
垂挂五件玉坠组成。均为白玉制作，
器表光亮。玉璧外周雕刻如意形云纹，
正面微雕十二生肖。
玉坠圆雕，有蛇、猴、蝎、蟾蜍、蜥蜴。

## Jade Animal Pendants

The seventh year of the Kaitai reign of the Liao Dynasty (AD 1018)
Length 14.8 cm
Unearthed in 1986 from the Tomb of the Princess of Chen,
Naiman Banner
Collection of the Archaeological Research Institute of Inner Mongolia

This set of pendants composed of a large jade ornament and five jade pendants strung with gilded silver chains attached to the large ornament. The pendants are all made of pure white hard jade. The rectangular jade ornament is carved with openwork designs of ribbon. The jade pendants are in the shapes of a capricornus, double fish with lotus leaf, double phoenixes, double dragons, and fish resting on lotus flowers.

## 动物形玉佩

辽开泰七年（公元 1018 年）
通长 14.8 厘米
1986 年奈曼旗辽陈国公主墓出土
内蒙古文物考古研究所藏

玉佩由一件玉饰以鎏金银链垂挂五件玉坠组成。
均为白玉制作，玉质坚硬蕴亮，
洁白无瑕。玉饰略呈长方形，
镂雕绶带纹。玉坠圆雕，有摩羯鱼、
荷叶双鱼、双凤、双龙、莲花卧鱼。

## Amber Double-Fish Box

The seventh year of the Kaitai reign of the Liao Dynasty (AD 1018)
Length 7.8 cm, width 4.7 cm
Unearthed in 1986 from the Tomb of the Princess of Chen,
Naiman Banner
Collection of the Archaeological Research Institute of Inner Mongolia

The hollow amber box is carved into a double-fish.
The fish eyes, head and fins are incised with simple lines.
A gold chain is connected to the fish mouth.
The tail has a hinge attached by a gold lock and nails.
When the two fish are close together the box can be locked.

## 双鱼形琥珀盒

辽开泰七年（公元 1018 年）
长 7.8、宽 4.7 厘米
1986 年奈曼旗辽陈国公主墓出土
内蒙古文物考古研究所藏

整体雕刻成并联的双鱼，腹空，
子母口扣合。鱼眼、鳃、
腹鳍、尾雕刻线条简练。鱼嘴部有穿孔，
内穿金链；尾部用金铆钉固定金合页、
金插销，双鱼扣合后可固定。

## Amber Swan-Shaped Pendant

The seventh year of the Kaitai reign of the Liao Dynasty (AD 1018)
Length 5.3 cm, Width 2.8 cm, Height 4 cm
Unearthed in 1986 from the Tomb of the Princess of Chen,
Naiman Banner
Collection of the Archaeological Research Institute of Inner Mongolia

This round oval pendant was carved into a sitting
swan with round eyes, a turned neck
resting his head on its wing. The oval belly is hollow.
A lotus leaf-shaped gold cap is on the back.
The cap has a small ring finial, which is connected to a gold
chain tied to the neck of the swan.

## 鸿雁形琥珀饰件

辽开泰七年（公元 1018 年）
长 5.3、宽 2.8、高 4 厘米
1986 年奈曼旗辽陈国公主墓出土
内蒙古文物考古研究所藏

整体雕刻成鸿雁形。呈卧伏状，
圆眼，屈颈回首，扁喙，
头贴于翼，椭圆体，两足曲于腹下。
腹空，上有荷叶形小金盖，
盖顶饰环形小钮，
上系金链，链另一端系于雁之颈部。

## Amber Burial Ornaments

The seventh year of the Kaitai reign of the Liao Dynasty (AD 1018)
Length 6.2 cm — 6.7 cm, width 4.3 cm — 4.8 cm
Unearthed in 1986 from the Tomb of the Princess of Chen,
Naiman Banner
Collection of the Archaeological Research Institute of Inner Mongolia

One piece has phoenix patterns in relief and the other has a carved dragon with the head connected to the tail. There is a hole pierced lengthwise and threaded by a gold chain. The two burial ornaments were found separately in the hands of the Princess of the Chen State. Since the ancient times, it has been a funeral custom that the dead hold something in their hands. Using ornaments as burial objects by the Qidan people was definitely influenced by the Han burial tradition.

## 琥珀握手

辽开泰七年（公元 1018 年）
两件。长 6.2 — 6.7、宽 4.3 — 4.8 厘米
1986 年奈曼旗辽陈国公主墓出土
内蒙古文物考古研究所藏

一件为浮雕双凤纹握手，一件为圆雕
蟠龙形握手，首尾相接，均两侧横穿一孔，内穿金链，
分别握于公主左右手。死者手握物品之丧葬
习俗由来以久，据《释名·释丧制》解释："以物著
尸手中，使握之也。"契丹族死者手握
物品之习俗显然是受汉族葬俗影响。

## Amber Tassel

琥珀璎珞

The seventh year of the Kaitai reign of the Liao Dynasty (AD 1018)
One set of two groups. Length 113 — 159 cm
Unearthed in 1986 from the Tomb of the Princess of Chen,
Naiman Banner
Collection of the Archaeological Research Institute of Inner Mongolia

One piece is composed of sixty amber beads and nine round
sculpted heart-shaped and dragon-shaped
charms in relief, assembled together by a thin silver thread.
The other piece consists of five strings of two
hundred and fifty-seven oblate or date-pit-shaped amber beads, five
charms with dragon and lotus flowers in relief and two pieces of
plain amber all threaded together. An ornamental
tassel with such a number of amber carvings and beads is rarely seen.

辽开泰七年（公元 1018 年）
一套二组。周长 113 — 159 厘米
1986 年奈曼旗辽陈国公主墓出土
内蒙古文物考古研究所藏

一组由 60 颗琥珀珠和九件圆雕鸡心形、
浮雕龙形琥珀饰件以细银丝相间穿缀组成，一组
由六串计 257 颗枣核形、扁圆形琥珀珠
和五件浮雕龙纹、莲花纹琥珀饰件及两件素面琥珀
以细银丝相间穿缀而成。以如此数量可观的
各种琥珀雕饰串联组成的佩挂饰物，实为罕见。

# Jade Arm Protector

The seventh year of the Kaitai reign of the Liao Dynasty (AD 1018)
Length 9 cm, width 3.4 cm, thickness 0.35 cm
Unearthed in 1986 from the Tomb of the Princess of Chen,
Naiman Banner
Collection of the Archaeological Research Institute of Inner Mongolia

This piece was made of white jade. It has an oval shape,
with the surface slightly convex and the back
concave. There are two oval holes in the sides with two gold
chains in each hole. The piece was used for a falcon to
rest on while protecting the arm. When it was discovered, this piece
was on the left arm of the consort of the princess.

# 玉臂鞲

辽开泰七年（公元 1018 年）
长 9、宽 3.4、厚 0.35 厘米
1986 年奈曼旗辽陈国公主墓出土
内蒙古文物考古研究所藏

白玉磨制。呈椭圆形片状，
正面略弧，背凹。左右两侧各有一椭圆形穿孔，
孔内各穿系两条金链。
玉臂鞲是驾鹰用具，
出土时套于驸马左臂之上。

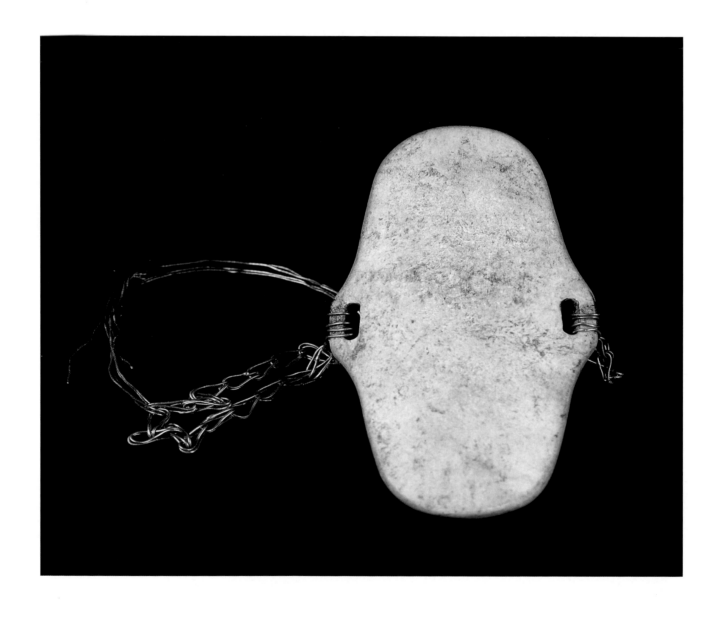

## Silver Pot

The seventh year of the Kaitai reign of the Liao Dynasty (AD 1018)
Height 10.1 cm, diameter of mouth 4.4 cm, and of base 5.6 cm, weight 135 g.
Unearthed in 1986 from the Tomb of the Princess of Chen,
Naiman Banner
Collection of the Archaeological Research Institute of Inner Mongolia

This piece was hammered separately and welded together.
This silver pot has a straight mouth, a broad shoulder,
a drum belly and a short ring foot. The tube-shaped spout is welded
on one side. The flat handle connects the neck to the lower belly.
There are two concave lines on the handle, which ends in the shape of
an apricot leaf. On the upper part of the handle, there is a welded
ring looped with a silver chain attached to the finial of the cover.

## 银壶

辽开泰七年（公元 1018 年）
通高 10.1、口径 4.4、底径 5.6 厘米　重 135 克
1986 年奈曼旗辽陈国公主墓出土
内蒙古文物考古研究所藏

分体打制，焊接成形。直口，广肩，鼓腹，
矮圈足。一侧焊接椭圆形管状直流，
另一侧颈、腹间焊接壶把，把柄宽扁，有两道凹槽，
下端呈杏叶形。把柄上部且焊接小环形钮，
内套银环，上系银链，与壶盖钮相连接。

## Silver Cup and Saucer

The seventh year of the Kaitai reign of the Liao Dynasty (AD 1018)
Height 7.8 cm, diameter of cup 8.4 cm, and of saucer 16 cm, weight 184 g.
Unearthed in 1986 from the Tomb of the Princess of Chen,
Naiman Banner
Collection of the Archaeological Research Institute of Inner Mongolia

This object was hammered separately into a cup,
a saucer and a high stem foot welded together.
The cup has a straight mouth and a flat bottom. The saucer
has a wide flared rim and curved belly with an
inscribed sign "人" at the exterior bottom. The outside
stem foot is incised with the signs "夼" and "冊". These
signs may be the marks of the artisan.

## 银盏托

辽开泰七年（公元 1018 年）
通高 7.8、口径 8.4、盘径 16 厘米　重 184 克
1986 年奈曼旗辽陈国公主墓出土
内蒙古文物考古研究所藏

分体打制，焊接成形。由杯、托盘和高圈足
三部分组成。杯，直口，平底。托盘，敞口，弧腹。
托盘外底用细线刻一"人"形符号，圈足
外壁两侧刻有"夼"形符号，另一侧刻"冊"形符号。
这些符号可能是制器工匠或作坊的标记。

## Engraved Bronze Basin

The seventh year of the Kaitai reign of the Liao Dynasty (AD 1018)
Height 19 cm, diameter of mouth 57 cm, and of base 33 cm
Unearthed in 1986 from the Tomb of the Princess of Chen,
Naiman Banner
Collection of the Archaeological Research Institute of Inner Mongolia

This hammered basin has a flared mouth, a square lip and
a curved belly. The incised bead pattern,
separated by geometrical designs, is decorated around the interior
of the rim. In the center there are six
engraved hexagonal patterns. This kind of pattern and the
vessel shape is often seen in the Islamic region.
Thus this piece should have come from Central Asia.

## 錾花铜盆

辽开泰七年（公元 1018 年）
高 19、口径 57、底径 33 厘米
1986 年奈曼旗辽陈国公主墓出土
内蒙古文物考古研究所藏

打制成型。口沿外撇，方唇，
腹部弧收成平底。口沿内壁錾刻联珠纹，
间隔几何纹，器内底正中錾刻
六角形图案。此盆器型和纹饰图案常见于
伊斯兰地区，应是中亚输入品。

## Glass Plate with Boss Decoration

The seventh year of the Kaitai reign of the Liao Dynasty (AD 1018)
Height 6.8 cm, diameter of mouth 25.5 cm, and of base 10 cm
Unearthed in 1986 from the Tomb of the Princess of Chen,
Naiman Banner
Collection of the Archaeological Research Institute of Inner Mongolia

This glass plate has a flared mouth with a round rim,
and a curved belly supported by a ring foot. The surface on
this transparent glass plate has effloresced. The fairly
thick plate is decorated with twenty-nine bosses on the exterior.
This piece is a masterpiece of the glassware of the
Byzantine times and is evidence of the trade exchange
between the East and West along the Silk Road.

## 乳钉纹玻璃盘

辽开泰七年（公元 1018 年）
高 6.8、口径 25.5、底径 10 厘米
1986 年奈曼旗辽陈国公主墓出土
内蒙古文物考古研究所藏

敞口，圆唇，弧腹，圈足。通体无色，
表面有风化层。器壁较厚，外饰一周 29 个锥形
乳钉纹。造型美观，做工精细，是拜占廷
玻璃器物之精品，也是丝绸之路上东西方
经济文化交流的实物见证。

## Glass Cup

The seventh year of the Kaitai reign of the Liao Dynasty (AD 1018)
Height 11.4 cm, diameter of mouth 9 cm, and of base 5.4 cm
Unearthed in 1986 from the Tomb of the Princess of Chen,
Naiman Banner
Collection of the Archaeological Research Institute of Inner Mongolia

The transparent glass cup, dark brown in color, has effloresced
on the surface. The mouth is slightly contracted and the
upper portion of the vessel is tubular. The lower belly is curved
leading to a false ring foot. A handle connects the rim with the
shoulder of the vessel. On the upper part of the handle,
there is a little round stud. This cup has a strong Western
and Middle East style. This product was
made in Iran between the 9th and the 10th centuries.

## 玻璃杯

辽开泰七年（公元 1018 年）
高 11.4、口径 9、底径 5.4 厘米
1986 年奈曼旗辽陈国公主墓出土
内蒙古文物考古研究所藏

深棕色透明，外表附有风化层。口微敛，
上腹器壁呈圆筒状，肩部外鼓，
下腹弧收，假圈足，
口和肩部连接扁圆形把手，上端有圆饼物。
扳手，外底部有粘棒疤痕。此杯带有浓郁的西亚、
中亚风格，是伊朗 9-10 世纪的产品。

## Glass Bottle with Boss Decoration

The seventh year of the Kaitai reign of the Liao Dynasty (AD 1018)
Height 17 cm, diameter of mouth 6 cm, and of base 8.7 cm
Unearthed in 1986 from the Tomb of the Princess of Chen,
Naiman Banner
Collection of the Archaeological Research Institute of Inner Mongolia

This transparent and colorless glass bottle has a flared V-shaped
mouth, a long neck and a drum belly supported by
a trumpet-shaped stem foot. There are five circles of bosses
around the belly. The handle has openwork designs.
The decorative boss patterns are usually seen on Egyptian
and Syrian glass wares of the 8th to the 10th centuries.
This might have been a product from Egypt or Syria.

## 乳钉纹玻璃瓶

辽开泰七年（公元 1018 年）
高 17、口径 6、底径 8.7 厘米
1986 年奈曼旗辽陈国公主墓出土
内蒙古文物考古研究所藏

通体无色，透明。侈口呈漏斗形，长颈，鼓腹，
喇叭状高圈足，腹壁饰五周乳钉纹。
花式镂空把手，用玻璃条堆砌。乳钉纹装饰，
在埃及和叙利亚 8-10 世纪的玻璃器上经常看到。
此瓶可能是埃及或叙利亚的产品。

## Incised Glass Bottle

The seventh year of the Kaitai reign of the Liao Dynasty (AD 1018)
Height 24.5 cm, diameter of mouth 74 cm and of base 11 cm
Unearthed in 1986 from the Tomb of the Princess of Chen,
Naiman Banner
Collection of the Archaeological Research Institute of Inner Mongolia

This transparent and colorless bottle has
efflorescence on the surface. This bottle has a flared
rim, a thin and long neck, a drum belly
and a flat bottom. On the neck and shoulder
are engraved some geometrical designs. This is one of the typical
Islamic glassware from the end of the 10th century.

## 刻花玻璃瓶

辽开泰七年（公元1018年）
高24.5、口径74、底径11厘米
1986年奈曼旗辽陈国公主墓出土
内蒙古文物考古研究所藏

通体无色，透明，表面有风化层。
宽折沿、细长颈、折肩、桶形腹、平底。
颈、腹部磨刻有几何形花纹。
此瓶为典型的伊斯兰玻璃器，
是公元10世纪末伊朗产品。

# White Glazed Covered Jar with Lotus Design

The seventh year of the Kaitai reign of the Liao Dynasty (AD 1018)
Total Height 11.4 cm, diameter of mouth 5.8 cm and of base 5.1 cm
Unearthed in 1986 from the Tomb of the Princess of Chen,
Naiman Banner
Collection of the Archaeological Research Institute of Inner Mongolia

This jar has a raised lid adorned with a pearl-shaped knob,
a contracted mouth, descending shoulder, a drum
belly and a concave base. Double leaf patterns and
double or triple lotus-petal designs are decorated in relief on
the lid, the shoulder and the belly of the jar. There is a
Chinese character "*Guan*"(official) clearly
incised on the bottom. This most likely is a Ding ware product.

## "官"字款莲纹白瓷盖罐

辽开泰七年（公元1018年）
通高11.4、口径5.8、底径5.1厘米
1986年奈曼旗辽陈国公主墓出土
内蒙古文物考古研究所藏

盖面隆起，盖顶饰宝珠形钮，子口。罐斜肩，
鼓腹向下斜收，底内凹成卧足。浮雕花纹，
盖面饰双重叶纹，肩部饰双重覆莲纹，
腹部饰三重仰莲纹，纹饰凸起，有立体感。白色胎质
细腻，施透明釉，略泛青色，釉面晶莹光亮，
施釉均匀。罐底部刻行书"官"字款。属定窑产品。

# White Glazed Mallow-Petal Bowl

The seventh year of the Kaitai reign of the Liao Dynasty (AD 1018)
Height 7.7 cm, diameter of mouth 14.8 cm, and of base 9 cm
Unearthed in 1986 from the Tomb of the Princess of Chen,
Naiman Banner
Collection of the Archaeological Research Institute of Inner Mongolia

This bowl has a flared mouth with a thin rim,
a deep belly and a ring foot.
The mallow-petal shaped rim has
twelve lobes. The refined
white clay is clearly glazed.
This bowl belongs to the Ding wares.

# 花式口白瓷碗

辽开泰七年（公元 1018 年）
高 7.7、口径 14.8、底径 9 厘米
1986 年奈曼旗辽陈国公主墓出土
内蒙古文物考古研究所藏

十二曲花瓣形，敞口，薄沿，
深腹，腹壁略呈瓜棱形，圈足。
胎质细白，
施透明釉，釉面白润光亮。
造型美观，属定窑产品。

# Celadon Plate with Chrysanthemum Design

The seventh year of the Kaitai reign of the Liao Dynasty (AD 1018)
Height 4.6 cm, diameter of mouth 17 cm, and of base 10.7cm
Unearthed in 1986 from the Tomb of the Princess of Chen,
Naiman Banner
Collection of the Archaeological Research Institute of Inner Mongolia

This hexagonal celadon plate has a wide flared mouth and a flat bottom with a ring foot. The grayish brown clay is glazed in green. A strip of curving grass pattern is incised in the interior of the rim. The inner bottom is incised with interlocking chrysanthemum designs. On the exterior bottom a Chinese character *"Guan"* (official) is incised in running script. This plate belongs to the Yue wares.

# 菊花纹青瓷盘

辽开泰七年（公元1018年）
高4.6、口径17、底径10.7厘米
1986年奈曼旗辽陈国公主墓出土
内蒙古文物考古研究所藏

六曲花瓣形，侈口，腹壁瓜棱形，
平底，圈足。胎质灰褐色，施青绿色釉。
口沿内壁刻划一周卷草纹，
盘内底刻缠枝菊花纹，盘底刻行书"官"字款，
刻痕较浅。属越窑青瓷。

## Wooden Cockscomb Pot

The seventh year of the Kaitai reign of the Liao Dynasty (AD 1018)
Height 29.2 cm, width 20.8 — 24.3 cm
Unearthed in 1986 from the Tomb of the Princess of Chen,
Naiman Banner
Collection of the Archaeological Research Institute of Inner Mongolia

This pot was made of two pieces of cypress wood, one side is smooth
and the other side is cut hollow, then the two were pieced together.
The body is oblate and rectangular with a square straight
mouth and a flat bottom. It is painted with dark brown color
and was oiled. The cockscomb pot was a typical daily utensil of the
Qidan people. The original version was a leather pouch convenient
to carry on a horse. Later there were porcelain pots or jugs.
This was the first time a wooden cockscomb pot was discovered
and it is evidence that the Qidan people once used wooden pots.

## 木鸡冠壶

辽开泰七年（公元 1018 年）
高 29.2、宽 20.8 — 24.3 厘米
1986 年奈曼旗辽陈国公主墓出土
内蒙古文物考古研究所藏

柏木制。用两块木料，一面修平，另一面凿空，然后
拼粘在一起。壶体宽扁，略呈长方形，
上部呈鸡冠状，方形直口，平底。外壁涂深赭色颜料
和清油。鸡冠壶是契丹族典型生活用品，最初为
皮囊式，便于马上携带，以后出现瓷质。木质鸡冠壶尚
属首次发现，说明契丹族曾使用过木质鸡冠壶。

## Wooden Bow Box

The seventh year of the Kaitai reign of the Liao Dynasty (AD 1018)
Length 74.5 cm, width 10 — 25 cm, thickness 2.9 — 4.4 cm
Unearthed in 1986 from the Tomb of the Princess of Chen,
Naiman Banner
Collection of the Archaeological Research Institute of Inner Mongolia

This box is made of cypress wood in the shape of a bow with
polished surface. The inside was scraped out
according to the shape of a bow. The two halves are connected
with a silver hinge and on the upper section there is
a silver buckle for carrying. It was painted in reddish brown
and with cloud designs outlined in ink.

## 木弓囊

辽开泰七年（公元 1018 年）
长 74.5、宽 10 — 25、厚 2.9 — 4.4 厘米
1986 年奈曼旗辽陈国公主墓出土
内蒙古文物考古研究所藏

柏木制。整体呈不规则的扁盒形，上宽下窄。
用两块木板先制成半张弓的形状，外侧修平，
打磨光滑，内侧两个对合面按弓的形状
凿出沟槽，用以置弓，对合后用银合页连接。
上部钉有银带扣，游猎出行时佩挂于身。
弓囊外表两面施红褐色，墨线勾绘云凤纹。

## Silver Plated Wooden Saddle

The seventh year of the Kaitai reign of the Liao Dynasty (AD 1018)
Height 18.8 — 26 cm, length 56 cm, width 41.2 cm
Unearthed in 1986 from the Tomb of the Princess of Chen,
Naiman Banner
Collection of the Archaeological Research Institute of Inner Mongolia

The saddle is made of cypress wood. The pommel, cantle and
fenders are attached together with wooden joints and
reinforced by bronze staples. The pommel and cantle are covered
with gilded silver leaf with cloud designs. Most of the
designs have flaked off. The Qidan saddle is well known for its high
quality and workmanship. It is regarded as the best in the world
together with Ding wares, Sichuan brocades and Duanxi ink-slabs.

## 包银木马鞍

辽开泰七年（公元1018年）
高18.8—26、长56、宽41.2厘米
1986年奈曼旗辽陈国公主墓出土
内蒙古文物考古研究所藏

鞍座用柏木制作。鞍座呈凹弧形，前桥直立，
后桥向后倾斜。前后木鞍桥和两侧木鞍座板是用
榫铆法拼合，再用铜条加固。前后鞍桥外侧
镶包云凤纹贴金银鞍饰，多已脱落。
契丹族马鞍用料考究，做工精细，
曾与定瓷、蜀锦、端砚，并列为天下第一。

## Gilded Silver Saddle Ornaments

The seventh year of the Kaitai reign of the Liao Dynasty (AD 1018)
Four pieces. Height of pommel 24.5 cm and of cantle 38 cm,
Length of half-moon shaped ornamental pieces 16.5 cm
Unearthed in 1986 from the Tomb of the Princess of Chen, Naiman Banner
Collection of the Archaeological Research Institute of Inner Mongolia

These saddle ornaments were made of
hammered and gilded silver
sheets. The silver fittings of the pommel and
cantle are engraved with bird
designs against the fishroe marks.

## 鎏金银鞍饰

辽开泰七年（公元 1018 年）
四件。前桥银饰高 24.5、后桥银饰高 38、半月形银饰长 16.5 厘米
1986 年奈曼旗辽陈国公主墓出土
内蒙古文物考古研究所藏

鞍桥外侧包镶饰件。
錾花，鎏金。
前后桥银饰均呈拱形，面凸，背凹。
正面錾刻花鸟纹，
鱼子纹地。

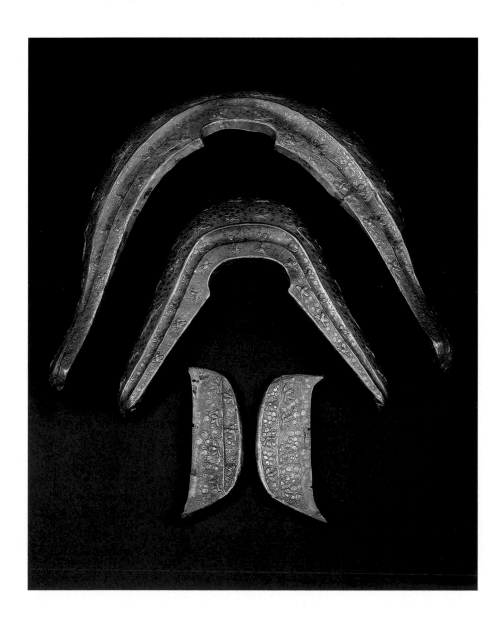

# Silver Bridle Inlaid with Jade Ornaments

The seventh year of the Kaitai reign of the Liao Dynasty (AD 1018)
Length 50 cm, width 30 cm
Unearthed in 1986 from the Tomb of the Princess of Chen,
Naiman Banner
Collection of the Archaeological Research Institute of Inner Mongolia

The bridle was made of silver strips 1.5 cm wide and 0.05 cm
thick and was inlaid with round carvings of jade horses
and lions along with silver buckle straps. They were first made in
small short pieces, then assembled together and
inlaid with jade ornaments. This kind of bridle with such excellent
ornaments and in such a good condition is rarely seen up to now.

# 镶玉银马络

辽开泰七年（公元 1018 年）
长约 50、宽 30 厘米
1986 年奈曼旗辽陈国公主墓出土
内蒙古文物考古研究所藏

由项带、额带、颊带、咽带、鼻带组成。
各条小带均用宽1.5、厚0.05厘米的薄银片制作，
带上钉缀马形、狻猊形圆雕玉饰和玉节约、银带扣、银带箍。
络头的配套方法是先将每条小带分件制作，
然后按部位组合连接起来，最后钉缀玉饰件。
如此装饰华丽、保存完好的马络较为少见。

# Gilded Iron Bit, Cheek-pieces and Silver Reins

The seventh year of the Kaitai reign of the Liao Dynasty (AD 1018)
Length of Bit 17 cm, of cheek-piece 16.5 cm, and of Reins 165 cm
Unearthed in 1986 from the Tomb of the Princess of Chen,
Naiman Banner
Collection of the Archaeological Research Institute of Inner Mongolia

This was made separately and assembled together
after the hammered small sections were made.
The bit has two sections resembling straight stick.
At one end there are two ring-like holes.
The cheek-pieces are long with phoenix head designs.
The reins were made of three pieces of silver straps.

鎏金铁马衔、镳，银马缰

辽开泰七年（公元 1018 年）
衔长 17、镳长 16.5、缰长 165 厘米
1986 年奈曼旗辽陈国公主墓出土
内蒙古文物考古研究所藏

分件打制，镶套组合。
衔两节，直棍式，
一端有两个环形孔。
镳长体，凤首。
马缰用三条薄银带连接组成。

## Silver Breast Collar and Gilded Iron Stirrup

The seventh year of the Kaitai reign of the Liao Dynasty (AD 1018)
Length of breast collar 168 cm, height of stirrup 19.5 cm, and its width 15 cm
Unearthed in 1986 from the Tomb of the Princess of Chen,
Naiman Banner
Collection of the Archaeological Research Institute of Inner Mongolia

The breast collar is composed of two long silver straps
and two short silver straps inlaid with jade.
A silver buckle is at the joints. The breast collar is adorned
with jade lions and horses. The stirrup has a
rectangular nose with a strap hole. The stirrup was
usually made of bronze and iron. But gilded stirrups are seldom seen.

## 银胸带、鎏金铁马镫

辽开泰七年（公元 1018 年）
胸带长 168，马镫通高 19.5、宽 15 厘米
1986 年奈曼旗辽陈国公主墓出土
内蒙古文物考古研究所藏

胸带也称攀胸，由两条长银带和两条短银带
用玉节约连接组成，连接部位钉有银带扣。
胸带上钉马形、狻猊形玉饰。马镫环梁，截面圆柱形，
上部有方形高鼻，正中有长方形带孔，
内穿银镫带。踏板椭圆形，饰镂孔花纹。
马镫多为铜、铁制品，鎏金铁马镫较为少见。

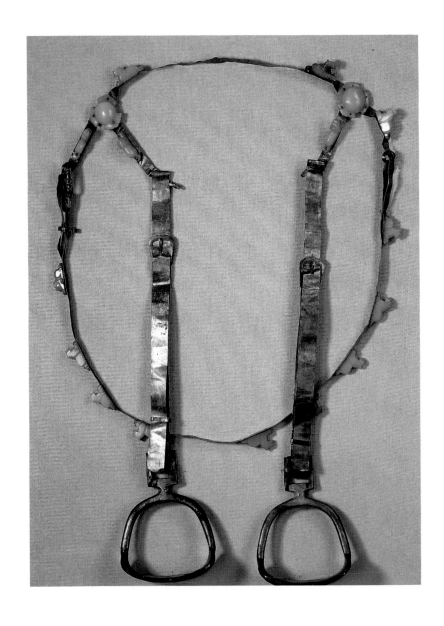

# Gold and Silver Belts with Ornaments

The seventh year of the Kaitai reign of the Liao Dynasty (AD 1018)
Total Length 320 cm, length of hanging ornaments 56 — 61cm
Unearthed in 1986 from the Tomb of the Princess of Chen,
Naiman Banner
Collection of the Archaeological Research Institute of Inner Mongolia

The belt and ornaments were made of thin silver sheets. The piece
was used as the horse decoration behind the saddle. Each side of the
piece consists of four long belts and a short one. There are eight
horse-shaped jade ornaments attached on the long belts. The belts
include another long silver belt with jade ornaments.
Both ends of the long belt hook onto the eight belts and make a knot.
The two short belts connect to the middle of the long belt in a T shape.

银蹀躞带、鞘带

辽开泰七年（公元1018年）
全长320厘米，下垂蹀躞带长56—61厘米
1986年奈曼旗辽陈国公主墓出土
内蒙古文物考古研究所藏

蹀躞带，用薄银片制作，垂挂于鞍座后部左右两侧，
每侧有四条长带和一条短带。长带上各钉八件马形玉饰。
两条短带分别与鞘带相连接。鞘带，由一条长银带和
两条短银带连成，带上钉玉节约和饰件。
长带两端连接于鞍座后两侧的蹀躞短带上，然后挽结成扣，
下端垂于马腹左右两侧。两条短带呈丁字形，
连接于长带中部两侧，相互对称，垂于马尻两侧。

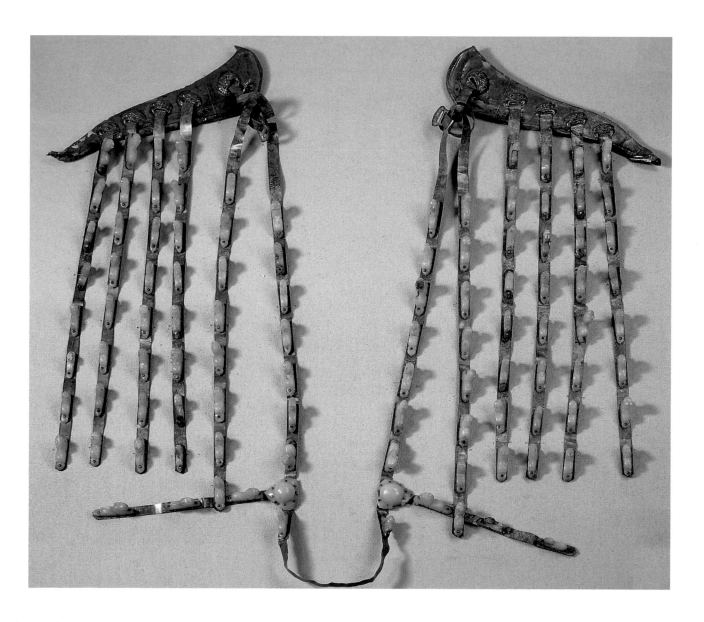

## Painted Silver Skirt

The seventh year of the Kaitai reign of the Liao Dynasty (AD 1018)
One pair of two pieces
Each length 59 cm, width 66 cm, thickness 0.05 cm, widtht 830 g.
Unearthed in 1986 from the Tomb of the Princess of Chen, Naiman Banner
Collection of the Archaeological Research Institute of Inner Mongolia

This is part of the horse saddle and made of very thin silver sheets
fitted onto the saddle. The shape is semicircular with
two pierced holes. On the front there are decorative patterns
of a scarlet bird, flaming pearl and curly clouds in bright colors.
This painted silver piece is a copy of leather one and is the
only one ever found.

## 彩绘银鞯

辽开泰七年（公元1018年）
一副两件。（单件）长59、宽66、厚0.05厘米　重830克
1986年奈曼旗辽陈国公主墓出土
内蒙古文物考古研究所藏

鞯也称"障泥"，用薄银片打制而成。
整体略呈半圆形，上部微凹，
有两个穿带孔。正面彩绘朱雀、
火焰珠、卷云纹，色彩艳丽。
彩绘银鞯应属仿皮制品，为首次发现。

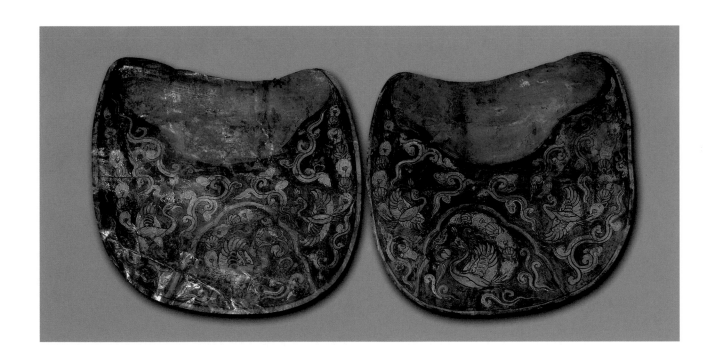

# Epitaph of the Tomb of the Princess of Chen

The seventh year of the Kaitai reign of the Liao Dynasty (AD 1018)
Height 28 cm, length of the sides 89.5 cm
Unearthed in 1986 from the Tomb of the Princess of Chen,
Naiman Banner
Collection of the Archaeological Research Institute of Inner Mongolia

This square piece was made of green sandstone and has a square top.
It is decorated with incised single-lined and double-lined frames,
cloud patterns, posy designs, entwined grass designs
and the twelve zodiac animals. Eight characters of
"Epitaph of the Princess of the Chen State" are incised
in seal script. The epitaph, in regular script,
has five hundred and thirteen characters in twenty-seven lines.

# 陈国公主墓志

辽开泰七年（公元 1018 年）
通高 28、边长 89.5 厘米
1986 年奈曼旗辽陈国公主墓出土
内蒙古文物考古研究所藏

绿色砂岩制。正方形。志盖方形盝顶。顶边有单线框，
内有双栏框两个。双栏内框内阴刻篆书"故陈国公主
墓志铭"3 行 8 字。内框与外框间，各边线刻三朵云纹，
四角各刻一朵四叶团花。外侧四个斜面上线刻
十二生肖像，四个斜角各刻一朵牡丹花，侧面刻缠枝
草叶纹。墓志铭，正面边框线刻几何纹，
侧面也刻缠枝草叶纹。铭文阴刻楷书 27 行，全文 513 字。

# 蒙古族

公元1206年，成吉思汗统一蒙古诸部，建立蒙古国，进而形成横跨欧亚的大汗国。以后，成吉思汗之孙忽必烈建立元王朝，统一了中国。因蒙古族实行秘葬，故其文物发现不多，但从展品中，仍可领略到成吉思汗及其子孙们的创造力。

# *Mongol*

Genghis Khan unified all the Mongolian tribes and established the Mongolian Empire in the year 1206, which then further developed into a great power covering the Euro-Asia areas. Kubilai Khan, Genghis' grandson, founded the Yuan dynasty and unified the entire China. Due to the secret burial custom within the Mongolian culture, discoveries of cultural relics from the tombs are rare. However from this exhibition, we have the opportunity to appreciate the great invention of Genghis Khan and his descendants.

## Silver Plaque with Gilded Bhaspa Script

Yuan Dynasty (AD 1271 — 1368)
Length 29 cm, width 8 cm
Collected in 1999 from Guchengcun, Xiachengwan,
Qingshuihe County
Collection of the Archaeological Research Institute of Inner Mongolia

This silver plaque, with gilded scripts in Bhaspa script, is rectangular in shape. There is a pierced hole with a movable ring. On one side of the ring are incised with five characters "number eighty of *Ding Zi*". There are five lines of thirty characters in Bhaspa script incised on both sides of the plaque. The inscription means that the name of the Emperor is sacred and inviolable. Anyone who is not respectful and obedient will be punished to death. This was an official identity plaque of personal status.

## 八思巴文金字银牌

元（公元 1271 年— 1368 年）
长 29、宽 8 厘米
1999 年清水河县下城湾古城村征集
内蒙古文物考古研究所藏

银质，文字鎏金。圆角长方形。上部有一圆形系挂穿孔，孔内嵌一圆环，可旋转活动。圆环一侧刻有"丁字八十号"五个汉字。银牌一面刻有两行、另一面刻三行八思巴文，共计 30 个字。据考释，意为：借助长生天的力量，皇帝的名字是神圣不可侵犯的，不尊敬服从的人将会被定罪致死。此牌是元代官府的身份牌，即元代四五品职官所佩带的"素金牌"。

# Silk Quilt Cover with Griffin Design

Yuan Dynasty (AD 1271 — 1368)
Length 204 cm, width 118 cm
Unearthed in 1976 from a hoard of the ancient city site at Jininglu,
Chahaeryouyiqian Banner
Collection of the Inner Mongolia Museum

This is a rectangular silk quilt cover. The main design, the "griffin,"
a creature with an eagle head and lion body,
is set against the hexagonal patterns edged with peony flowers.
The whole design symbolizes wealth, luck and longevity.
the griffin was a particularly common creature
among Middle East countries. This is evidence of
the cultural exchanges between China and foreign countries.

# "格力芬"丝织被面

元（公元1271年—1368年）
长204、宽118厘米
1976年察哈尔前旗元集宁路古城遗址窖藏出土
内蒙古博物馆藏

长方形织锦被面，主题图案为鹰首羊身的"格力芬"，
底纹为龟背纹，四周边饰牡丹花。
整幅被面图案寓意富贵、吉祥、长寿。
"格力芬"为流行于中亚的一种怪兽纹。
此物是中外文化交流的珍贵实物资料。

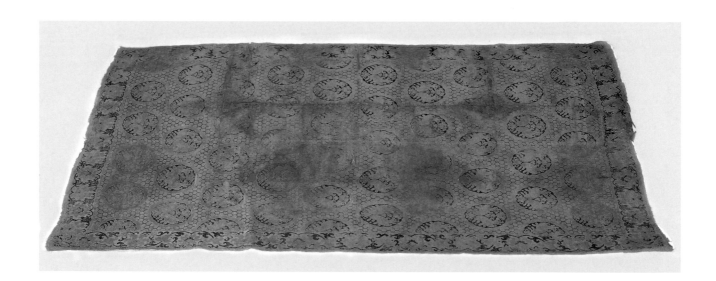

## Gilded Silver High Stemcup

Yuan Dynasty (AD 1271 — 1368)
Height 14 cm, diameter of mouth 11 cm, and of belly 7 cm, weight 190.5 g.
Unearthed in 1978 from Mingshuicun, Dasuji Village,
Da'erhan Maoming'an United Banner
Collection of the Inner Mongolia Museum

This cup has a flared mouth, a curved rim, a deep belly and a round bottom supported by a strumpet shaped high stem foot. Around the rim there is a circle of incised lotus flowers and on the outside of the cup is decorated with three groups of lotus flowers and leaves. Entwined grass designs are incised along the lower edge of the stem.

## 鎏金高足银杯

元（公元 1271 年—1368 年）
高 14、口径 11、腹径 7 厘米　重 190.5 克
1978 年达尔罕茂明安联合旗大苏吉乡明水村出土
内蒙古博物馆藏

敞口，卷沿，圆唇，深腹，
圆底，喇嘛状高圈足。
口沿錾刻一周莲花纹，腹部饰三组莲花纹，
莲花荷叶相映成趣，圈足底边錾刻卷草纹。

## Gold Single-Lugged Cup

Yuan Dynasty (AD 1271 — 1368)
Height 5 cm, diameter of mouth 12 cm and of bottom 7.9 cm, weight 189 g.
Unearthed in 1976 from Wujiadicun, Wuguquan Village,
Xinghe County
Collection of the Inner Mongolia Museum

This cup has a flower shape,
curved belly and a flat bottom.
On one side of the cup there is a crescent-shaped
handle and a loop underneath. Entwined honeysuckle
and peony designs run along the cup rim,
on the handle and on the base of the interior.

## 鋬耳金杯

元（公元 1271 年—1368 年）
高 5、口径 12、底 7.9 厘米　重 189 克
1976 年兴和县五股泉乡五甲地村出土
内蒙古博物馆藏

敞口，口沿有一周凸棱，弧腹，
平底。口沿一侧连接一月牙形鋬耳，
鋬耳下连一圆环。
杯底和鋬耳上均錾刻缠枝牡丹和忍冬纹，
口沿外侧饰忍冬纹。

## Blue and White Porcelain Stemcup

Yuan Dynasty (AD 1271 — 1368)
Height 9.5 cm, diameter of mouth 11.4 cm and of base 3.8 cm
Unearthed in 1978 from a hoard at Hajingou, Dayingzi Village,
Chifeng City
Collection of the Inner Mongolia Museum

This cup has a flared mouth, a flat bottom and
a bamboo-joint stem foot with decorations in underglaze blue.
A design of curling grass is around the inside rim and
a striding dragon is on the interior cup.
On the stem foot is a stylized banana leaf
pattern filled with cloud designs.
A striding dragon and fire patterns decorate the exterior of the cup.

## 青花高足杯

元（公元 1271 年—1368 年）
高 9.5、口径 11.4、足径 3.8 厘米
1978 年赤峰市大营子乡哈金沟窖藏出土
内蒙古博物馆藏

敞口，弧腹，平底，竹节状高圈足。
通体施青白釉，釉下绘青花图案。
沿内侧饰卷草纹，
腹内壁饰一条飞舞的龙纹，
高足饰变形蕉叶纹，内填如意形云纹。
腹外一条舞龙绕壁一周，火焰纹点缀其间。

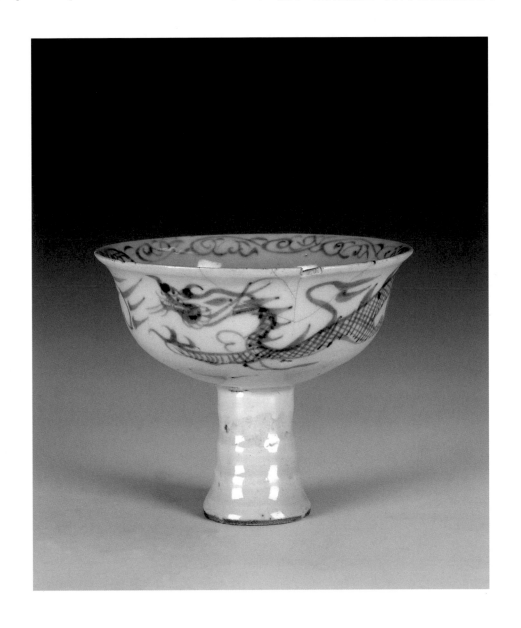

## Bronze Seal

The first year of Tianyuan, Northern Yuan Dynasty (AD 1379)

Height 9.2 cm, length of the side 8.4 cm

Unearthed in 1984 from the Heichengzi Site, Ejina Banner

Collection of the Archaeological Research Institute of Inner Mongolia

With a rectangular knob, this square seal is carved in Bhaspa script. On the right side of the back is the translation carved in Han script. The left side is carved with the date of its production: "Made by the Board of Rites in February of the first year of the Tianyuan." This is a precious piece of relic of the Northern Yuan period.

## "永昌等处行枢密院断事官府印"铜印

北元 天元元年（公元 1379 年）

通高 9.2、边长 8.4 厘米

1984 年额济纳旗黑城子遗址出土

内蒙古文物考古研究所藏

方体，长方形立钮。

印文为八思巴文字"永昌等处行枢密院断事官府印"。

背面右侧阴刻汉字同印文，

左侧刻"天元元年二月礼部造　日"。

为北元时期的珍贵文物。

## Stone Slab with Incised Carving

Yuan Dynasty (AD 1271 — 1368)

Length 71.5 cm, width 48 cm, thickness 12 cm

Unearthed in 1990 from the Zhenzishan Burial Site, Duolun County

Collection of the Archaeological Research Institute of Inner Mongolia

The dark blue stone is carved with simple lines in relief and made with skillful workmanship. The scene of the painting depicts five boys trying to pick out their kite from a tree. There are two women standing in front of the house watching. The motif of this painting refers to a wish for the young generations to succeed in the imperial examinations, become high officials and bring honor and wealth to the family.

## 五子登科画像石

元（公元 1271 年—1368 年）

长 71.5、宽 48、厚 12 厘米

1990 年多伦县砧子山墓地出土

内蒙古文物考古研究所藏

青灰色石料，用剔地浅浮雕手法雕刻，手法简练而娴熟。
画面主题是表现五个童子摘取挂在树上的风筝。
画面右中刻住宅门前一童子手托线团，一童子双手拽线，眼望着挂在柳树上的风筝；树下一童子蹲踞，另一童子抱树干，正欲向上攀登；树上还有一童子正在摘取风筝。
住宅门前还站立两妇人，正在观看。这幅画的寓意，就是"五子登科"，意为祈求子孙后代登科及第、全家富贵繁昌。

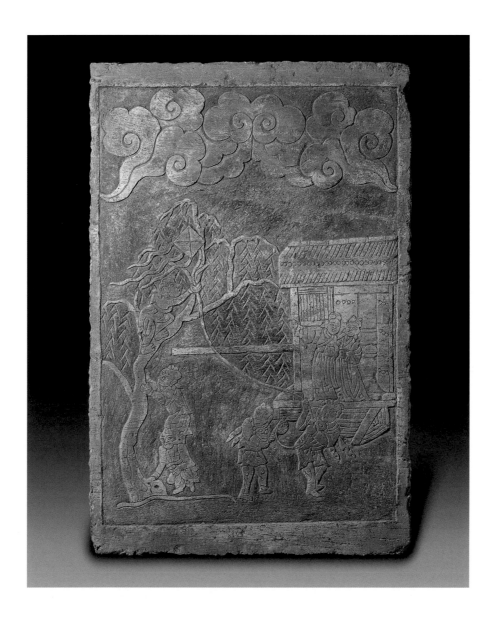

## Tomb Stone

Yuan Dynasty (AD 1271 — 1368)
Length 105 cm, width 34 cm, height 44 cm
Unearthed in 1996 from Muhuersuoboga, E'erdunaobaosumu,
Da'erhan Maoming'an United Banner
Collection of the Archaeological Research Institute of Inner Mongolia

This rectangular tomestone was made of light-gray granite.
The front face is square. On the front and the sides
are carved with a cross sign with a lotus flower below
and a rosette design above.
One the back of the stone, in a semicircle, is a line
of incised ancient Syrian characters.
Entwined grass patterns are incised along both sides.

## 景教墓顶石

元（公元 1271 年—1368 年）
长 105、宽 34、高 44 厘米
1996 年达尔罕茂明安联合旗额尔敦敖包苏木木胡儿索卜嘎出土
内蒙古文物考古研究所藏

灰白色花岗岩雕琢制作。
略呈前大后小长方体。前端正方形，
正面和左右侧面各阴刻一"十"字架，
下刻一朵莲花；上面刻一宝相花。
后端呈半圆形，背上阴刻一行古叙利亚文，
左右两侧面各刻两行蔓草纹。

展 品 目 录 索 引

| 品　名 | 年　代 | 尺寸／重量 | 出土地点 | 收　藏 | 页码 |
|---|---|---|---|---|---|
| 玉玦 | 新石器时代兴隆洼文化（约公元前6000年） | 直径2.9－4.2厘米 | 1989年林西县白音长汗遗址出土 | 内蒙古文物考古研究所藏 | 64 |
| 玉蝉 | 新石器时代兴隆洼文化（约公元前6000年） | 长3.2、宽1.8厘米 | 1989年林西县白音长汗遗址出土 | 内蒙古文物考古研究所藏 | 65 |
| 玉管 | 新石器时代兴隆洼文化（约公元前6000年） | 长4、3.7厘米 | 1989年林西县白音长汗遗址出土 | 内蒙古文物考古研究所藏 | ＊ |
| 玉锥 | 新石器时代兴隆洼文化（约公元前6000年） | 长6.7、宽1.8厘米 | 1989年林西县白音长汗遗址出土 | 内蒙古文物考古研究所藏 | ＊ |
| 人面形蚌饰 | 新石器时代兴隆洼文化（约公元前6000年） | 长4.1、宽3.5厘米 | 1989年林西县白音长汗遗址出土 | 内蒙古文物考古研究所藏 | ＊ |
| 人面形石佩饰 | 新石器时代兴隆洼文化（约公元前6000年） | 长4、宽3厘米 | 1989年林西县白音长汗遗址出土 | 内蒙古文物考古研究所藏 | 66 |
| 石雕人像 | 新石器时代兴隆洼文化（约公元前6000年） | 长16、宽11.5、高35.5厘米 | 1989年林西县白音长汗遗址出土 | 内蒙古文物考古研究所藏 | 67 |
| 筒形陶罐 | 新石器时代兴隆洼文化（约公元前6000年） | 高43、口径43、底径22厘米 | 1989年林西县白音长汗遗址出土 | 内蒙古文物考古研究所藏 | 68 |
| 勾云形玉佩 | 新石器时代红山文化（公元前4000年） | 长15.5、宽6厘米 | 1980年科尔沁左翼中旗胜利乡塔拉土村征集 | 通辽市博物馆藏 | ＊ |
| 勾云形玉佩 | 新石器时代红山文化（公元前4000年） | 长12.7、宽11.7厘米 | 1981年巴林右旗巴彦汉苏木那日斯台遗址出土 | 巴林右旗博物馆藏 | ＊ |
| 勾云形玉佩 | 新石器时代红山文化（公元前4000年） | 长18.2、宽10.9、厚0.4厘米 | 1981年巴林右旗巴彦汉苏木那日斯台遗址出土 | 巴林右旗博物馆藏 | 69 |
| 勾云形玉器 | 新石器时代红山文化（公元前4000年） | 长6.8、宽2.5厘米 | 1981年巴林右旗巴彦汉苏木那日斯台遗址出土 | 巴林右旗博物馆藏 | ＊ |
| 玉猪龙 | 新石器时代红山文化（公元前4000年） | 通高16.8、宽11.5、厚2.8厘米 | 1974年巴林右旗羊场乡额尔根勿苏村征集 | 巴林右旗博物馆藏 | 70 |
| 玉龙 | 新石器时代红山文化（公元前4000年） | 高7.3、厚2.2厘米 | 1976年敖汉旗下洼镇河西遗址出土 | 敖汉旗博物馆藏 | ＊ |
| 黄玉龙 | 新石器时代红山文化（公元前4000年） | 长17厘米 | 1986年翁牛特旗广德公乡黄谷屯征集 | 翁牛特旗博物馆藏 | 71 |

＊ 未收入本图册

| 品　名 | 年　代 | 尺寸／重量 | 出土地点 | 收　藏 | 页码 |
|---|---|---|---|---|---|
| 玉鸮 | 新石器时代红山文化<br>（公元前 4000 年） | 通长 6.1、直径 6、<br>厚 1.8 厘米 | 1981 年巴林右旗<br>巴彦汉苏木那日斯台遗址出土 | 巴林右旗博物馆藏 | 72 |
| 玉燕 | 新石器时代红山文化<br>（公元前 4000 年） | 长 3、宽 2.5 厘米 | 1981 年巴林右旗<br>巴彦汉苏木那日斯台遗址出土 | 巴林右旗博物馆藏 | ＊ |
| 玉蚕 | 新石器时代红山文化<br>（公元前 4000 年） | 长 9.3、宽 3.4 厘米 | 1981 年巴林右旗<br>巴彦汉苏木那日斯台遗址出土 | 巴林右旗博物馆藏 | ＊ |
| 三联玉璧 | 新石器时代红山文化<br>（公元前 4000 年） | 长 11.9、宽 3.9 厘米 | 1981 年巴林右旗<br>巴彦汉苏木那日斯台遗址出土 | 巴林右旗博物馆藏 | ＊ |
| 人面形玉饰 | 新石器时代红山文化<br>（公元前 4000 年） | 长 4.2、宽 3.8 厘米 | 1987 年巴林右旗<br>巴彦塔拉苏木苏达来征集 | 巴林右旗博物馆藏 | ＊ |
| 马蹄形玉箍 | 新石器时代红山文化<br>（公元前 4000 年） | 长 14.1、直径 7.4 厘米 | 1964 年巴林左旗<br>杨家营子镇葛家营子征集 | 巴林左旗博物馆藏 | ＊ |
| 马蹄形玉箍坯料 | 新石器时代红山文化<br>（公元前 4000 年） | 长 16.7、宽 12<br>－10.2、厚 7 厘米 | 1980 年敖汉旗<br>大甸子乡大瓜翅遗址出土 | 敖汉旗博物馆藏 | ＊ |
| 玉匕形器 | 新石器时代红山文化<br>（公元前 4000 年） | 长 14.1、宽 2.6 厘米 | 1982 年巴林右旗<br>查干诺苏木征集 | 巴林右旗博物馆藏 | ＊ |
| 玉匕 | 新石器时代红山文化<br>（公元前 4000 年） | 长 16.5 厘米 | 巴林左旗征集 | 巴林左旗博物馆藏 | ＊ |
| 玉斧 | 新石器时代红山文化<br>（公元前 4000 年） | 长 13.2、宽 6 厘米 | 1981 年巴林右旗<br>巴彦汉苏木那日斯台遗址出土 | 巴林右旗博物馆藏 | ＊ |
| 鸟形石玦 | 新石器时代红山文化<br>（公元前 4000 年） | 长 5.5、宽 4.9 厘米 | 1981 年巴林右旗<br>巴彦汉苏木那日斯台遗址出土 | 巴林右旗博物馆藏 | ＊ |
| 猪首形彩陶罐 | 新石器时代小河沿文化<br>（约公元前 3000 年） | 高 18.6、口径 8.2－10.2、<br>底径 8.5 厘米 | 1985 年赤峰市松山区<br>红花沟镇四分地村征集 | 赤峰市文物店藏 | 73 |
| 鳞纹彩陶罐 | 新石器时代红山文化<br>（公元前 4000 年） | 高 36、口径 27、<br>底径 10 厘米 | 1976 年阿鲁科尔沁旗<br>赛罕塔拉塔本陶拉盖遗址出土 | 阿鲁科尔沁旗博物馆藏 | ＊ |
| 彩陶钵 | 新石器时代仰韶文化<br>（约公元前 4000 年） | 高 15.5、口径 39 厘米 | 1991 年凉城县<br>王墓山下遗址出土 | 内蒙古文物考古研究所藏 | ＊ |
| 环首青铜短剑 | 商代早期<br>（公元前 16 世纪－前 15 世纪） | 通长 24.6 厘米 | 1980 年伊金霍洛旗<br>朱开沟墓葬出土 | 内蒙古文物考古研究所藏 | 77 |

＊ 未收入本图册

| 品　名 | 年　代 | 尺寸／重量 | 出土地点 | 收　藏 | 页码 |
|---|---|---|---|---|---|
| 环首青铜刀 | 商代早期<br>（公元前 16 世纪－前 15 世纪） | 通长 34.1、<br>柄长 10.5 厘米 | 1980 年伊金霍洛旗<br>朱开沟墓葬出土 | 内蒙古文物考古研究所藏 | 78 |
| 虎纹青铜直内戈 | 商代早期<br>（公元前 16 世纪－前 15 世纪） | 通长 28.5、<br>援长 21 厘米 | 1980 年伊金霍洛旗<br>朱开沟墓葬出土 | 内蒙古文物考古研究所藏 | 79 |
| 青铜鍪 | 商代早期<br>（公元前 16 世纪－前 15 世纪） | 长 18.2、宽 18.2 厘米 | 1980 年伊金霍洛旗<br>朱开沟遗址出土 | 内蒙古文物考古研究所藏 | ＊ |
| 双鸟首青铜短剑 | 春秋晚期<br>（约公元前 5 世纪） | 通长 27.8 厘米 | 1979 年凉城县<br>毛庆沟墓地出土 | 内蒙古文物考古研究所藏 | ＊ |
| 鹰形金冠饰 | 战国晚期<br>（约公元前 3 世纪） | 通高 7.1、<br>直径 16.5 厘米 | 1972 年杭锦旗<br>阿门其日格乡阿鲁柴登出土 | 内蒙古博物馆藏 | 80 |
| 镶绿松石金耳坠 | 战国晚期<br>（约公元前 3 世纪） | 长 8.2 厘米 | 1972 年杭锦旗<br>阿门其日格乡阿鲁柴登出土 | 内蒙古博物馆藏 | 84 |
| 金项圈 | 战国<br>（公元前 476 年－前 221 年） | 展开长 145 厘米 | 1972 年杭锦旗<br>阿门其日格乡阿鲁柴登出土 | 内蒙古博物馆藏 | ＊ |
| 虎咬牛纹金饰牌 | 战国晚期<br>（约公元前 3 世纪） | 长 12.7、宽 7.4 厘米<br>重 203.8 克 | 1972 年杭锦旗<br>阿门其日格乡阿鲁柴登出土 | 内蒙古博物馆藏 | 83 |
| 虎鸟纹金带饰 | 战国晚期<br>（约公元前 3 世纪） | 长 4.2、宽 3.4 厘米 | 1972 年杭锦旗<br>阿门其日格乡阿鲁柴登出土 | 内蒙古博物馆藏 | 81 |
| 佩饰<br>（项饰、腰带饰、链环） | 春秋晚期<br>（约公元前 5 世纪） | 虎纹铜饰牌长 10.7、宽 6.1 厘米<br>双鸟纹铜饰牌长 5、宽 3 厘米 | 1979 年凉城县<br>毛庆沟墓地出土 | 内蒙古文物考古研究所藏 | 85 |
| 虎纹青铜带饰 | 战国<br>（公元前 476 年－前 221 年） | 通长 10.3 厘米 | 1979 年凉城县<br>毛庆沟墓地出土 | 内蒙古文物考古研究所藏 | ＊ |
| 盘角羊首青铜辕饰 | 战国晚期<br>（约公元前 3 世纪） | 通长 19.5、<br>銎内径 5.8 厘米 | 1974 年准格尔旗<br>玉隆太征集 | 内蒙古博物馆藏 | 86 |
| 鹤头形青铜竿头饰 | 战国<br>（公元前 476 年－前 221 年） | 通长 24 厘米 | 1962 年准格尔旗<br>瓦尔吐沟征集 | 内蒙古博物馆藏 | 87 |
| 蹲踞状青铜鹿 | 战国晚期<br>（约公元前 3 世纪） | 最高 7.7－8 厘米 | 1962 年准格尔旗<br>速机沟窖藏出土 | 内蒙古博物馆藏 | 88 |
| 穿带青铜背壶 | 秦－西汉<br>（公元前 221 年－公元 8 年） | 高 48 厘米 | 1975 年准格尔旗<br>秦汉广衍故城出土 | 内蒙古博物馆藏 | 91 |

＊ 未收入本图册

| 品 名 | 年 代 | 尺寸／重量 | 出土地点 | 收 藏 | 页码 |
|---|---|---|---|---|---|
| 双耳青铜镀 | 西汉<br>（公元前206年－公元8年） | 通高24厘米 | 1974年伊克昭盟地区征集 | 内蒙古文物考古研究所藏 | ＊ |
| 双耳圈足青铜镀 | 西汉<br>（公元前206年－公元8年） | 通高15.8厘米 | 1974年伊克昭盟地区征集 | 内蒙古文物考古研究所藏 | 89 |
| 象牙尺 | 西汉<br>（公元前206年－公元8年） | 长22.9、宽2.3厘米 | 1992年磴口县<br>纳林套海汉墓出土 | 内蒙古文物考古研究所藏 | 92 |
| 建宁三年墓碑 | 东汉建宁三年<br>（公元170年） | 残长73、宽48、<br>厚16厘米 | 1993年包头市南郊<br>黄河乳牛场召湾村墓葬出土 | 内蒙古文物考古研究所藏 | 93 |
| 凉州刺史墓志 | 夏龙昇二年<br>（公元408年） | 边长54、厚5厘米 | 1992年乌审旗<br>纳林河乡郭梁村墓葬出土 | 内蒙古文物考古研究所藏 | 94 |
| 鹿纹柄青铜短剑 | 春秋<br>（公元前770年－前476年） | 通长26厘米 | 1993年宁城县<br>小黑石沟遗址出土 | 内蒙古文物考古研究所藏 | 96 |
| 双涡纹首青铜短剑 | 春秋<br>（公元前770年－前476年） | 长26.6厘米 | 1992年宁城县<br>小黑石沟遗址出土 | 内蒙古文物考古研究所藏 | ＊ |
| 金环饰青铜短剑 | 春秋<br>（公元前770年－前476年） | 通长29厘米 | 1998年宁城县<br>小黑石沟遗址出土 | 内蒙古文物考古研究所藏 | 97 |
| 动物纹青铜短剑 | 春秋<br>（公元前770年－前476年） | 通长28.5厘米 | 1975年宁城县<br>小黑石沟遗址出土 | 赤峰市博物馆藏 | 98 |
| 立人柄曲刃青铜短剑 | 春秋<br>（公元前770年－前476年） | 通长31.6、<br>柄长10厘米 | 1958年宁城县<br>南山根遗址出土 | 内蒙古博物馆藏 | 101 |
| T形柄曲刃青铜短剑 | 春秋<br>（公元前770年－前476年） | 通长41.5厘米 | 1985年宁城县<br>小黑石沟遗址出土 | 宁城县博物馆藏 | 99 |
| 双联青铜剑鞘 | 春秋<br>（公元前770年－前476年） | 鞘长38.5、宽10厘米 | 1985年宁城县<br>小黑石沟遗址出土 | 宁城县博物馆藏 | ＊ |
| 金饰兽首青铜刀 | 春秋<br>（公元前770年－前476年） | 通长28.8厘米 | 1998年宁城县<br>小黑石沟遗址出土 | 内蒙古文物考古研究所藏 | 102 |
| 齿柄青铜刀 | 春秋<br>（公元前770年－前476年） | 通长37、<br>刀长31.2厘米 | 1985年宁城县<br>小黑石沟遗址出土 | 内蒙古文物考古研究所藏 | 103 |
| 亻宁立虎首青铜刀 | 春秋<br>（公元前770年－前476年） | 通长21.8厘米 | 1992年宁城县<br>小黑石沟遗址出土 | 内蒙古文物考古研究所藏 | 104 |

＊ 未收入本图册

| 品　名 | 年　代 | 尺寸／重量 | 出土地点 | 收　藏 | 页码 |
|---|---|---|---|---|---|
| 骨柄青铜刀 | 春秋<br>（公元前 770 年 - 前 476 年） | 通长 21、<br>骨柄长 13 厘米 | 1993 年宁城县<br>小黑石沟遗址出土 | 内蒙古文物考古研究所藏 | ＊ |
| 双兽头环首青铜刀 | 春秋<br>（公元前 770 年 - 前 476 年） | 通长 20.4 厘米 | 1985 年宁城县<br>小黑石沟遗址出土 | 宁城县博物馆藏 | ＊ |
| 羊首青铜刀 | 商代晚期<br>（约公元前 11 世纪） | 长 37、宽 4.3 厘米 | 1987 年巴林左旗<br>福山地乡塔子沟征集 | 巴林左旗博物馆藏 | 105 |
| 銎内青铜戈 | 春秋<br>（公元前 770 年 - 前 476 年） | 通长 27、<br>銎径 1.2 - 2 厘米 | 1985 年宁城县<br>小黑石沟遗址出土 | 内蒙古文物考古研究所藏 | ＊ |
| 管銎青铜钺 | 春秋<br>（公元前 770 年 - 前 476 年） | 通长 13.5、<br>管銎长 12 厘米 | 1985 年宁城县<br>小黑石沟遗址出土 | 宁城县博物馆藏 | 106 |
| 矛头形管銎青铜斧 | 春秋<br>（公元前 770 年 - 前 476 年） | 通长 14.7、銎长 7.2 厘米 | 1985 年宁城县<br>小黑石沟遗址出土 | 宁城县博物馆藏 | ＊ |
| 锥形青铜器 | 春秋<br>（公元前 770 年 - 前 476 年） | 长 19.2 厘米 | 1985 年宁城县<br>小黑石沟遗址出土 | 宁城县博物馆藏 | ＊ |
| 青铜扁盒 | 春秋<br>（公元前 770 年 - 前 476 年） | 长 13.8、厚 2.7 厘米 | 1985 年宁城县<br>小黑石沟遗址出土 | 宁城县博物馆藏 | ＊ |
| 青铜盔 | 春秋<br>（公元前 770 年 - 前 476 年） | 高 20.2、口径 21.5 厘米 | 1982 年宁城县<br>小黑石沟遗址出土 | 宁城县博物馆藏 | ＊ |
| 人面纹护胸青铜牌饰 | 春秋<br>（公元前 770 年 - 前 476 年） | 长 23、宽 8.3 厘米 | 1985 年宁城县<br>小黑石沟遗址出土 | 宁城县博物馆藏 | 107 |
| 青铜马衔 | 春秋<br>（公元前 770 年 - 前 476 年） | 通长 23.5 厘米 | 1963 年宁城县<br>南山根墓葬出土 | 赤峰市博物馆藏 | 108 |
| 青铜车轭 | 春秋<br>（公元前 770 年 - 前 476 年） | 长 48、高 18.6 厘米 | 1985 年宁城县<br>小黑石沟遗址出土 | 宁城县博物馆藏 | 109 |
| 鹿形铜饰 | 西周<br>（约公元前 11 世纪 - 前 771 年） | 高 20、长 31.5 厘米 | 1988 年克什克腾旗<br>龙头山遗址出土 | 内蒙古文物考古研究所藏 | 110 |
| 豹形青铜饰牌 | 春秋<br>（公元前 770 年 - 前 476 年） | 长 9.8 厘米 | 1985 年宁城县<br>小黑石沟遗址出土 | 宁城县博物馆藏 | ＊ |
| 马形金牌饰 | 春秋<br>（公元前 770 年 - 前 476 年） | 长 4.6、宽 4.5 厘米 | 1986 年宁城县<br>小城子出土 | 宁城县博物馆藏 | 111 |

＊ 未收入本图册

| 品　名 | 年　代 | 尺寸／重量 | 出土地点 | 收　藏 | 页码 |
|---|---|---|---|---|---|
| 猪形青铜饰牌 | 战国<br>（公元前 475 年 - 前 221 年） | 长 6.1- 5.2、<br>高 3.2 - 3.8 厘米 | 1990 年敖汉旗<br>新惠乡铁匠沟 1 号墓出土 | 敖汉旗博物馆藏 | 112 |
| 几何纹双钮铜镜 | 春秋<br>（公元前 770 年 - 前 476 年） | 直径 17.3、厚 0.9 厘米 | 1998 年宁城县<br>小黑石沟遗址出土 | 内蒙古文物考古研究所藏 | 113 |
| "师道"簋 | 西周中期<br>（约公元前 11 世纪 - 前 10 世纪） | 通高 23.4、口径 19.6、<br>底径 20.6 厘米 | 1996 年宁城县<br>小黑石沟遗址出土 | 宁城县博物馆藏 | 115 |
| "许季姜"簋 | 西周晚期<br>（约公元前 9 世纪上半叶 - 前 771 年） | 高 25、口径 21.4、<br>底径 21 厘米 | 1987 年宁城县<br>小黑石沟石椁墓出土 | 内蒙古博物馆藏 | 117 |
| "滕"盉 | 春秋早期<br>（约公元前 770 年 - 前 7 世纪上半叶） | 通高 21.3、<br>腹径 18.5 厘米 | 1985 年宁城县<br>小黑石沟遗址出土 | 宁城县博物馆藏 | 119 |
| 青铜罍 | 西周<br>（约公元前 11 世纪 - 前 771 年） | 高 40 厘米 | 1985 年宁城县<br>小黑石沟石椁墓出土 | 内蒙古博物馆藏 | 121 |
| 十字徽帜青铜甗 | 商代<br>（公元前 16 世纪 - 前 11 世纪） | 通高 66、口径 41 厘米 | 1981 年翁牛特旗<br>头牌子乡出土 | 翁牛特旗文物管理站藏 | ＊ |
| 双耳青铜鼎 | 春秋<br>（公元前 770 年 - 前 476 年） | 高 17、口径 12 厘米 | 1998 年宁城县<br>小黑石沟遗址出土 | 内蒙古文物考古研究所藏 | ＊ |
| 刖人守门青铜方鼎 | 西周<br>（约公元前 11 世纪 - 前 771 年） | 通高 19、<br>口径 9.7 - 12.7 厘米 | 1985 年宁城县<br>小黑石沟遗址出土 | 宁城县博物馆藏 | 123 |
| 兽耳青铜鬲 | 春秋<br>（公元前 770 年 - 前 476 年） | 高 21.5、<br>口径 15.8 厘米 | 1985 年宁城县<br>小黑石沟遗址出土 | 宁城县博物馆藏 | ＊ |
| 青铜匜 | 西周<br>（约公元前 11 世纪 - 前 771 年） | 通高 19.5、长 41 厘米 | 1985 年宁城县<br>小黑石沟遗址出土 | 宁城县博物馆藏 | ＊ |
| 联体青铜豆 | 春秋<br>（公元前 770 年 - 前 476 年） | 通高 14.6、<br>通径 37.8 厘米 | 1985 年宁城县<br>小黑石沟遗址出土 | 宁城县博物馆藏 | ＊ |
| 口缘饰兽青铜豆 | 春秋<br>（公元前 770 年 - 前 476 年） | 高 24.6、<br>口径 17.6 厘米 | 1996 年宁城县<br>小黑石沟墓地出土 | 宁城县博物馆藏 | 124 |
| 祖柄青铜勺 | 春秋<br>（公元前 770 年 - 前 476 年） | 通长 20、<br>勺径 8.5 厘米 | 1963 年宁城县<br>南山根墓葬出土 | 赤峰市博物馆藏 | 126 |
| 单耳四足青铜盘 | 春秋<br>（公元前 770 年 - 前 476 年） | 高 7.4、<br>口径 28.3 - 22.6 厘米 | 1996 年宁城县<br>小黑石沟遗址出土 | 宁城县博物馆藏 | ＊ |

＊ 未收入本图册

| 品 名 | 年 代 | 尺寸／重量 | 出土地点 | 收 藏 | 页码 |
|---|---|---|---|---|---|
| 瓦棱纹青铜罐 | 春秋<br>（公元前770年－前476年） | 高10－12.5、<br>口径6.1厘米 | 1996年宁城县<br>小黑石沟遗址出土 | 宁城县博物馆藏 | ＊ |
| 六连青铜盖罐 | 春秋<br>（公元前770年－前476年） | 长50、高11.5厘米 | 1996年宁城县<br>小黑石沟遗址出土 | 宁城县博物馆藏 | ＊ |
| 鼓形青铜器 | 春秋<br>（公元前770年－前476年） | 通长27.2、<br>口径12厘米 | 1996年宁城县<br>小黑石沟遗址出土 | 宁城县博物馆藏 | 125 |
| 鼓形陶器 | 春秋<br>（公元前770年－前476年） | 高25.8、口径14.8、<br>底径15厘米 | 1996年宁城县<br>小黑石沟遗址出土 | 内蒙古文物考古研究所藏 | ＊ |
| 筒形彩绘陶罐 | 夏<br>（约公元前21世纪－前16世纪） | 高22、口径11.2、<br>底径12.5厘米 | 1974年敖汉旗<br>大甸子墓地出土 | 赤峰市博物馆藏 | 127 |
| 勾云纹彩绘陶罐 | 夏<br>（约公元前21世纪－前16世纪） | 高20、口径18.5、<br>底径9.7厘米 | 1974年敖汉旗<br>大甸子墓地出土 | 赤峰市博物馆藏 | 129 |
| 嵌贝彩绘陶鬲 | 夏<br>（约公元前21世纪－前16世纪） | 高29.5、口径22厘米 | 1974年敖汉旗<br>大甸子墓地出土 | 赤峰市博物馆藏 | 131 |
| 陶鼎 | 战国<br>（公元前475年－前221年） | 通高25.6、<br>口径13.6厘米 | 1998年宁城县<br>小黑石沟墓葬出土 | 内蒙古文物考古研究所藏 | ＊ |
| 陶豆 | 战国<br>（公元前475年－前221年） | 通高42.4、口径8、<br>底径11厘米 | 1998年宁城县<br>小黑石沟墓葬出土 | 内蒙古文物考古研究所藏 | 132 |
| 陶豆 | 战国<br>（公元前475年－前221年） | 通高37.6、口径12.8、<br>底径12厘米 | 1998年宁城县<br>小黑石沟墓葬出土 | 内蒙古文物考古研究所藏 | ＊ |
| 陶壶 | 战国<br>（公元前475年－前221年） | 通高35.6、口径12、<br>底径9厘米 | 1998年宁城县<br>小黑石沟墓葬出土 | 内蒙古文物考古研究所藏 | 133 |
| 陶匜 | 战国<br>（公元前475年－前221年） | 高4.4、口径14.4厘米 | 1998年宁城县<br>小黑石沟墓葬出土 | 内蒙古文物考古研究所 | ＊ |
| 狩猎纹骨板 | 东汉<br>（公元25年－220年） | 长15、宽2.5、<br>厚0.3厘米 | 1960年新巴尔虎右旗<br>扎赉诺尔鲜卑墓出土 | 内蒙古博物馆藏 | 137 |
| 三鹿纹金饰牌 | 东汉<br>（公元25年－220年） | 长6.8、宽4.5厘米，<br>重21.6克 | 1983年察哈尔右翼后旗<br>三道湾墓地出土 | 乌兰察布盟博物馆藏 | ＊ |
| 双鹿纹金饰牌 | 东汉<br>（公元25年－220年） | 长7.1、宽5.3厘米，<br>重44.5克 | 1983年察哈尔右翼后旗<br>三道湾墓地出土 | 乌兰察布盟博物馆藏 | ＊ |

＊ 未收入本图册

| 品　　名 | 年　　代 | 尺寸／重量 | 出土地点 | 收　　藏 | 页码 |
|---|---|---|---|---|---|
| 马鹿首金步摇冠饰 | 北朝<br>（公元 386 年 - 581 年） | 高 19.5 厘米　重 92 克 | 1981 年达尔罕茂明安联合旗<br>西河子村出土 | 内蒙古博物馆藏 | 139 |
| 牛首金步摇冠饰 | 北朝<br>（公元 386 年 - 581 年） | 高 18.5 厘米　重 70 克 | 1981 年达尔罕茂明安联合旗<br>西河子村出土 | 内蒙古博物馆藏 | 138 |
| 金冠顶饰 | 北朝<br>（公元 386 年 - 581 年） | 高 6 厘米　重 18 克 | 1979 年科尔沁左翼中旗<br>哈日干吐苏木毛加吐出土 | 通辽市博物馆藏 | ＊ |
| 金龙项饰 | 北朝<br>（公元 386 年 - 581 年） | 长 128 厘米　重 213.8 克 | 1981 年达尔罕茂明安联合旗<br>西河子村出土 | 内蒙古博物馆藏 | 141 |
| 卧羊形金戒指 | 北朝<br>（公元 386 年 - 581 年） | 高 2 厘米 | 1955 年土默特左旗<br>美岱村出土 | 内蒙古博物馆藏 | ＊ |
| 人面形金饰牌 | 北朝<br>（公元 386 年 - 581 年） | 长 9、宽 6 厘米<br>重 91.5 - 99.2 克 | 1990 年科尔沁左翼中旗<br>腰林毛都苏木北哈拉吐出土 | 通辽市博物馆藏 | 142 |
| 人物双狮纹金饰牌 | 北朝<br>（公元 386 年 - 581 年） | 长 10、宽 5.8 厘米<br>重 130.8 克 | 1990 年科尔沁左翼中旗<br>腰林毛都苏木北哈拉吐出土 | 通辽市博物馆藏 | 143 |
| 瑞兽纹金饰牌 | 北朝<br>（公元 386 年 - 581 年） | 长 9.7 厘米、重 63 克 | 1983 年科尔沁左翼中旗<br>希伯花苏木木西六家子出土 | 通辽市博物馆藏 | ＊ |
| 子母马纹金饰牌 | 北朝<br>（公元 386 年 - 581 年） | 长 6.8、宽 5.7 厘米<br>重 41.8 克 | 1983 年科尔沁左翼中旗<br>希伯花苏木木西六家子出土 | 通辽市博物馆藏 | ＊ |
| 蹲踞式马纹金挂饰 | 北朝<br>（公元 386 年 - 581 年） | 长 8、宽 5 厘米<br>重 91.5 克 | 1983 年科尔沁左翼中旗<br>希伯花苏木木西六家子出土 | 通辽市博物馆藏 | ＊ |
| 兽纹金饰牌 | 北朝<br>（公元 386 年 - 581 年） | 长 8.1、宽 4.7 厘米<br>重 36 克 | 1983 年科尔沁左翼中旗<br>希伯花苏木木西六家子出土 | 通辽市博物馆藏 | ＊ |
| 双马纹金饰牌 | 北朝<br>（公元 386 年 - 581 年）. | 长 8.8、宽 4.1 厘米<br>重 31.5 克 | 1983 年科尔沁左翼中旗<br>希伯花苏木木西六家子出土 | 通辽市博物馆藏 | ＊ |
| 陶罐 | 东汉<br>（公元 25 年 - 220 年） | 最高 20 厘米 | 1960 年新巴尔虎右旗<br>扎赉诺尔鲜卑墓出土 | 内蒙古博物馆藏 | ＊ |
| 骨镞 | 东汉<br>（公元 25 年 - 220 年） | 长 12.9 - 6.4 厘米 | 1960 年新巴尔虎右旗<br>扎赉诺尔鲜卑墓出土 | 内蒙古博物馆藏 | ＊ |
| 弓弭 | 东汉<br>（公元 25 年 - 220 年） | 最长 25 厘米 | 1960 年新巴尔虎右旗<br>扎赉诺尔鲜卑墓出土 | 内蒙古博物馆藏 | ＊ |

＊ 未收入本图册

| 品　名 | 年　代 | 尺寸／重量 | 出土地点 | 收　藏 | 页码 |
|---|---|---|---|---|---|
| 青铜鍑 | 东汉<br>（公元 25 年 - 220 年） | 通高 19.5、口径 12.5、<br>底径 8.8 厘米 | 1982 年和林格尔县<br>三道营乡另皮窑出土 | 内蒙古博物馆藏 | ＊ |
| 舞乐陶俑 | 北魏<br>（公元 386 年 - 534 年） | 高 15.5 - 19.8 厘米 | 1975 年呼和浩特市<br>大学路北魏墓出土 | 内蒙古博物馆藏 | 145 |
| 镇墓陶俑 | 北魏<br>（公元 386 年 - 534 年） | 高 39.5、43.5 厘米 | 1975 年呼和浩特市<br>大学路北魏墓出土 | 内蒙古博物馆藏 | 146 |
| 摩羯形金耳坠 | 辽会同四年<br>（公元 941 年） | 通长 4.4、宽 4.4 厘米 | 1992 年阿鲁科尔沁旗<br>辽耶律羽之墓出土 | 内蒙古文物考古研究所藏 | 149 |
| 金戒指 | 辽会同四年<br>（公元 941 年） | 戒面长 1.9 - 3.2 厘米 | 1992 年阿鲁科尔沁旗<br>辽耶律羽之墓出土 | 内蒙古文物考古研究所藏 | ＊ |
| 龙首形金镯 | 辽会同四年<br>（公元 941 年） | 宽 1.2、直径 6.1、<br>厚 0.1 厘米 | 1992 年阿鲁科尔沁旗<br>辽耶律羽之墓出土 | 内蒙古文物考古研究所藏 | ＊ |
| 水晶包金心形饰件 | 辽<br>（公元 916 年 - 1125 年） | 高 5.2 厘米 | 1993 年阿鲁科尔沁旗<br>扎嘎斯台苏木花根塔拉辽墓出土 | 阿鲁科尔沁旗博物馆藏 | ＊ |
| 水晶包金管饰件 | 辽<br>（公元 916 年 - 1125 年） | 长 10 厘米 | 1993 年阿鲁科尔沁旗<br>扎嘎斯台苏木花根塔拉辽墓出土 | 阿鲁科尔沁旗博物馆藏 | ＊ |
| 玛瑙、水晶璎珞 | 辽会同四年<br>（公元 941 年） | 周长 78 厘米 | 1992 年阿鲁科尔沁旗<br>辽耶律羽之墓出土 | 内蒙古文物考古研究所藏 | 147 |
| 玉熊 | 辽<br>（公元 916 年 - 1125 年） | 长 6.8、宽 3.8 厘米 | 1978 年巴林右旗<br>巴彦汉苏木友爱村窖藏出土 | 巴林右旗博物馆藏 | 150 |
| 水晶鱼 | 辽<br>（公元 916 年 - 1125 年） | 长 4、宽 1.7 厘米 | 喀喇沁旗<br>宫家营子乡吉旺营子辽墓出土 | 赤峰市博物馆藏 | 151 |
| 水晶鼠 | 辽<br>（公元 916 年 - 1125 年） | 长 3.6、宽 2.3 厘米 | 喀喇沁旗<br>宫家营子乡吉旺营子辽墓出土 | 赤峰市博物馆藏 | 154 |
| 盘龙纹铜镜 | 辽会同四年<br>（公元 941 年） | 直径 28 厘米 | 1992 年阿鲁科尔沁旗<br>辽耶律羽之墓出土 | 内蒙古文物考古研究所藏 | 153 |
| 海兽纹铜镜 | 辽<br>会同四年（公元 941 年） | 直径 18、厚 1.2 厘米 | 1992 年阿鲁科尔沁旗<br>辽耶律羽之墓出土 | 内蒙古文物考古研究所藏 | ＊ |
| 人形金饰件 | 辽<br>（公元 916 年 - 1125 年） | 高 9.2 厘米 | 1993 年阿鲁科尔沁旗<br>扎嘎斯台苏木花根塔拉辽墓出土 | 阿鲁科尔沁旗博物馆藏 | 155 |

＊ 未收入本图册

| 品　名 | 年　代 | 尺寸／重量 | 出土地点 | 收　藏 | 页码 |
|---|---|---|---|---|---|
| 海东青鎏金铜饰件 | 辽会同四年（公元941年） | 高24.3、宽30.5、厚0.03厘米 | 1992年阿鲁科尔沁旗辽耶律羽之墓出土 | 内蒙古文物考古研究所藏 | 156 |
| 鎏金门神铜饰件 | 辽会同四年（公元941年） | 高40.8、宽23.6、厚0.03厘米 | 1992年阿鲁科尔沁旗辽耶律羽之墓出土 | 内蒙古文物考古研究所藏 | 157 |
| 鎏金木雕坐狮 | 辽会同四年（公元941年） | 通高15.6、宽7厘米 | 1992年阿鲁科尔沁旗辽耶律羽之墓出土 | 内蒙古文物考古研究所藏 | ＊ |
| 彩绘双扇木门 | 辽会同四年（公元941年） | (单扇门)长28、宽20.8、厚1.7厘米 | 1992年阿鲁科尔沁旗辽耶律羽之墓出土 | 内蒙古文物考古研究所藏 | 158 |
| 双鱼形鎏金银壶 | 唐（公元618－907年） | 高28.5、口径5、腹径20.4、底径15厘米 | 1976年喀喇沁旗锦山镇窖藏出土 | 喀喇沁旗文管所藏 | 159 |
| 花式口金杯 | 辽会同四年（公元941年） | 高3、口径7.7、底径4.2厘米 重61.2克 | 1992年阿鲁科尔沁旗辽耶律羽之墓出土 | 内蒙古文物考古研究所藏 | 161 |
| 摩羯纹金花银碗 | 辽会同四年（公元941年） | 高6.5、口径20、底径10.2厘米 | 1992年阿鲁科尔沁旗辽耶律羽之墓出土 | 内蒙古文物考古研究所藏 | 163 |
| 鎏金錾花银盘 | 辽会同四年（公元941年） | 高3.5、口径18.4、底径11.5厘米 | 1992年阿鲁科尔沁旗辽耶律羽之墓出土 | 内蒙古文物考古研究所藏 | 164 |
| 狮纹鎏金錾花银盘 | 唐（公元618年－907年） | 高2.4、口径46.6厘米 | 1976年喀喇沁旗锦山镇窖藏出土 | 喀喇沁旗文管所藏 | 167 |
| 海棠形錾花银盘 | 辽（公元916年－1125年） | 长31、宽18.3、高1.8厘米 | 1978年巴林右旗巴彦汉苏木友爱村窖藏出土 | 巴林右旗博物馆藏 | ＊ |
| 双摩羯形鎏金银提梁壶 | 辽（公元916年－1125年） | 通高33、口径5.4、底径15.3厘米 | 1979年赤峰市城子乡洞山村窖藏出土 | 赤峰市博物馆藏 | 165 |
| 长颈银壶 | 辽（公元916年－1125年） | 高65.3、底径20.7厘米 | 1966年克什克腾旗热水镇二八地村辽墓出土 | 赤峰市博物馆藏 | ＊ |
| 金花银渣斗 | 辽会同四年（公元941年） | 高12、口径15.4、腹径10.5、底径8.3厘米 | 1992年阿鲁科尔沁旗辽耶律羽之墓出土 | 内蒙古文物考古研究所藏 | 169 |
| 银文房四宝（笔管、洗、砚、盘） | 辽（公元916年－1125年） | 笔管长25、洗高3.8、口径9.6、砚高2.1、通长21.1、盘高2.8、长24、宽12.9厘米 | 1988年敖汉旗新地乡英凤沟4号墓出土 | 敖汉旗博物馆藏 | ＊ |
| 莲花鹊尾银香炉 | 辽大康七年（公元1081年） | 通长36.5厘米 | 1993年宁城县头道营子乡埋王沟墓葬出土 | 内蒙古文物考古研究所藏 | 171 |

＊ 未收入本图册

| 品　名 | 年　代 | 尺寸／重量 | 出土地点 | 收　藏 | 页码 |
|---|---|---|---|---|---|
| 鎏金银覆面 | 辽代<br>（公元916年－1125年） | 高21、宽19.3厘米 | 1988年敖汉旗<br>新地乡英凤沟4号墓出土 | 敖汉旗博物馆藏 | ＊ |
| 刻花长颈白瓷瓶 | 辽<br>（公元916年－1125年） | 通高52.8、口径13.8、<br>足径10厘米 | 1985年巴林右旗<br>巴彦尔灯苏木布和特哈达辽墓出土 | 巴林右旗博物馆藏 | 173 |
| 盘口穿带白瓷瓶 | 辽会同四年<br>（公元941年） | 高37.3、口径12.8、<br>足径12.5厘米 | 1992年阿鲁科尔沁旗<br>辽耶律羽之墓出土 | 内蒙古文物考古研究所藏 | ＊ |
| "盈"字款白瓷碗 | 辽会同四年<br>（公元941年） | 高8.4、口径23.6、<br>足径10.8厘米 | 1992年阿鲁科尔沁旗<br>辽耶律羽之墓出土 | 内蒙古文物考古研究所藏 | 174 |
| 葵口白瓷碗 | 辽会同四年<br>（公元941年） | 高10、口径25.6、<br>底径10厘米 | 1992年阿鲁科尔沁旗<br>辽耶律羽之墓出土 | 内蒙古文物考古研究所藏 | ＊ |
| 莲花纹"官"字款执壶、温碗、盏<br>等一组酒具（4件） | 辽<br>（公元916年－1125年） | 壶高22.5、口径4.8、底径8.6厘米<br>碗高7.8、口径19.6、底径8厘米<br>盏高6、口径8.8、底径4.6厘米<br>托盘高3.8、口径15.2、底径8.3厘米 | 1989年敖汉旗<br>贝子府镇驿马吐墓出土 | 敖汉旗博物馆藏 | ＊ |
| 葫芦形白瓷执壶 | 辽<br>（公元916年－1125年） | 通高23.2、口径2.8、<br>底径8.2厘米 | 1988年巴林右旗<br>羊场乡辽墓出土 | 巴林右旗博物馆藏 | 175 |
| 定窑钼器 | 辽<br>（公元916年－1125年） | 高5.7、口径8.3、<br>底径4.5厘米 | 1978年敖汉旗<br>南塔子乡北三家辽墓出土 | 敖汉旗博物馆藏 | ＊ |
| 迦叶白瓷像 | 辽<br>（公元916年－1125年） | 高26.5厘米 | 1986年库伦旗<br>奈林稿苏木前勿力布格村征集 | 通辽市博物馆藏 | 176 |
| 阿难白瓷像 | 辽<br>（公元916年－1125年） | 高27厘米 | 1986年库伦旗<br>奈林稿苏木前勿力布格村征集 | 通辽市博物馆藏 | 177 |
| 双耳四系青瓷盖罐 | 辽会同四年<br>（公元941年） | 通高34.2、口径9.8、<br>底径10.5厘米 | 1992年阿鲁科尔沁旗<br>辽耶律羽之墓出土 | 内蒙古文物考古研究所藏 | ＊ |
| 搅胎瓷盒 | 辽<br>（公元916年－1125年） | 高6.5、口径12.5、<br>底径5.5厘米 | 1990年敖汉旗<br>玛尼罕乡皮匠营子七家村辽墓出土 | 敖汉旗博物馆藏 | ＊ |
| 葫芦形黄釉瓷壶 | 辽<br>（公元916年－1125年） | 高26.7、口径3.2、<br>底径8.3厘米 | 1978年库伦旗<br>水泉乡昆都岭村征集 | 通辽市博物馆藏 | ＊ |
| 印花紫定碗 | 辽<br>（公元916年－1125年） | 高5.2－5.6、口径16.5－17.1、<br>底径5.4厘米 | 1975年奈曼旗<br>白音昌乡石碑村征集 | 通辽市博物馆藏 | 178 |
| 喇叭口浅褐釉瓷壶 | 辽会同四年<br>（公元941年） | 口径14.3、底径10.5厘米 | 1992年阿鲁科尔沁旗<br>辽耶律羽之墓出土 | 内蒙古文物考古研究所藏 | ＊ |

＊ 未收入本图册

| 品　名 | 年　代 | 尺寸／重量 | 出土地点 | 收　藏 | 页码 |
|---|---|---|---|---|---|
| 暗花黑釉葫芦瓶 | 辽<br>（公元916年－1125年） | 高35.7、口径3、<br>底径9.4厘米 | 1987年敖汉旗<br>新惠乡呼仁宝和村出土 | 敖汉旗博物馆藏 | 179 |
| 龙首绿釉鸡冠壶 | 辽<br>（公元916年－1125年） | 高23.5、底径7.5厘米 | 1965年翁牛特旗<br>广德公乡辽墓出土 | 赤峰市博物馆藏 | 180 |
| 刻花绿釉鸡冠壶 | 辽<br>（公元916年－1125年） | 高23、足径9厘米 | 1965年翁牛特旗<br>广德公乡辽墓出土 | 赤峰市博物馆藏 | ✱ |
| 双猴绿釉鸡冠壶 | 辽<br>（公元916年－1125年） | 长16、宽9、高27厘米 | 1989年翁牛特旗<br>广德公乡辽墓出土 | 翁牛特旗文物管理站藏 | 181 |
| 牡丹花绿釉鸡冠壶 | 辽<br>（公元916年－1125年） | 高23.2、底径8.2厘米 | 巴林左旗征集 | 巴林左旗博物馆藏 | ✱ |
| 灰陶鸡冠壶 | 辽<br>（公元916年－1125年） | 高26、足径12.8厘米 | 1964年喀喇沁旗<br>楼子店乡上烧锅辽墓出土 | 赤峰市博物馆藏 | ✱ |
| 摩羯形三彩壶 | 辽<br>（公元916年－1125年） | 高22.3、长30、<br>足径9厘米 | 1975年科尔沁左翼中旗<br>征集 | 通辽市博物馆藏 | 183 |
| 摩羯形三彩壶 | 辽<br>（公元916年－1125年） | 高25.5、足径9厘米 | 1982年宁城县<br>榆树林子乡辽墓出土 | 赤峰市博物馆藏 | ✱ |
| 鸳鸯形三彩壶 | 辽<br>（公元916年－1125年） | 高20、口径8.2、<br>底径9厘米 | 1977年赤峰市<br>松山区征集 | 赤峰市博物馆藏 | 184 |
| 龙纹三彩执壶 | 辽<br>（公元916年－1125年） | 高18.8、口径3.5、<br>底径7.8厘米 | 1977年赤峰市<br>松山区征集 | 赤峰市文物店藏 | 185 |
| 三彩埙 | 辽咸雍六年<br>（公元1070年） | 高6.3、直径8.3厘米 | 1992年宁城县<br>头道营子乡埋王沟墓葬出土 | 内蒙古文物考古研究所藏 | 188 |
| 八角形三彩砚 | 辽咸雍六年<br>（公元1070年） | 高12.6、直径22厘米 | 1992年宁城县<br>头道营子乡埋王沟墓葬出土 | 内蒙古文物考古研究所藏 | 187 |
| 鹿纹穹庐式骨灰罐 | 辽<br>（公元916年－1125年） | 通高25.5、底径31厘米 | 1973年巴林左旗<br>哈达英格乡哈达图村墓葬出土 | 巴林左旗博物馆藏 | 189 |
| 仓式茶釉骨灰罐 | 辽<br>（公元916年－1125年） | 通高43、腹径31厘米 | 1972年巴林左旗<br>福山地乡塔子沟墓葬出土 | 巴林左旗博物馆藏 | ✱ |
| 鎏金铜铎 | 辽<br>（公元916年－1125年） | 高42、长径30、<br>短径20厘米 | 1993年阿鲁科尔沁旗<br>辽耶律羽之家族墓地出土 | 内蒙古文物考古研究所藏 | 190 |

✱ 未收入本图册

| 品　名 | 年　代 | 尺寸／重量 | 出土地点 | 收　藏 | 页码 |
|---|---|---|---|---|---|
| 陀罗尼咒金板 | 辽重熙十八年<br>（公元 1049 年） | 长 16.7、宽 9.6、<br>厚 0.03 厘米 | 1989 年巴林右旗<br>辽庆州释迦佛舍利塔塔刹出土 | 巴林右旗博物馆藏 | 191 |
| 陀罗尼咒银板 | 辽重熙十八年<br>（公元 1049 年） | 长 21.2、宽 11.6、<br>厚 0.03 厘米 | 1989 年巴林右旗<br>辽庆州释迦佛舍利塔塔刹出土 | 巴林右旗博物馆藏 | ＊ |
| 十方佛彩绘舍利塔 | 辽重熙十八年<br>（公元 1049 年） | 通高 45.5、底径 13 厘米 | 1989 年巴林右旗<br>辽庆州释迦佛舍利塔塔刹相轮橖出土 | 巴林右旗博物馆藏 | 192 |
| 七佛贴金舍利塔 | 辽重熙十八年<br>（公元 1049 年） | 通高 23、底径 9.1 厘米 | 1989 年巴林右旗<br>辽庆州释迦佛舍利塔塔刹相轮橖出土 | 巴林右旗博物馆藏 | 193 |
| 七佛彩绘贴金舍利塔 | 辽重熙十八年<br>（公元 1049 年） | 通高 22.8、底径 22.8 厘米 | 1989 年巴林右旗<br>辽庆州释迦佛舍利塔塔刹相轮橖出土 | 巴林右旗博物馆藏 | 196 |
| 七佛素彩舍利塔 | 辽重熙十八年<br>（公元 1049 年） | 高 23、底径 8.7 厘米 | 1989 年巴林右旗<br>辽庆州释迦佛舍利塔塔刹相轮橖出土 | 巴林右旗博物馆藏 | ＊ |
| 凤衔珠银鎏金舍利塔 | 辽重熙十八年<br>（公元 1049 年） | 通高 40.5、底径 10.7 厘米 | 1989 年巴林右旗<br>辽庆州释迦佛舍利塔塔刹相轮橖出土 | 巴林右旗博物馆藏 | 195 |
| 梅花蜂蝶蓝色罗地绣巾 | 辽重熙十八年<br>（公元 1049 年） | 长 65、宽 50 厘米 | 1989 年巴林右旗<br>辽庆州释迦佛舍利塔塔刹相轮橖出土 | 巴林右旗博物馆藏 | 197 |
| 联珠云龙纹橙色罗地绣巾 | 辽重熙十八年<br>（公元 1049 年） | 长 79.2、宽 58.5 厘米 | 1989 年巴林右旗<br>辽庆州释迦佛舍利塔塔刹相轮橖出土 | 巴林右旗博物馆藏 | 198 |
| 联珠人物红罗地绣经袱 | 辽重熙十八年<br>（公元 1049 年） | 长 27.5、宽 27 厘米 | 1989 年巴林右旗<br>辽庆州释迦佛舍利塔塔刹相轮橖出土 | 巴林右旗博物馆藏 | 199 |
| 释迦佛涅槃彩绘汉白玉雕像 | 辽重熙十八年<br>（公元 1049 年） | 通高 36、长 60、宽 33 厘米 | 1989 年巴林右旗<br>辽庆州释迦佛舍利塔内出土 | 巴林右旗博物馆藏 | 200 |
| 金面具、银丝网络(部分) | 辽开泰七年<br>（公元 1018 年） | 长 21.7、宽 18.8 厘米<br>重 293.5 克 | 1986 年奈曼旗<br>辽陈国公主墓出土 | 内蒙古文物考古研究所藏 | 201 |
| 鎏金银冠 | 辽开泰七年<br>（公元 1018 年） | 通高 31.5、宽 31.4、口径 19.5 厘米<br>重 587 克 | 1986 年奈曼旗<br>辽陈国公主墓出土 | 内蒙古文物考古研究所藏 | 203 |
| 金花银靴 | 辽开泰七年<br>（公元 1018 年） | 高 34.6、底长 30.4 厘米 | 1986 年奈曼旗<br>辽陈国公主墓出土 | 内蒙古文物考古研究所藏 | 204 |
| 金花银枕 | 辽开泰七年<br>（公元 1018 年） | 枕面长 36、宽 49.6、<br>高 0.9－14 厘米　重 1510 克 | 1986 年奈曼旗<br>辽陈国公主墓出土 | 内蒙古文物考古研究所藏 | 205 |

＊ 未收入本图册

| 品　名 | 年　代 | 尺寸／重量 | 出土地点 | 收　藏 | 页码 |
|---|---|---|---|---|---|
| 玉銙丝鞓蹀躞带 | 辽开泰七年<br>（公元1018年） | 通长156厘米 | 1986年奈曼旗<br>辽陈国公主墓出土 | 内蒙古文物考古研究所藏 | ＊ |
| 银、铜銙银鞓蹀躞带 | 辽开泰七年<br>（公元1018年） | 通长137.5厘米 | 1986年奈曼旗<br>辽陈国公主墓出土 | 内蒙古文物考古研究所藏 | 206 |
| 玉銙银带 | 辽开泰七年<br>（公元1018年） | 通长163.7厘米 | 1986年奈曼旗<br>辽陈国公主墓出土 | 内蒙古文物考古研究所藏 | 207 |
| 双龙纹金镯 | 辽开泰七年<br>（公元1018年） | 镯径5.5－7.7厘米<br>（单件）重66.5克 | 1986年奈曼旗<br>辽陈国公主墓出土 | 内蒙古文物考古研究所藏 | 208 |
| 八曲式金盒 | 辽开泰七年<br>（公元1018年） | 高1.7、直径5.5厘米<br>重85克 | 1986年奈曼旗<br>辽陈国公主墓出土 | 内蒙古文物考古研究所藏 | 211 |
| 錾花金针筒 | 辽开泰七年<br>（公元1018年） | 通长11.7、<br>直径1.2厘米 | 1986年奈曼旗<br>辽陈国公主墓出土 | 内蒙古文物考古研究所藏 | ＊ |
| 玉柄银刀 | 辽开泰七年<br>（公元1018年） | 刀通长26.8、<br>银鞘长32厘米 | 1986年奈曼旗<br>辽陈国公主墓出土 | 内蒙古文物考古研究所藏 | ＊ |
| 玉柄银锥 | 辽开泰七年<br>（公元1018年） | 锥通长17.8、<br>银鞘长15厘米 | 1986年奈曼旗<br>辽陈国公主墓出土 | 内蒙古文物考古研究所藏 | 209 |
| 琥珀柄银刀 | 辽开泰七年<br>（公元1018年） | 刀通长30.4、<br>鞘长32厘米 | 1986年奈曼旗<br>辽陈国公主墓出土 | 内蒙古文物考古研究所藏 | ＊ |
| 交颈鸳鸯玉坠 | 辽开泰七年<br>（公元1018年） | 长6、宽2、高2.8厘米 | 1986年奈曼旗<br>辽陈国公主墓出土 | 内蒙古文物考古研究所藏 | 212 |
| 交颈鸿雁玉坠 | 辽开泰七年<br>（公元1018年） | 长6.5、宽1.6、高2.5厘米 | 1986年奈曼旗<br>辽陈国公主墓出土 | 内蒙古文物考古研究所藏 | ＊ |
| 双鱼玉佩 | 辽开泰七年<br>（公元1018年） | 通长10.5厘米 | 1986年奈曼旗<br>辽陈国公主墓出土 | 内蒙古文物考古研究所藏 | ＊ |
| 动物形玉佩 | 辽开泰七年<br>（公元1018年） | 通长15厘米 | 1986年奈曼旗<br>辽陈国公主墓出土 | 内蒙古文物考古研究所藏 | 214 |
| 动物形玉佩 | 辽开泰七年<br>（公元1018年） | 通长14.8厘米 | 1986年奈曼旗<br>辽陈国公主墓出土 | 内蒙古文物考古研究所藏 | 215 |
| 鱼形玉盒 | 辽开泰七年<br>（公元1018年） | 通长23.5厘米 | 1986年奈曼旗<br>辽陈国公主墓出土 | 内蒙古文物考古研究所藏 | 213 |

＊ 未收入本图册

| 品 名 | 年 代 | 尺寸／重量 | 出土地点 | 收 藏 | 页码 |
|---|---|---|---|---|---|
| 螺形玉佩 | 辽开泰七年<br>（公元1018年） | 通长23厘米 | 1986年奈曼旗<br>辽陈国公主墓出土 | 内蒙古文物考古研究所藏 | ＊ |
| 玉臂鞲 | 辽开泰七年<br>（公元1018年） | 长9、宽3.4、厚0.35厘米 | 1986年奈曼旗<br>辽陈国公主墓出土 | 内蒙古文物考古研究所藏 | 222 |
| 琥珀珍珠头饰 | 辽开泰七年<br>（公元1018年） | 通长30厘米 | 1986年奈曼旗<br>辽陈国公主墓出土 | 内蒙古文物考古研究所藏 | ＊ |
| 龙纹琥珀佩饰 | 辽开泰七年<br>（公元1018年） | 长6.7、宽4.7、厚2.6厘米 | 1986年奈曼旗<br>辽陈国公主墓出土 | 内蒙古文物考古研究所藏 | ＊ |
| 荷叶双雁纹琥珀佩饰 | 辽开泰七年<br>（公元1018年） | 长7.3、宽4.7、厚2.1厘米 | 1986年奈曼旗<br>辽陈国公主墓出土 | 内蒙古文物考古研究所藏 | ＊ |
| 琥珀小瓶 | 辽开泰七年<br>（公元1018年） | 通高6.2、宽4.7厘米 | 1986年奈曼旗<br>辽陈国公主墓出土 | 内蒙古文物考古研究所藏 | ＊ |
| 琥珀蚕蛹 | 辽开泰七年<br>（公元1018年） | (单件)长4.5、<br>宽1.5-1.9厘米 | 1986年奈曼旗<br>辽陈国公主墓出土 | 内蒙古文物考古研究所藏 | ＊ |
| 双鱼形琥珀盒 | 辽开泰七年<br>（公元1018年） | 长7.8、宽4.7厘米 | 1986年奈曼旗<br>辽陈国公主墓出土 | 内蒙古文物考古研究所藏 | 216 |
| 鸿雁形琥珀饰件 | 辽开泰七年<br>（公元1018年） | 长5.3、宽2.8、<br>高4厘米 | 1986年奈曼旗<br>辽陈国公主墓出土 | 内蒙古文物考古研究所藏 | 217 |
| 琥珀握手 | 辽开泰七年<br>（公元1018年） | 长6.2－6.7、<br>宽4.3－4.8厘米 | 1986年奈曼旗<br>辽陈国公主墓出土 | 内蒙古文物考古研究所藏 | 219 |
| 琥珀佩饰 | 辽开泰七年<br>（公元1018年） | 周长约160厘米 | 1986年奈曼旗<br>辽陈国公主墓出土 | 内蒙古文物考古研究所藏 | ＊ |
| 琥珀璎珞 | 辽开泰七年<br>（公元1018年） | 周长113、159厘米 | 1986年奈曼旗<br>辽陈国公主墓出土 | 内蒙古文物考古研究所藏 | 221 |
| 银壶 | 辽开泰七年<br>（公元1018年） | 通高10.1、口径4.4、<br>底径5.6厘米　重135克 | 1986年奈曼旗<br>辽陈国公主墓出土 | 内蒙古文物考古研究所藏 | 223 |
| 银盏托 | 辽开泰七年<br>（公元1018年） | 通高7.8、口径8.4、<br>盘径16厘米　重184克 | 1986年奈曼旗<br>辽陈国公主墓出土 | 内蒙古文物考古研究所藏 | 224 |
| 金花银钵 | 辽开泰七年<br>（公元1018年） | 高6.1、口径16.8厘米 | 1986年奈曼旗<br>辽陈国公主墓出土 | 内蒙古文物考古研究所藏 | ＊ |

＊ 未收入本图册

| 品　名 | 年　代 | 尺寸／重量 | 出土地点 | 收　藏 | 页码 |
|---|---|---|---|---|---|
| 鎏金银勺 | 辽开泰七年<br>（公元 1018 年） | 通长 28 厘米 | 1986 年奈曼旗<br>辽陈国公主墓出土 | 内蒙古文物考古研究所藏 | ＊ |
| 银勺 | 辽开泰七年<br>（公元 1018 年） | 通长 21.8 厘米 | 1986 年奈曼旗<br>辽陈国公主墓出土 | 内蒙古文物考古研究所藏 | ＊ |
| 银唾盂 | 辽开泰七年<br>（公元 1018 年） | 高 16、口径 24.5 厘米 | 1986 年奈曼旗<br>辽陈国公主墓出土 | 内蒙古文物考古研究所藏 | ＊ |
| 铜镜 | 辽开泰七年<br>（公元 1018 年） | 直径 44 厘米 | 1986 年奈曼旗<br>辽陈国公主墓出土 | 内蒙古文物考古研究所藏 | ＊ |
| 錾花铜盆 | 辽开泰七年<br>（公元 1018 年） | 高 19、口径 57、<br>底径 33 厘米 | 1986 年奈曼旗<br>辽陈国公主墓出土 | 内蒙古文物考古研究所藏 | 225 |
| 玉砚 | 辽开泰七年<br>（公元 1018 年） | 高 2.6 – 4.1、<br>长 12、宽 7.1 厘米 | 1986 年奈曼旗<br>辽陈国公主墓出土 | 内蒙古文物考古研究所藏 | ＊ |
| 玉水盂 | 辽开泰七年<br>（公元 1018 年） | 高 2.3、口径 5.6-6.9 厘米 | 1986 年奈曼旗<br>辽陈国公主墓出土 | 内蒙古文物考古研究所藏 | ＊ |
| 乳钉纹玻璃盘 | 辽开泰七年<br>（公元 1018 年） | 高 6.8、口径 25.5、<br>底径 10 厘米 | 1986 年奈曼旗<br>辽陈国公主墓出土 | 内蒙古文物考古研究所藏 | 226 |
| 玻璃杯 | 辽开泰七年<br>（公元 1018 年） | 高 11.4、口径 9、<br>底径 5.4 厘米 | 1986 年奈曼旗<br>辽陈国公主墓出土 | 内蒙古文物考古研究所藏 | 227 |
| 乳钉纹玻璃瓶 | 辽开泰七年<br>（公元 1018 年） | 高 17、口径 6、<br>底径 8.7 厘米 | 1986 年奈曼旗<br>辽陈国公主墓出土 | 内蒙古文物考古研究所藏 | 228 |
| 刻花玻璃瓶 | 辽开泰七年<br>（公元 1018 年） | 高 24.5、口径 74、<br>底径 11 厘米 | 1986 年奈曼旗<br>辽陈国公主墓出土 | 内蒙古文物考古研究所藏 | 229 |
| 高颈玻璃瓶 | 辽开泰七年<br>（公元 1018 年） | 高 31.8、口径 8.5、<br>腹径 20 厘米 | 1986 年奈曼旗<br>辽陈国公主墓出土 | 内蒙古文物考古研究所藏 | ＊ |
| "官"字款莲纹白瓷盖罐 | 辽开泰七年<br>（公元 1018 年） | 通高 11.4、口径 5.8、<br>底径 5.1 厘米 | 1986 年奈曼旗<br>辽陈国公主墓出土 | 内蒙古文物考古研究所藏 | 231 |
| 花式口白瓷碗 | 辽开泰七年<br>（公元 1018 年） | 高 7.7、口径 14.8、<br>底径 9 厘米 | 1986 年奈曼旗<br>辽陈国公主墓出土 | 内蒙古文物考古研究所藏 | 232 |
| 花式口青瓷碗 | 辽开泰七年<br>（公元 1018 年） | 高 7、口径 19 厘米 | 1986 年奈曼旗<br>辽陈国公主墓出土 | 内蒙古文物考古研究所藏 | ＊ |

＊ 未收入本图册

| 品　名 | 年　代 | 尺寸／重量 | 出土地点 | 收　藏 | 页码 |
|---|---|---|---|---|---|
| 菊花纹青瓷盘 | 辽开泰七年<br>（公元1018年） | 高4.6、口径17、<br>底径10.7厘米 | 1986年奈曼旗辽<br>陈国公主墓出土 | 内蒙古文物考古研究所藏 | 233 |
| 双蝶纹青瓷盘 | 辽开泰七年<br>（公元1018年） | 高5.1、口径16.4、<br>底径10厘米 | 1986年奈曼旗<br>辽陈国公主墓出土 | 内蒙古文物考古研究所藏 | ＊ |
| 绿釉长颈盖壶 | 辽开泰七年<br>（公元1018年） | 通高58.4、口径12.8、<br>底径10.8厘米 | 1986年奈曼旗<br>辽陈国公主墓出土 | 内蒙古文物考古研究所藏 | ＊ |
| 木鸡冠壶 | 辽开泰七年<br>（公元1018年） | 高29.2、<br>宽20.8－24.3厘米 | 1986年奈曼旗<br>辽陈国公主墓出土 | 内蒙古文物考古研究所藏 | 234 |
| 木弓囊 | 辽开泰七年<br>（公元1018年） | 长74.5、宽10－25、<br>厚2.9－4.4厘米 | 1986年奈曼旗<br>辽陈国公主墓出土 | 内蒙古文物考古研究所藏 | 235 |
| 包银木马鞍 | 辽开泰七年<br>（公元1018年） | 高26－18.8、长56、<br>宽41.2厘米 | 1986年奈曼旗<br>辽陈国公主墓出土 | 内蒙古文物考古研究所藏 | 237 |
| 鎏金银鞍饰 | 辽开泰七年<br>（公元1018年） | 前桥银饰高24.5、<br>后桥银饰高38、<br>半月形银饰长16.5厘米 | 1986年奈曼旗<br>辽陈国公主墓出土 | 内蒙古文物考古研究所藏 | 239 |
| 镶玉银马络 | 辽开泰七年<br>（公元1018年） | 长约50、宽30厘米 | 1986年奈曼旗<br>辽陈国公主墓出土 | 内蒙古文物考古研究所藏 | 240 |
| 鎏金铁马衔、镳，银马缰 | 辽开泰七年<br>（公元1018年） | 衔长17、镳长16.5、<br>缰长165厘米 | 1986年奈曼旗<br>辽陈国公主墓出土 | 内蒙古文物考古研究所藏 | 241 |
| 银胸带、鎏金铁马镫 | 辽开泰七年<br>（公元1018年） | 胸带长168、<br>马镫通高19.5、宽15厘米 | 1986年奈曼旗<br>辽陈国公主墓出土 | 内蒙古文物考古研究所藏 | 242 |
| 银踯躞带、鞦带 | 辽开泰七年<br>（公元1018年） | 全长320厘米，<br>下垂踯躞带长56－61厘米 | 1986年奈曼旗<br>辽陈国公主墓出土 | 内蒙古文物考古研究所藏 | 243 |
| 彩绘银鞦 | 辽开泰七年<br>（公元1018年） | （单件）长59、宽66、<br>厚0.05厘米　重830克 | 1986年奈曼旗<br>辽陈国公主墓出土 | 内蒙古文物考古研究所藏 | 245 |
| 陈国公主墓志 | 辽开泰七年<br>（公元1018年） | 通高28、<br>边长89.5厘米 | 1986年奈曼旗<br>辽陈国公主墓出土 | 内蒙古文物考古研究所藏 | 247 |
| 八思巴文金字银牌 | 元<br>（公元1271年－1368年） | 长29、<br>宽8厘米 | 1999年清水河县<br>下城湾古城村征集 | 内蒙古文物考古研究所藏 | 249 |
| 迦陵频迦银带扣 | 元<br>（公元1271年－1368年） | 长5.9、宽5.4、<br>高2.3厘米 | 1983年敖汉旗兴窝铺乡<br>盛家窝铺村窖藏出土 | 内蒙古博物馆藏 | ＊ |

＊ 未收入本图册

| 品　名 | 年　代 | 尺寸／重量 | 出土地点 | 收　藏 | 页码 |
|---|---|---|---|---|---|
| 狮子衔绶纹银带扣 | 元<br>（公元 1271 年 – 1368 年） | 长 5、宽 4.8 厘米 | 1976 年敖汉旗<br>四家子镇大南城窖藏出土 | 内蒙古博物馆藏 | ＊ |
| 银锭 | 元<br>（公元 1271 年 – 1368 年） | 长 13、最宽 9.5 厘米 | 1977 年阿鲁科尔沁旗<br>天口镇征集 | 内蒙古博物馆藏 | ＊ |
| "格力芬"丝织被面 | 元<br>（公元 1271 年 – 1368 年） | 长 204、宽 118 厘米 | 1976 年察哈尔右翼前旗<br>元集宁路古城遗址窖藏出土 | 内蒙古博物馆藏 | 250 |
| 鎏金高足银杯 | 元<br>（公元 1271 年 – 1368 年） | 高 14、口径 11、腹径 7 厘米<br>重 190.5 克 | 1978 年达尔罕茂明安联合旗<br>大苏吉乡明水村出土 | 内蒙古博物馆藏 | 251 |
| 鎏金錾花银杯、盘 | 元<br>（公元 1271 年 – 1368 年） | 杯高 2.6、口径 9.1、盘高 0.8、<br>口径 16.8 厘米 | 1997 年达尔罕茂明旗<br>巴音脑包苏木石板墓出土 | 内蒙古文物考古研究所藏 | ＊ |
| 鏊耳金杯 | 元<br>（公元 1271 年 – 1368 年） | 高 5、口径 12、底 7.9 厘米<br>重 189 克 | 1976 年兴和县五股泉乡<br>五甲地村出土 | 内蒙古博物馆藏 | 252 |
| 青花高足杯 | 元<br>（公元 1271 年 – 1368 年） | 高 9.5、口径 11.4、<br>足径 3.8 厘米 | 1978 年赤峰市大营子乡<br>哈金沟窖藏出土 | 内蒙古博物馆藏 | 253 |
| "内府"白瓷瓶 | 元<br>（公元 1271 年 – 1368 年） | 高 35、口径 5.8、<br>底径 14.7 厘米 | 1982 年开鲁县三义井乡<br>元代窖藏出土 | 内蒙古博物馆藏 | ＊ |
| "内府官用"漆盘 | 元<br>（公元 1271 年 – 1368 年） | 高 4、口径 22.5、<br>径 13.7 厘米 | 1958 年察哈尔右翼前旗<br>元集宁路古城出土 | 内蒙古博物馆藏 | ＊ |
| 石雕龙纹香炉 | 元<br>（公元 1271 年 – 1368 年） | 通高 26 厘米 | 1991 年呼和浩特市<br>郊区星星板村征集 | 内蒙古博物馆藏 | ＊ |
| "永昌等处行枢密院断事官府印"<br>铜印 | 北元<br>天元元年（公元 1379 年） | 通高 9.2、边长 8.4 厘米 | 1984 年额济纳旗<br>黑城子遗址出土 | 内蒙古文物考古研究所藏 | 255 |
| 五子登科画像石 | 元<br>（公元 1271 年 – 1368 年） | 长 71.5、宽 48、厚 12 厘米 | 1990 年多伦县<br>砧子山墓地出土 | 内蒙古文物考古研究所藏 | 257 |
| 景教墓顶石 | 元<br>（公元 1271 年 – 1368 年） | 长 105、宽 34、高 44 厘米 | 1996 年达尔罕茂明安联合旗<br>额尔敦敖包苏木<br>木胡儿索卜嘎出土 | 内蒙古文物考古研究所藏 | 259 |
| 高翅鎏金银冠（公主） | 辽开泰七年<br>（公元 1018 年） | 冠体高 26、冠箍口径 19.5、<br>立翅高 30、宽 12.5 厘米<br>重 807 克 | 1986 年奈曼旗<br>辽陈国公主墓出土 | 内蒙古文物考古研究所藏 | ＊ |
| 银丝网络（公主） | 辽开泰七年<br>（公元 1018 年） | 全长 168 厘米 | 1986 年奈曼旗<br>辽陈国公主墓出土 | 内蒙古文物考古研究所藏 | ＊ |

＊ 未收入本图册

| 品 名 | 年 代 | 尺寸／重量 | 出土地点 | 收 藏 | 页码 |
|---|---|---|---|---|---|
| 金銙银蹀躞带 | 辽开泰七年（公元1018年） | 长156厘米 | 1986年奈曼旗辽陈国公主墓出土 | 内蒙古文物考古研究所藏 | ＊ |
| 金带銙 | 辽开泰七年（公元1018年） | 长10.2、宽6.2厘米 | 1986年奈曼旗辽陈国公主墓出土 | 内蒙古文物考古研究所藏 | ＊ |
| 绣花金荷包 | 辽开泰七年（公元1018年） | 包长13.4、宽7.8厘米，金链长9.2厘米 | 1986年奈曼旗辽陈国公主墓出土 | 内蒙古文物考古研究所藏 | ＊ |
| 工具形玉佩 | 辽开泰七年（公元1018年） | 长18.2厘米 | 1986年奈曼旗辽陈国公主墓出土 | 内蒙古文物考古研究所藏 | ＊ |
| 琥珀珍珠耳坠 | 辽开泰七年（公元1018年） | 长13厘米 | 1986年奈曼旗辽陈国公主墓出土 | 内蒙古文物考古研究所藏 | ＊ |
| 胡人驯狮琥珀佩饰 | 辽开泰七年（公元1018年） | 长8.4、宽6、厚3.4厘米 | 1986年奈曼旗辽陈国公主墓出土 | 内蒙古文物考古研究所藏 | ＊ |
| 金花银盒 | 辽开泰七年（公元1018年） | 通高21、口径25.4厘米重1800克 | 1986年奈曼旗辽陈国公主墓出土 | 内蒙古文物考古研究所藏 | ＊ |
| 玛瑙碗 | 辽开泰七年（公元1018年） | 高3.1、口径7.4、底径4.4厘米 | 1986年奈曼旗辽陈国公主墓出土 | 内蒙古文物考古研究所藏 | ＊ |
| 水晶花口杯 | 辽开泰七年（公元1018年） | 高2.3、口径3.6 – 5.3厘米 | 1986年奈曼旗辽陈国公主墓出土 | 内蒙古文物考古研究所藏 | ＊ |
| 系链水晶杯 | 辽开泰七年（公元1018年） | 连盖通高3.5、口径2.8厘米 | 1986年奈曼旗辽陈国公主墓出土 | 内蒙古文物考古研究所藏 | ＊ |
| 五瓣花形金杯 | 辽会同四年（公元941年） | 高4.9、口径7.3、底径4厘米 | 1992年阿鲁科尔沁旗辽耶律羽之墓出土 | 内蒙古文物考古研究所藏 | ＊ |
| 金花银"万岁台"砚盒 | 辽会同四年（公元941年） | 长18.4、宽11 – 13.6、通高7.6厘米 | 1992年阿鲁科尔沁旗辽耶律羽之墓出土 | 内蒙古文物考古研究所藏 | ＊ |
| 鎏金錾花银杯 | 辽会同四年（公元941年） | 高6.4、口径7.3、腹径5.2厘米 | 1992年阿鲁科尔沁旗辽耶律羽之墓出土 | 内蒙古文物考古研究所藏 | ＊ |
| 鎏金錾花银盘 | 辽会同四年（公元941年） | 高3.5、口径15.9、腹径12.4厘米 | 1992年阿鲁科尔沁旗辽耶律羽之墓出土 | 内蒙古文物考古研究所藏 | ＊ |
| 鎏金錾花银盒 | 辽会同四年（公元941年） | 通高8.9、口径14.6厘米 | 1992年阿鲁科尔沁旗辽耶律羽之墓出土 | 内蒙古文物考古研究所藏 | ＊ |

＊ 未收入本图册

| 品　名 | 年　代 | 尺寸／重量 | 出土地点 | 收　藏 | 页码 |
|---|---|---|---|---|---|
| 鎏金錾花银罐 | 辽会同四年<br>（公元941年） | 高14.8、口径7.6、<br>腹径12.2、底径7.1厘米 | 1992年阿鲁科尔沁旗<br>辽耶律羽之墓出土 | 内蒙古文物考古研究所藏 | ＊ |
| 褐釉皮囊式鸡冠壶 | 辽会同四年<br>（公元941年） | 高28.8、腹径24、<br>底径10.8厘米 | 1992年阿鲁科尔沁旗<br>辽耶律羽之墓出土 | 内蒙古文物考古研究所藏 | ＊ |
| 白瓷皮囊式鸡冠壶 | 辽会同四年<br>（公元941年） | 高30.4、腹径24、<br>底径11.4厘米 | 1992年阿鲁科尔沁旗<br>辽耶律羽之墓出土 | 内蒙古文物考古研究所藏 | ＊ |
|  |  |  |  |  |  |
|  |  |  |  |  |  |
|  |  |  |  |  |  |
|  |  |  |  |  |  |
|  |  |  |  |  |  |
|  |  |  |  |  |  |
|  |  |  |  |  |  |
|  |  |  |  |  |  |
|  |  |  |  |  |  |
|  |  |  |  |  |  |
|  |  |  |  |  |  |

＊ 未收入本图册

# 内蒙古自治区考古文物出土

额济纳旗

巴彦淖尔盟

阿拉善盟

磴口县

杭锦旗

伊金霍洛旗

伊克昭盟

准格

乌审旗

图

呼伦贝尔盟

新巴尔虎右旗

兴安盟

哲里木盟

锡林郭勒盟

巴林左旗　　　　　　　科尔沁左翼中旗
　　　　　　阿鲁科尔沁旗
林西县　　巴林右旗
　　　　　翁牛特旗　　奈曼旗　　开鲁县
克什克腾旗

　　　　赤峰市　敖汉旗　　库伦旗
多伦县
　　　喀喇沁旗

茂明安联合旗　　　　　宁城县
察哈尔右翼后旗
和浩特市
　凉城县　　兴和县
各尔
　　察哈尔右翼前旗
清水河县

| | 国　界 |
| --- | --- |
| | 省　界 |
| | 盟　界 |
| | 塔　址 |
| | 城　址 |
| | 窖　藏 |
| | 遗　址 |
| | 墓　葬 |
| | 辽　陈国公主墓 |
| | 辽　耶律羽之墓 |
| | 征　集 |
| | 市、县、旗所在地 |

| 主　编 | 陈燮君　汪庆正 |
| :--- | :--- |
| **Chief Editor** | *Chen Xiejun　Wang Qingzheng* |
| 责任编辑 | 茅子良　张　岚 |
| **Executive Editor** | *Mao Ziliang　Zhang Lan* |
| 翻　译 | 周志聪 |
| **Translator** | *Zhou Zhicong* |
| 校　对 | 陶喻之　许筱江 |
| **Reviser** | *Tao Yuzhi　Xu Xiaojiang* |
| 摄　影 | 汪雯梅　盛黎明 |
| **Photographer** | *Wang Wenmei　Shen Liming* |
| 装帧设计 | 姚伟延 |
| **Catalogue Design** | *Yao Weiyan* |
| 技术编辑 | 吴蕃中　陈　昕 |
| **Technical Editor** | *Wu Fanzhong　Chen Xin* |

**图书在版编目（CIP）数据**

草原瑰宝——内蒙古文物考古精品／上海博物馆编，
上海：上海书画出版社，2000.6
ISBN 7-80635-587-1

I. 草...　II. 上...　III. 文物－内蒙古
IV. k872.26

中国版本图书馆 CIP 数据核字（2000）第 62182 号

草原瑰宝——内蒙古文物考古精品

上海博物馆编

上海书画出版社出版发行

（上海市钦州南路 81 号　邮政编码 200233）

上海公牛广告有限公司设计

杭州海洋电脑制版有限公司制版

深圳中华商务联合印刷有限公司印刷

2000 年 6 月第一版　第一次印刷

开本　635 × 960 毫米　1/8　印张 36

ISBN 7-80635-587-1/J · 1311

定价　350.00 元